IT'S NOT ROCKET
A walk through
By: Kai

Written for my girls, Krista Hatcher Miller and Von de Leigh Hatcher, and for my grandchildren, born and yet to be born.

INTRO:

IT'S NOT ROCKET SCIENCE, VOLUME 1, contains essays on various subjects. This book contains points to ponder from the New Testament. Most of these thoughts are from the margins of my Bible and were written either as a result of my own personal devotions, or from sermons I've heard over the years.

Each one of these points could be developed into an essay (or a sermon). My prayer is the reader will not just skim over them, but take each one and develop the idea more fully as it pertains to the reader's particular situation. **Ponder these thoughts!** Meditate on them.

Living for God is really easy! It doesn't take a highly intellectual person to figure it out. *IT'S NOT ROCKET SCIENCE!* What *is* difficult, however, is getting my carnal self under subjection to God. The battle is between my ears.

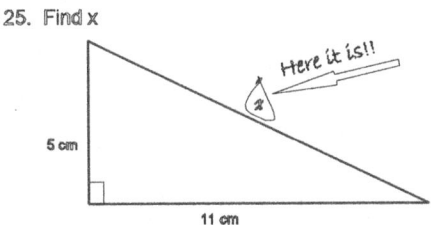

A secondary theme of these writings is about the *trajectory of the heart.* Is my heart pointed in the right direction? Proverbs 4:23 states, "Keep thy heart with all diligence; for out of it are the issues of life."

I have tried to personalize these thoughts. I have no right to preach to others. I can only preach to myself. Unless noted, scriptural quotes are from the King James Version.

Grab a cup of coffee and a lap blanket. Sit down in a comfortable chair. Get out your Bible. Read the verse and the comments in this book. Look up the other scripture references. Think about it and pray. God will give you a personal "a-hah" moment! Let's do some soul searching together, shall we?

Let's take Mary's lead and meditate on some truths! *"... Mary kept all these things, and **pondered them in her heart**"* (Luke 2:19).

I want to give a special thanks to **Michelle Goudeau** for helping me proof this book.

Disclaimer: My husband and I have pastored or assisted the pastor in churches in three continents and in three states. I may relate some experiences in my writings. All names have been changed to protect the guilty! My immediate family members, on the other hand, don't get off that easily. They are guilty as charged.

© 2014-2019 by Karen R. (Bernard) Hatcher

TABLE OF CONTENTS

NEW TESTAMENT POINTS TO PONDER 5
Focus of the Biographies 5
Groups of Paul's Epistles (Letters) 5
Genealogy of Jesus 5
MATTHEW 6
MARK 27
LUKE 37
JOHN 53
ACTS 73
ROMANS 96
I CORINTHIANS 117
II CORINTHIANS 136
GALATIANS 150
EPHESIANS 158
PHILIPPIANS 166
COLOSSIANS 172
I THESSALONIANS 179
II THESSALONIANS 183
I TIMOTHY 185
II TIMOTHY 192
TITUS 196
PHILEMON 199
HEBREWS 200
JAMES 212
I PETER 218

II PETER	224
I JOHN	227
II JOHN	232
III JOHN	233
JUDE	234
REVELATION	236
VOCABULARY	246

NEW TESTAMENT POINTS TO PONDER

Breakdown of the New Testament
1. Matthew, Mark, Luke & John are biographical sketches of the life of Jesus.
2. Acts is a historical record of the birth of the church, thus the only book telling us how people initially got saved.
3. Romans through Jude are letters to Christians, instructing them on daily Christian living. These books instruct us how to stay saved. There is no record of people receiving initial salvation in these writings.
4. Revelation reveals the true nature of Jesus and gives insight to the end of time.

Focus of the Biographies
(See also notes at Numbers 2 in *It's Not Rocket Science, Volume 3*.)
1. Matthew was written to the Jews. They longed for a king. *Theme: Jesus is the perfect King!* As the son of David, Jesus was entitled to the throne. This biography corresponds with the banner of the lead tribe encamped around the east side of the Tabernacle (Judah, the lion).
2. Mark was written to the Romans. They liked having servants. *Theme: Jesus is the perfect servant!* As a servant, His lineage was not important, and not recorded. This biography corresponds with the banner of the lead tribe encamped around the south side of the Tabernacle (Ephraim, the ox).
3. Luke was written to the Greeks. They were focused on developing the mind & body. *Theme: Jesus is the perfect man!* This biography corresponds with the banner of the lead tribe encamped around the west side of the Tabernacle (Rueben, the man).
4. John was written much later than the other gospels. By the time John was written, many false doctrines regarding Jesus had begun to be taught. John was written to everyone in general. *Theme: Jesus is God!* This biography corresponds with the banner of the lead tribe encamped around the north side of the Tabernacle (Dan, the eagle).

Groups of Paul's Epistles (Letters)
1. I, II Thessalonians was written during Paul's second missionary tour.
2. Galatians, I, II Corinthians & Romans was written during Paul's third tour.
3. Colossians, Philemon, Ephesians & Philippians was written during Paul's first imprisonment.
4. I Timothy & Titus was written after Paul's first imprisonment.
5. II Timothy was written during Paul's second imprisonment.

Genealogy of Jesus
1. Matthew records the genealogy through Joseph, the "adopted" father of Jesus.

There are 41 generations from Abraham to Jesus. It is through this line Jesus, being of David's line (Matthew 1:1), has a right to be King. Jechonias (also called Jehoiachin, Jeconiah, Coniah) was an evil king and his line was cursed by God so no descendent of his could be king (Jeremiah 22:24-30). Therefore, Jesus could NOT have been Joseph's natural son and still be king. Joseph did not "beget" Jesus, but was the legal father of Jesus. God honored Joseph's legal right and gave Joseph instructions concerning the family (Matthew 2:13, 19).

2. Luke records Jesus' genealogy through Mary, the natural mother of Jesus. There are 77 generations total. Jewish tradition does not usually include women in genealogical links. Joseph is listed here as Heli's son, but he was actually Heli's son-in-law. This precedent of name substitution was established in Numbers 27:1-11 and Numbers 36:1-12. It is through Mary's line Jesus is established as the son of God.

King James Version
King James of England had the Bible translation into English. The English language was a bit different than what is spoken today. Most languages, such as French and Spanish, have a "formal" and an "informal" speech. In fact, the Korean language has seven forms of speech. The form used depends upon the speaker's relationship to the person to whom he is speaking! The words "thee" and "thou" were the *informal* word for "you" in the time of King James. God wants a close, intimate relationship with us. He is not an "arms-length" God. He wants to embrace us and wants us to embrace Him!

Parables of Jesus
A parable is an earthly story with a heavenly meaning. The parables of Jesus teach us about Christian behavior:
1. how to be a Christian in various situations;
2. to use talents well;
3. to remain watchful; and finally
4. about judgment.

MATTHEW

Written to the Jews. Theme: Jesus is the King of the Jews and is sovereign. As the son of David, Jesus is entitled to the throne.

Matthew 1:3, 5. Rahab and Ruth were both Gentile women who ended up being in the lineage of Jesus! Rahab had a bad reputation. Women aren't usually listed in Jewish genealogy. Why here? Apparently, neither my past nor my pedigree is of significance to God! (Interesting tidbit: If modern genealogy reports are to be believed, Zara, son of Judah, is my ancestor on my father's side! His line left the

Israelites at some point while they were in Egypt and traveled north to Europe.)

Matthew 1:21. Joseph was not Jesus' biological father; however, God gave to Joseph the name to call Mary's baby. Mary was the "chosen vessel" (Luke 1:28), but God honored Joseph as the spiritual head of the house. God also warned Joseph (not Mary) in a dream to go to Egypt to escape Herod's massacre of baby boys. Joseph was also told when it was safe to come back to Israel (Matthew 2:19; 22). God established man as the head of the household as part of the woman's curse in Genesis 3:6. If God follows His own rules, who am I to buck them?

Matthew 3:11. John the Baptist was the forerunner of Jesus. He preached all of the same elements in the New Testament salvation plan. He preached repentance, water baptism and the Holy Spirit. The Holy Spirit wasn't available yet because Jesus hadn't ascended (John 7:39). Baptism wasn't done in the name of Jesus because Jesus hadn't yet been buried (Romans 6:4; Colossians 2:12). However, John's message was the precursor to the new covenant.

Matthew 3:15-16. Isn't it interesting to observe after a spiritual milestone, a huge trial follows? It seems to happen every time. Jesus was baptized of John, but not because He needed to for salvation. Jesus was baptized (1) as an example; (2) as the ultimate High Priest, a washing was required; and (3) to conclude the law of Moses before another covenant could begin. Baptism identified Jesus as the one of whom John spoke. Baptism signified the beginning of Jesus' public ministry. Immediately after His baptism, the *Spirit* led Jesus into the wilderness (Matthew 4:1). Not all of our wilderness experiences are from the devil. God leads us there sometimes to fine-tune us. After His fast, when Jesus was physically weak, Satan challenged His identity. He was tempted (Matthew 4:3-6) by the (1) lust of the flesh (food); (2) lust of the eye (power); and (3) pride of life (control). All temptations fall under one of these three categories (I John 2:16). In this weakened state, Satan appealed to all three of these categories. As usual, Satan twisted scriptures around. He told Jesus if He was the son of God, He could cast Himself down and the angels would protect Him. That is not true. Angels do not protect the disobedient and rebellious. Satan is really good at deception. He is good at taking the scripture and twisting it around to mean something other than what it means. It sounds good, but I really do need to examine what God Himself says and not take Satan's (or someone else's) word for it.

Matthew 5 contains the Be-Attitudes. These are the attitudes I must possess to be successful in my Christian walk. "Blessed" means "empowered to succeed" and also "to be envied". If I hunger and thirst after these attributes, God will fill me up (Matthew 5:6). Hunger and thirst are different. Usually around the third day of fasting or starvation, the hunger pains dissipate and may even go away. Thirst, however, cannot be quenched without water. Thirst doesn't go away! (Psalm 42). The same applies spiritually. I know of people who have a heart for God, but the hunger for spiritual things has gone away. They don't live for God, but are "thirsty" for Him. These are the people who talk about wanting more of God. They get enough of a drink to feel satisfied for the moment, but aren't getting enough spiritual nutrients to sustain them, and either end up being a yo-yo Christian, or talk the talk without walking the walk.

Matthew 5:13. We are the salt of the earth. What does that mean? Salt makes things more palatable. Salt also is a preservative and helps food stay fresh longer. Imagine how bland our food would be if there was no salt! Salt enhances all flavors. Just a touch of salt takes a dish from "blah" to "yum". I'm the salt of the earth. Have I lost my flavor? If I am a hypocrite, I have lost my flavor and the world will turn away from God because of me. I take this scripture in Matthew to work two ways:
1. We are the salt of the earth *to God*. We give Him a reason to tolerate the sinful state of mankind. We delay (preserve) His judgment and anger for a later date. This is why I believe as soon as we are called away (rapture), the world will plunge into utter darkness very quickly. Once all true Christians are removed from the earth, there is nothing to keep the earth from total decay. We restrain total lawlessness (II Thessalonians 2:6-7).
2. We are the salt of the earth *to man*. Salt makes God palatable or desirable to a sinful man. Just reading the Bible and understanding it is very difficult. The Ethiopian eunuch had a very hard time figuring out what Isaiah was saying. God saw the *<u>trajectory</u> of his heart* was pointed in the right direction. God saw he was hungry to know more about God, so God sent Philip to explain what he was reading (Acts 8:30-40). The vast majority of people never open up the Bible. If they do, many get so confused, they give up. However, when they come in contact with a true Christian, *who is living out the Bible*, they are intrigued. When they see the blessings of God on my life and when they see the practical application of the Bible in my life, they are intrigued. My life makes God more real and more palatable to them.

Matthew 5:22-30. The seed of murder or adultery can reside in the heart, even if it is not acted out. The problem is not my arms, legs, etc., which actually commit a sin, but my problem is *the <u>trajectory</u> of my heart*. The body merely carries out the work of the heart.

Matthew 5:44-48. I **MUST** love others. Why? So I will be a child of God. I am commanded to love others. Why? So, I can be like God. Everybody can love the "good people", or those whom they like! It takes something supernatural to love those we dislike and those who do us wrong. Joseph blessed his brothers who had done wrong and caused him thirteen years of pain (Genesis 42:25).

Matthew 5:45. Nestled in the discourse on loving others is the comment we like to pull out about troubles falling on both the good and evil people. Note this verse also states good times and blessings will come to both the good and evil people as well.

Just because someone appears to be blessed of God doesn't mean God approves of their life. Jacob and Esau's blessing from their father started out exactly the same (Genesis 27:28, 39). We know from their story Jacob ended up becoming "Israel", meaning a prince with God (Genesis 32:28) and Esau was labeled as being profane (Hebrews 12:16). It's not how I start that matters. It is how I end. I must put my spiritual blinders on and keep on living right without regard to what others are doing. God will ultimately judge us all.

Matthew 6:2-3, 5, 9-13, 17. Giving is not an option (Matthew 6:2-3). Prayer is not an option (Matthew 6:5). Fasting is not an option (Matthew 6:17).

Matthew 6:9-13. Jesus gave us a step-by-step manual for prayer. I can't go wrong if I follow His pattern!
1. ACKNOWLEDGE. *Our father which art in heaven.* (Psalm 22:3) God is sovereign. God is the boss. My acknowledgment helps me to remember God is in control, God knows best, and God has a right to do whatever He pleases in my life.
2. PRAISE. *Hallowed be thy name.* (Psalm 63:3; Heb. 13:15) Begin all prayer with praise. Whatever my petition may be, I first praise God. With praise, I esteem God for His greatness and virtues.
3. GOD'S WILL. *Thy will be done on earth as it is in heaven.* God's will is automatically done in Heaven. Period. He wouldn't have it any other way. God's will is not done on earth because He gave mankind the choice of whether or not to follow Him. Above my wants and my way of thinking, is God's will. I always predicate my petition with God's will. God knows what is best for me. (See essay entitled "Not My Will but Thine Be Done" in *It's Not Rocket Science, Volume 1.*)
4. *Give us this day our daily bread.* This can be divided into two parts.
    a. PETITION. (James 4:2-3) This aspect of prayer deals with our personal needs. Take them to the Lord, and leave them there. "Cast" them upon Him. (See essay entitled "Is God Deaf?" in *It's Not Rocket Science, Volume 1.)*
    b. READ THE BIBLE. (II Timothy 3:16). It may be surprising to suggest reading the Bible during prayer. However, the Word is enlightening to the eyes (Psalm 19:8). When you read the Bible, things are made clear.
5. *Forgive us our debts as we forgive our debtors.* This is also two-fold:
    a. CONFESSION. (Psalm 139:23-24; Psalm 66:18) I must deal with my sin. If I hide sin in my heart God will not hear me. (See essay entitled "Is God Deaf?" in *It's Not Rocket Science, Volume 1.)*
    b. FORGIVENESS. (Hebrews 12:15) Nothing will block my spiritual progress more fatally than an unforgiving spirit. Forgiveness is a complete pouring-out of any feeling that might develop against anyone during the day. Even a small root of bitterness will quickly grow into a serious problem (Hebrews 12:15). (See essays entitled "Make the Hurt

Go Away" and "Offense" in *It's Not Rocket Science, Volume 1.*)
6. INTERCESSION. *Lead us not into temptation but deliver us from evil.* Intercession involves the most intense dimension of prayer. Intercession for others is God's love flowing through me. God will lead and develop my prayer. I intercede for "us", meaning ...
   a. others (I Timothy 2:1-2; Matthew 9:37-38)
   b. and for myself (Matthew 26:41).
7. PRAISE. *For thine is the kingdom and the power and the glory forever.* (Exodus 15:2; Psalm 30:1). Conclude every prayer with praise. Again, we exalt the nature of God.
8. Other notes on prayer time.
   a. MEDITATION. (Psalm 1:1-2; Psalm 77:12) When I make time to "think on these things". God will open my understanding.
   b. THANKSGIVING. (I Thessalonians 5:18; Philippians 4:6) Although this will probably occur throughout prayer, I spend a special time thanking God out loud for his provision and goodness to me.
   c. PRAY THE WORD. Apply the precepts of the Bible to your life. Personalize the scripture. I substitute MY name and MY situation in the wording of the scripture. Who knows what God wants better than God Himself? The scriptures were inspired by God. Therefore, I have confidence when I pray the word, I am praying God's will.
   d. SINGING. (Psalm 100:2; Ephesians 5:19) Singing refreshes and comforts the soul.
   e. LISTENING. (I Kings 19:11-12) Prayer is not all talking to God. Prayer is also listening for direct orders from God. He will speak His thoughts into my thoughts.
9. **Prayer protocol & safeguards:** (See essay entitled "Prayer is the Place Where Burdens Change Shoulders" in *It's Not Rocket Science, Volume 1.*)
   a. I must repent and clean out my heart so my prayers are not ignored (Psalm 66:18; I Peter 3:7)
   b. I must use any personal insights or impressions for prayer only, not for gossip. Example: If I smell strong alcohol on someone's breath, it is not for me to go tell others the person is an alcoholic. It is for me to pray for them!
   c. I must be full of grace. God is patient and I must be as well (both with myself and with others).
   d. I must be a committed pray-er and not a crises pray-er (Leviticus 6:12; Luke 18:1; I Thessalonians 5:17). Just as the fire on the altar was to never go out in the Old Testament, neither should my prayers. I should pray enough so I am comfortable talking with God. If I just go to Him in times of crises, my relationship is skewed. I must have a continual prayer life. This keeps me strong.

Matthew 6:22-23. I must be careful what I allow my eyes to see. I must guard my eyes.

In many cases, seeing is the first temptation. There are plenty of things I can't avoid seeing because I live in a world of sin. However, I don't have to *intentionally* allow myself to see something which could possibly pose a temptation to me. This applies to both books and movies too!
1. Examples: Genesis 3:6; Joshua 7:21; II Samuel 11:2. They saw, and they took.
2. I must make a covenant with my eyes (Job 31:1; Psalm 101:3; Psalm 119:37; Ecclesiastes 7:29; Isaiah 33:15; Ezekiel 23:14).
3. Satan tempted Jesus through the eye (Matthew 4:8).
4. Why make a covenant with my eye? The eye is the first line of defense (or temptation) for the whole body. Couple Matthew 15:19-20 and Mark 7:21-23 together with Luke 11:34-35.

Matthew 6:33. It's not that I don't need earthly things, but if I seek after the eternal, heavenly things, God will see to it my temporal needs are met. God knows what I need and will supply it (Philippians 4:19). What I think I need (or want) and what God knows I need may be different things! I *trust* God. God knows what I need before I even ask (Matthew 6:8)! He knows what I need better than I do.

Matthew 7:1-5. I must take care of my own issues before I start trying to fix others. What right do I have to judge someone else when I've got flaws myself? This is why daily repentance is necessary.

Matthew 7:13-23. I must actively search for truth. Most people take the easy route and just believe whatever someone else tells them is the truth. I will stand before God on judgment day. I am responsible for my own self. People will argue with God and state they have prayed and received miracles in His name. That is not an indication of my salvation. God will answer the prayers of faith whether from a saint or sinner! I must do what the Bible says. No number of miracles takes the place of obedience. It is the fruit I bear, not the miracles God does which tells the tale. People call Him "Lord", but Jesus asked why bother if you don't obey (Luke 6:46)? Not everyone who says they're a Christian will be saved (Jeremiah 14:14; Matthew 7:21; Luke 13:25-27); even those who accept Jesus as Lord and those who received the Holy Spirit at one time (I Corinthians 12:3). I've got to obey the word. I've got to walk the walk and not just talk the talk.

Matthew 7:24-27. Good things and bad things happen to both the good people and the bad people (Matthew 5:45; Ecclesiastes 8:14). The difference is the foundation. If my foundation is built upon the ROCK (Jesus, truth), my life will stand in the storm of trials. If my foundation is built upon sand, I won't. I have a question: What is sand? Sand is ground up particles of rock. If my foundation is built on part-truth ~ truth that has been broken down, I will fail. Satan's primary weapon is the breaking down of truth. He is a master at twisting scripture. He did it to Eve and he did it to Jesus. Eve failed because she didn't know the truth (God's specific instructions). God didn't tell them not to *touch* the tree. He told them not to *eat* of the tree. Once

Satan realized Eve wasn't sure about what God had said, he was able to get her to rationalize her way into sin. Jesus passed the test because He *did know* what the scriptures said and what they meant.

Matthew 8:21-22. Jesus sounded really harsh when He told the man to "let the dead bury the dead". That is out of character for a loving God, so we must immediately reject the idea Jesus was being mean. This was not a calloused answer. "Life" can get in the way. There is always something that needs to be done. I can't put God on hold while I take care of the mundane things of life. I must do God's will and He will take care of the other stuff (Matthew 6:33). When it came time for my parents to depart to South Korea as missionaries, my mother had a similar dilemma. Her mother was dying of cancer. Should my parents delay their mission? My grandmother told my mother, "Go. I am ready to meet the Lord. There are people in South Korea who will die without God while you are waiting for me to die. Go and tell them about Jesus." Approximately 6 months after our departure, we received notice my grandmother had passed away from this life. Only eternity will tell how many people had a witness during that 6-month period of time.

Matthew 8:23-24. I am safer in the boat with Jesus than on the shore without Him (Matthew 8:23-24)! I'd rather live for God and let God speak peace into my life when the storms of life come my way. The storms are coming anyway, whether I'm living for God or not. I don't understand why people backslide in a trial. Do they really think things would be better without God?

Matthew 8:24. I want to learn to see things through God's eyes. I, in my humanity, see a storm, but God sees the storm as nap time!

Matthew 8:31-32. When the demons asked Jesus if they could go into the pigs, Jesus agreed and the pigs were killed. Satan always kills (John 10:10). Why would Jesus allow the livelihood of the residents to be destroyed? Again, when things seem out of character for God, or contradictory to another scripture, its best to investigate the circumstances. We can't arbitrarily accuse God of wrongdoing. First of all, God had declared swine were to be considered "unclean" to the Jews (Deuteronomy 14:8-10). They were violating the law given to Moses by owning pigs! They should not have been raising pigs. They were in the wrong business. Secondly, there was a pagan temple in Gadara where pigs were sacrificed to heathen gods. Not only were these people raising a crop they had no business raising, they were raising the pigs for the express purpose of providing a sacrifice to a heathen god. They were violating the first commandment by assisting others in worship to another god! They were so far removed from a relationship with God they not only failed to recognize their sin, but their economy was more important to them than the healing of the man possessed of the devil (Matthew 8:34)! When I vote for politicians, I can't just vote based on my economics. I need to vote for people who will uphold the most Biblical principles.

Matthew 9:20-22. The woman with the "issue of blood" didn't actually *touch* Jesus. She touched the HEM of His garment. She touched what was touching Him. People who have never been taught about God don't know how to touch Him. I must be touching Him, so when they touch me, they will feel His virtue. I very well may be the only "Jesus" they initially see.

Matthew 9:28. This is one of the two prayer requests Jesus had.
1. Pray for missionaries (Luke 10:2)
2. Pray I don't fall into temptation (Luke 22:40)

Matthew 9:29. Change is an issue of my faith. I will never change that which I tolerate in myself, my family, or in my job. I counseled a lady who didn't want her husband to get in church because she didn't think they could afford to pay tithes. She was griping about how hard it was to live with his sins, but yet didn't want him to get in church!! I just shook my head in amazement. The change I want to come will only come according to MY faith. Do I want to change? Do I believe God can change me? Am I ready for God to change me? If I am willing to tolerate it, God isn't going to change it.

Matthew 10:14. There are too many hungry people out there for me to fool around with those who aren't hungry. I'm glad I don't have to have it all figured out! God will help me to cross whatever bridge I need to cross when I get there (Matthew 10:19). He sends me forth. He will vindicate me. I am to sow the seed and not worry about those who refuse it. People don't reject me, they are rejecting Him (Matthew 10:20, 40).

Matthew 10:30. Isn't it amazing so many melodies can come out of just 12 notes (including half notes) in a musical scale? Wow. God most definitely had an imagination when He made music. I wonder how many songs (each with a different melody) have been written since the beginning of time? Since God has the hairs on our heads numbered, surely, He has a count. If God keeps a record of the number of hairs I have, surely, He notices other things about me ~ such as whether or not I'm having a bad day! God knows where I am at all times. He has not forsaken me. I may think He has, but He's just standing somewhere in the shadows, waiting for an invitation to take over.

Matthew 10:37. To interpret this verse to mean we can't love our family would be contradictory to other scriptures. We just can't put anyone else *before* God. Our loved ones can't take priority over God. We can't excuse the sin of our loved ones or make allowances for them to sin. Eli had a double standard for his sons and God was not happy. (I Samuel 2:12-17).

Matthew 13:3-9. The parable of the sower is a well-known parable and many sermons have been preached about it. Prepping the soil is paramount to having good soil. I don't want to be that person whose soil is hard, thorny, or devoid of nutrition. In order for me to have soil the seed of the word of God can grow and flourish in, I must prep my heart. I must spend some time getting out the roots of bitterness, the thorns of jealousy, the stones from hurts, the acid of hatred, etc., out. That takes some soul searching and some hard praying. It is not easy. Breaking up ground for planting is hard, back-breaking work. It hurts when the shovel tills the ground. It hurts to dig these things up in my heart. However, it must be done. I must have good ground. I must get the *trajectory of my heart* in the right direction.

Matthew 13:29-30. Over 500 people saw Jesus after His resurrection (I Corinthians 15:6). Only 120 tarried in the upper room (Acts 1:15). That is a 24% retention rate. A little less than 1/4 of the people who were eye-witnesses to the resurrected Christ were willing to do 'whatever it took" to develop a closer relationship. Not everyone who "believes" really and truly believes. The wheat and the weeds grow together. There is a weed that looks almost identical to monkey grass. I have to wait until that weed matures and grows up taller than the monkey grass to be able to tell the difference. Once I pull it up, I can see the root system is different. My root system MUST be rooted and grounded in truth. I can't worry about what others say. I merely trust God. He will sort it all out in the end. I just need to make sure I'm the wheat and not a weed. What is my root system like? Am I rooted and grounded in Biblical truths or are my roots shallow in human philosophies and reasoning (Colossians 2:8)?

Matthew 14:17-20. Sometimes miracles are progressive. Had Jesus multiplied enough bread and fish to feed that multitude at one time, there would have been a mountain of bread and fish on the ground! They didn't have enough baskets to handle that much food! There were over 5,000 little miracles that day! Sometimes, God chooses to perform a huge miracle in increments. Dianne was born to one of our parishioners. Dianne had no arteries and her heart was shaped like a donut instead of having four chambers. She was not expected to live past a few weeks. Her young parents sat in our office and planned her funeral. That night, Marie held the baby as we all prayed and travailed before God. Marie said she felt something like electricity hit her head and flow down her hands to Dianne. We were all convinced the baby was healed. The mom took her to the doctor and he said, "I don't know how she is still alive, but she can't last three more months. The veins will not be able to provide enough blood to her growing body." Fast-forward three months. The baby was still alive and the doctor shook his head again and made the same prediction. This scenario has repeated itself over and over again during the past twenty years! She is still alive, but they don't know how! God has healed her for the moment each time. This is every bit a miracle as it would have been had God healed completely and totally twenty years ago.

Matthew 14:28-30. All is well when I have my eyes on Jesus. If I am in a storm, I must focus on Jesus. He will either calm the waves, or take my hand. When I focus on my storm, it is impossible to walk through it. Jesus will invite me to get out of my boat. The only way I can walk out of my comfort zone is to keep my focus on Him. What other option do I have? Sink? I don't want to sink! I want to glide above the surface of my storm. I still have to go through it, but by keeping my focus on Jesus, I can walk on it, not sink under it. (See also notes by Psalm 13 in *It's Not Rocket Science, Volume 3*.)

Matthew 16:16-18. Peter blurted out Jesus was the Messiah. The church's foundation is the revelation Jesus is God in work clothes. Satan has no power over God. Satan will come against me, but will not win (Jeremiah 1:19; 15:20).

Matthew 17:17. Jesus got frustrated! He said, "How long do I have to put up with you?" It's nice to know He understands how we feel when we rant and rave in frustration! Joshua got frustrated with Israel (Joshua 18:3). People can be very frustrating. Leading a group of people is a frustrating experience. Not everyone is on the same page all of the time. When we do get "in one mind and one accord", God can really move in a miraculous way (Acts 1:14; 2:1-2).

Matthew 19:16-17. In taking a close look at the story of the "rich young ruler", I see that it was his attitude Jesus zeroed in on. He started off by complimenting Jesus, by calling Him "Good Master". In response to the young man's question, Jesus asked him a question. Jesus called his bluff by asking if the young man was indeed calling Jesus "God". Jesus likes to make us think for ourselves. It is not enough to just accept traditional teachings of the scripture. I need to know *for myself*. ***It isn't Rocket Science***, but it does require *I* know the scriptures.

Matthew 19:18-19. It is interesting to note Jesus only mentioned the human relationship commandments.

Matthew 19:20-23. The young man insisted he had kept all of the commandments. His attitude was "What else do I *have to do*?" The correct attitude is: "What can I do to get closer to God?" He was looking for Jesus to validate him. Jesus was and still is looking for more than just a rule-keeper. Jesus told him to obey Him and give his wealth. This test would reveal the true ***trajectory of the heart*** of this young man. (See essay entitled "Me 'N' You Stick Together Like Glue" in *It's Not Rocket Science, Volume 1*.)
1. If he gave his wealth to family & friends, he would have the opportunity to get it back. Jesus wanted him to burn his bridges.
2. Giving money to strangers sounds insane to family & friends. Was he willing to obey Jesus at that cost?
3. This was a test to see if the young man would blindly obey and trust Jesus. The military requires blind obedience and trust of its officers! So does God! Why is it easier to trust the military and not God?

Matthew 19:24. There are a couple of explanations of this verse and they both make the same point. Both of these scenarios are possible, but very difficult. Jesus was saying it is possible for the rich man to enter into heaven, but he had a lot of obstacles to overcome.
1. "Camel" referred to a rope too large to go through the eye of a needle. The rope had to be first unraveled and separated into strands before it could be used as thread. This was a huge project and only a serious seamstress was willing to tackle the job.
2. "Eye of the needle". Refers to a small opening in the wall for "after-hours" only. A merchant who arrived at a city after the gates were closed, had to take his wares through this small opening in order to be protected by the city walls. To do so, his camel had to be first unloaded. The wares had to be hand-carried through the opening. Then, the camel had to be made to sit down on all fours and scoot through the opening. The wares then had to be reloaded onto the camel before the merchant could proceed to his destination. What a difficult process!

Matthew 19:26. God wants to know (or actually, He already knows, but He wants ME to know) what I am willing to "bring to the table". I've got to do my part. He will do the rest (the impossible). There is no miracle without my efforts or involvement. (Ref. John 6:5). After my involvement, not only will He perform the miracle, He will do it "over the top" (John 6:13).

Matthew 20:16; 22:14. Comparing is not wise. I must work for God, do what He has called me to do, and be content (II Corinthians 10:12).

Matthew 20:22. I must be careful what I ask for. God just might answer my prayer but it may be not at all what I thought I was asking for! God knows the big picture. I don't ever want God to answer a prayer if it would be to my detriment, both spiritually and physically. Sure, I would love to be a millionaire, but if a lot of money would cause me to veer away from God, I don't really want it.

Matthew 20:23. There is a place of fellowship with His suffering (Philippians 3:10). When we suffer with someone, we develop a kinship. Victims of disasters have a special bonding. We all want to share in the glory and blessings of serving God, but it is when we go through some of the same sufferings Jesus went through that we develop a deeper bond with Him. Do I want to feel rejection? Oh, no, but when I do, I am reminded of the rejection Jesus felt on the cross. Even his closest friends, the disciples who had been with Him through miracle after miracle, turned their backs on Him. Do I want to be publicly ridiculed and humiliated for my stand on holiness and righteousness? Oh no, but when I do, I am relating to the public humiliation He endured all of His life as a bastard child and on the cross. Our shared emotional experience binds me to Him even more! If Jesus could overcome, so can I with His help!

Matthew 20:26. God respects those who will humble themselves enough to serve others. This is the opposite of pride. Humility is not thinking less of yourself. Humility is thinking of yourself less. There is a difference.

Matthew 21:16. Was Jesus misquoting Psalm 8:2? Is the Bible contradicting itself? NO! To think those two questions are even possible would be to discount the whole Bible. Jesus is really saying there is strength in my praise! When I praise even though I am having difficulties, I will receive strength to plow through them and be an overcomer.

Matthew 21:24. I love that Jesus generally answered a question by asking a question, thereby forcing the questioner to answer his own question!

Matthew 22:10-14. Who are the chosen ones? The ones wearing the wedding garment. What is the wedding garment? The Robe of Righteousness (Isaiah 61:10). How is my robe made white? Through the blood of the Lamb (Revelation 7:14). It is not that God has predestined who would or would not be saved. I make that choice. When I choose to separate myself unto God, He chooses me. The path to salvation is what is predestined.

Matthew 23 synopsis: Don't split hairs over "issues". The question is not "What can I get away with and still be saved?", but a prayerful "How can I get closer to God?" Vs. 26: True holiness is the cleanness of the INSIDE. The _**trajectory of the heart**_ makes the outside man clean, not vice versa. The scriptures most definitely teach separation from the world, but it does no good to clean up the outside if the inside is dirty. Vs. 37: God is saying "I wanted to hold you, bless and protect you, but you chose to operate outside my umbrella of protection. My life of separation is for naught if my attitudes/heart is in the wrong place. (See I Corinthians 13:1-3).
Definition of a hypocrite, as defined by Jesus. Hypocrites:
1. Don't practice what they preach (vs 3).
2. Demand too much of others (vs 4).
3. Boast (vs 5).
4. Expect special seating at events (vs 6).
5. Love having a title (vs 7).
6. Exalt themselves (vs 12).
7. Take advantage of the unfortunate (vs 14).
8. Travel under the pretense of a mission's trip, yet the converts are worse off (vs 15).
9. Proud of their offerings & tithing to the point they think they own the church (vs 17).
10. Live by the "rules", but neglect the "heart" issues (vs 23).

Matthew 23:2. The Pharisees were masters at NOT practicing what they preached. They had "head knowledge" but not "heart knowledge". That is a very, very dangerous position to take, because I end up deceiving myself. I'm certainly not deceiving God! He knows if my actions match my rhetoric!

Matthew 23:12. If I don't humble myself, God will humble me.

Matthew 23:26. True holiness: The inside, when clean, will clean up the outside, not vice-versa. I don't get good to get God. I get God to get good. Having said that, if my outside doesn't clean up after I follow the plan of salvation, then something is wrong. I am rejecting the prompting and leading of the Spirit of God. That will result in a DI-gression, not a progression of my spiritual state. I will quickly become a follower of Christ by mouth and not by actions.

Matthew 23:28-33. Jesus exposed the *trajectory of their hearts.* Jesus ended up calling them out and letting them know exactly what their fate would be. Exposure is, in my opinion, the last act of mercy before mercy steps aside and allows judgment to come. I've seen God deal with so many people in different ways - powerful services, sermons, etc., trying to get them to repent. After they refuse Him so many times, God has no choice but to expose their sin publicly. If that doesn't bring repentance, they have damned themselves. The pharisees had a long history of not listening to the prophets sent by God. They wouldn't even listen to God Himself.

Matthew 24:5. *Many* will be deceived. The only way to make sure I'm not one of the deceived is to get in the scripture and don't let anyone talk me into doing anything the contrary. Logic doesn't come in to play here. Obedience does.

Matthew 24:10. *Many* will backslide because of offences. I can't allow what someone does to me affect my relationship with God.

Matthew 24:24. Careful ~ even the most spiritual of us all is subject to deception. I've got to keep my eye focused on Jesus and His word and not on others.

Matthew 24:30-31. The pharisees kept asking for a sign from Heaven to prove Jesus was God, even though they had all of the prophecies from the Old Testament (John 2:8). They'll finally get their sign, but it will be too late for them. Their unbelief will cost them.

Matthew 24:50-51. The hypocrite has a place to go. I'm not going to worry about them. I'm not going to stress over a hypocrite who has the pastor or other church members fooled. God will take care of him/her in due time.

Matthew 25:1-14. *ALL* 10 virgins (even the ones who ran out of oil) were pure, moral, and set apart. They were "good people". They had to have known the bridegroom or they would not have been invited to the wedding! All 10 slept, but when they had the "wake-up call", 5 of them realized they didn't have enough oil to keep their lamps lit. The 5 who were not adequately prepared, blamed their lamps (vs 8)! Human nature is to always blame something or someone else. They frantically tried to get things right, but the bridegroom came, and the door was shut before they could get back with their oil. The bridegroom claimed to not know them (vs 12). Why? This speaks of relationship. Relationship is a 2-way street. If they had known Him, they would have known to be prepared. It is only by the Holy Spirit that I can call Him "Lord" (I Corinthians 12:3). The Foolish Five had had *some* oil, but it ran out. People who once received the Holy Spirit and then backslide know enough to call Him "Lord", but they no longer have what it takes to make it to Heaven. Just as a soldier on guard duty must stay focused and diligent; just as a driver must not get sleepy behind the wheel, I must keep myself on guard and prepared for the coming of the Lord (or for my death). I can't afford to go to sleep spiritually, nor can I afford to not be prayed up and full of the oil of the Holy Spirit. It is the Holy Spirit which will enable me to break gravity (Romans 8:11) and go to Heaven.

Matthew 25:15-30. God only demands of me what I am capable of doing. He didn't give each servant an equal number of talents. He doled the talents out, expecting the servants to do something productive with the money. The master gave his servants a long time (vs 19) to produce results. What assets has God given me? How can I use those assets for His glory? Some people are so very creative but if they are not using that creativity for God, they have nothing to return to Him at the end of the day. My work here on earth is either temporal or eternal. Only what is done for Christ is eternal. I will have to use my skills ~ actually, they're not *my* skills, but the skills God has doled out to me ~ to make a living for myself and my family here on earth, but if I'm not also using those skills to further the kingdom of God, God is not pleased (vs 30).

Matthew 25:24. Isn't it interesting the servant who was lazy and did nothing accused the master of being a hard man! So, it is in church situations. The people who sit on a pew and do nothing are the first ones to criticize leadership. The issue with this servant isn't that he only had one skill set. The issue is he was lazy and wasn't productive (vs 26). Laziness and wickedness go hand in hand. Am I a griper and grumbler in the church? I need to find something to do. If I refuse, God will ultimately move me out of the way. I must be a *productive* saint. This entire chapter is telling me how to be prepared for the coming of the Lord. The parable of the 10 virgins is about being *spiritually ready*. The talents parable is about being a *worker*. I must be both. Faith without works is dead and works without faith is pharisee-ism. Pastor: Sure, the pew-warmers may give in the offering, but they drag the church down if they're not working for God. Even Jesus said to shake the dust off your feet if someone was not receptive. There are too many HUNGRY people out there for us to be bogged down with the gripers and grumblers. They are time consuming, draining, and pointless (if they refuse to change). Be patient and merciful, but at some point, wash your hands (with love).

Matthew 25:35-46. God takes how I treat my fellow man personally (I Samuel 8:7; Isaiah 25:4). I need to be conscious of that. Do I have road rage? Do I cut someone off? I'm cutting God off. Am I ugly to the sales clerk? I am being ugly to God. Am I snooty and look down on the homeless? I'm looking down at God. I am an extension of God. I am a billboard for God. Just as He treats me, so must I treat others (Isaiah 25:4). He has shown me much mercy and grace. I will show the same to others.

Matthew 26:1-5. It is very easy to skim or gloss over little nuggets sandwiched between eye-catching passages. The subject of this passage is the beginning of the serious plot to take Jesus, however, Jesus revealed to His disciples exactly when He would be betrayed: 2 days after the Passover (vs 2). God reveals secrets to His friends. (See essay entitled "Me 'N' You Stick Together Like Glue" in *It's Not Rocket Science, Volume 1.*) How many times has God tried to tell me something and I have been too consumed with the "big" picture that I fail to recognize He's already revealed it all to me? God told Moses Pharaoh's heart would repeatedly harden, but Moses was "shocked" when it happened and questioned God (Exodus 5:22-23)! God knows the end result. God tells us the end result. All we have to do is trust Him and go along for the ride! A second point that strikes me in this passage is the priests were concerned about taking Jesus on a feast day, because of the people. Why does a specific day matter? When I was a child, there was the "blue law", which stated no retail establishment could be open on a Sunday. I live in an area where certain days of the year are considered sacred, and one must not sin on those days! Wwhhhaaattt? *Every* day is a day to live for God! *Every* day is holy unto God. I must live a separated life, free from sin *every* day. It's good to know if I do trip up and commit a sin, God is faithful to forgive when I repent (I John 1:9).

Matthew 26:7-13. Much has been said about the woman with the alabaster box. Did you ever notice in vs 8, it is recorded that ALL of the disciples were upset with her offering? Judas was the only one who took that indignation to the next level, but all of the disciples were offended she "wasted" her precious oil on Jesus! They all had a good idea. Sell it and give it to the poor! Helping the poor is very scriptural. They had learned that lesson, however, they were misguided due to their ignorance. Ignorance gets me in trouble more often than I care to admit! It really wasn't their place to judge her, was it? This offering was between the woman and Jesus. They were merely bystanders. It would have been Jesus' place to rebuke her, not the disciples'. It is human nature to barge into someone else's business, but I really need to just mind my own. Judas took his indignation too far. It is fine to get angry if I don't let that anger push me into sin (Ephesians 4:26). Jesus confirmed with them for the 2nd time He would be betrayed and also told them He would die (vs 2). Sometimes God gives us revelation a little bit at a time. We have a hard time digesting the entire message at once. He was gently, lovingly trying to prepare them for the huge trial which is coming. Remember, they were still thinking of the glorious, triumphant Messiah who would deliver them from their Roman oppressors. It hadn't quite dawned on the disciples Jesus was the fulfillment of the overlooked scriptures concerning the suffering Messiah who would be punished for their sins. Jesus tried to gently ease them into the difficult times ahead. How many times do I miss His clues? God doesn't just allow me to be thrown unawares into a trial. He will prepare me, if I will take the time to listen. Jesus correctly predicted the offering of this woman would be told throughout the ages (vs 13). My offering matters to God. My sacrifice is duly noted by God. I'm not worried about the accolades I don't receive here on earth. God knows.

Matthew 26:14-16. Judas' betrayal was premeditated and carefully schemed. There was plenty of time for his conscious to prick him. There was plenty of time for him to change his mind and repent. There is a difference between a rash, spur-of-the moment sin and a willful, wanton sin. If the *trajectory of my heart* is right, I will readily repent of the rash sin. The premeditated sins show a disregard for God's law and show how off my trajectory is. It is a much more serious matter because I don't recognize how off course I have gotten. It is a much longer road to get back to God. Jesus had to die to fulfil the prophecies (vs 24), but Judas didn't have to be the one to betray Him. Jesus' public exposure of Judas gave him one more chance to repent of his intent (vs 25). Likewise, it is true the world will disintegrate to the point it will welcome the Antichrist, but that doesn't have to happen on my shift!

Matthew 26:17-20. Jesus celebrated religious holidays. These holidays were simply days set apart to REMEMBER something about God and His character. The days weren't "holy", per se, but days set apart and designed to make mankind stop and remember. The Passover was for the Israelites to remember God had miraculously delivered them from the tyranny of Egyptian bondage. Many went through the motions of the rituals without remembering, though. The Pharisees even declared they had never been in bondage (John 8:33)! This shows me the Pharisees had "commercialized" the Passover and had forgotten its true meaning. Yet, Jesus soberly commemorated it. Days such as Christmas and Easter are meant to commemorate certain events. The secular world has twisted them into a different meaning, but it is still appropriate to celebrate the incarnation: the birth and resurrection of Jesus. Both of those events are big deals in a Christian's life!

Matthew 26:24-25. Jesus never set out to humiliate Judas, even though Jesus knew Judas was the one who would betray Him. Jesus gave Judas a chance to reconsider his plans. Judas claimed innocence and so Jesus was forced to identify Judas as the betrayer. Ultimate mercy and last chance are usually exposure. If exposure doesn't cause repentance, I become a reprobate. "Lord, help me not to feign innocence when I know I am guilty."

Matthew 26:34-56. Jesus warned Peter and tried to get him to prepare for his upcoming trial. Synopsis:
- Peter, you are in a perilous position.
- Jesus called a prayer meeting.
- Peter didn't pray.
- Jesus warned again if you don't pray, you'll be too weak to overcome your trial.
- Peter slept through the warning.
- Peter fell into temptation.
- Jesus prayed three times. Peter denied three times.
- When Jesus prayed, the angels ministered unto Him (Luke 22-43).

Had Peter and the others prayed, they would have had the strength necessary to overcome the night's trial.

Matthew 26:38. Have you ever experienced sorrow "unto death"? Have you ever lost something or someone and hurt so badly, you thought your heart would explode in your chest? Jesus knows the feeling. He understands. He can help you with that pain. Jesus was so stressed out he sweated blood (hematidrosis). What was He so stressed over? He knew He would experience pain, but He had surely experienced that before in His life. Jesus had done carpentry work. Surely, He had hammered his thumb or cut his hand before. He understood pain. He also knew He would experience sin for the first time ever. He had never *not* had God's presence in His life. He was afraid of the unknown.

Matthew 26:39, 42. It is okay to ask God to deliver me from a trial as long as I ultimately surrender to His will. God doesn't mind me praying specific prayers for a specific result. I must remember He knows what is ultimately the best path and I must surrender to that, even if it means some temporary, although extreme, discomfort. It may be the death of a loved one or my own sickness. If an unfortunate event results in someone's salvation, isn't that more important than my selfish prayers? I have to trust God.

Matthew 26:44. Two thoughts on this verse: (1) This time, Jesus let them sleep. At what point will God stop trying to shake me awake? At what point will God give up? I must be careful not to spurn Him so much He just leaves me be. (2) There is a time when I must persevere and fight my own battles *by myself*. I can't depend on others to pray FOR me or even WITH me. It is nice when they do, but I can't depend on others and neglect to pray myself. Jesus had to do Gethsemane alone.

Matthew 26:45-46. There is a time to get up from praying, and start doing. When the action begins to take place, I don't have time to stop and pray. My praying needs to be done AHEAD of my trial. It is so very important to maintain a consistent prayer life. Many people, even Christians, get into a crises mode and discover they don't know how to pray. Many Christians are so involved with church activities, they forget to pray until the crises hits. Decorating for a banquet, practicing music, or baking for a bake sale does not prepare me for my upcoming trial. Prayer does. I can't neglect to pray. I am going to have another trial. Trials don't stop because I've conquered the last one! At any given time in my life, I am in one of three places: (1) I've just come out of a trial, (2) I'm in a trial, or (3) I'm getting ready to go into a trial. Trials are pesky things that keep popping up. Once my trial hits me, I have to walk through it or be devoured by it. Stay Prepared.

Matthew 26:51-52. Jesus rebuked the disciple who cut off the ear of the high priest's servant. The disciple had good intentions! He was trying to defend Jesus. He reverted to his upbringing of self-defense instead of God-defense. He probably was trying to cut off the man's head and got the ear instead. Even though he "meant well", Jesus rebuked him. Why? Because you always *reap what you sow*. Two wrongs don't make a right. If I do wrong, even though it is a well-meaning act, I must suffer the consequences of my wrong action. Time and time again in the Old Testament, God used neighboring nations to chastise the nation of Israel, but then God had to punish those nations for their sin of coming against Israel. The prevalent teaching is the ends justify the means. This is not Biblical and in fact, is actually anti-Biblical. Ephesians 4:26 states "be ye angry and sin not". I must make sure when I see an injustice, I do not try to correct it with a sin. I'm going to let God be God. He doesn't need me to right a wrong (verse 53).

Matthew 26:53-54. Just because you can, doesn't mean you should. Jesus could have called down angels to deliver Him from the mob. He could have just "poof", disappeared. However, that would have aborted the ultimate plan for the salvation of mankind. He could have, and actually wanted to (remember, He prayed He would be spared - vs 39), but He knew He shouldn't and therefore, didn't. Sometimes I may be within my rights to say something or to do something. That doesn't mean I should do or say that thing. I need to learn and know when to do and when to refrain.

Matthew 26:55. People are very fickle. Don't trust accolades by man. Do what is right. Do what is good. Do what is Biblical. I won't ever be able to please everyone. Jesus couldn't. What makes me think I can? Therefore, I must please God. That is the only thing that matters. What (or who) is important today will not be important tomorrow. One hundred years from now, what will matter? Only that I pleased God.

Matthew 26:56. *ALL* of the disciples forsook Jesus. Even John. Remember that. *All* of them failed. *However,* everyone but Judas eventually came back. It's not my failures that matter; my bounce back matters. In the heat of the moment, I may fail. I don't want to and I pray I don't, but I am human and failure is a strong possibility.

I must shake off that failure, repent, and get back to where I need to be in God. He's got a big heart! He'll forgive and forget my sin (I John 1:9; Jeremiah 31:34)! I must end my race well (Matthew 10:22).

Matthew 26:58. Curiosity got the best of Peter and he hung around. He kept denying he knew Jesus (vs 69-74), but ultimately repented and became a powerhouse for God (Acts 2). I need to be patient with those who backslide but still want to "hang around". They just might "come around"!

Matthew 26:60. Jesus was killed by lies. These false witnesses couldn't even get their stories straight (Mark 14:58-59). Nevertheless, the court accepted their testimony. Satan is the originator of all lies (John 8:44). He will try to kill each one of us with a lie. "You're all alone. You don't deserve God. No one loves you. God won't forgive you." These are some of the favorite lies Satan used to kill.

Matthew 27:3-4. Isn't it interesting that those whom Judas thought was on his team, ultimately threw him under the bus? When I set about to please the "in" crowd and things go badly, they aren't going to stick with me. They're going to distance themselves from me. Judas set out to make some money and do the religious rulers a big favor. When he realized he had sinned against God, he attempted to undo his mistake. The religious rulers had already dismissed him as a piece of trash. They had used him and were through with him. Oh, if he had only repented before God! It is never enough to repent before man. Man might not forgive me. Man might turn against me. I must repent before God! If I have done someone wrong, I must ask their forgiveness, but all wrongs are ultimately sins against God (Psalm 51:4). I must repent before God as well. Judas was sorry, but never repented. Repentance means to make a U-turn. Repentance goes beyond being sorry. Repentance causes me to change my course. Had he repented, he could have experienced "the promise" in Acts 2, and what a testimony he could have had!

Matthew 27:12-14. Jesus knew when to keep His mouth shut. Our mouths get us into so much trouble. A dog can whip a skunk, but it is just not worth it. Likewise, sometimes it just may be prudent to be quiet and hold my peace, even though inwardly I know I'm right.

Matthew 27:18. Jealousy is murderous.

Matthew 27:19-26. Pilate was warned through his wife not to pass judgment against Jesus. Judas was warned in Matthew 26:24. The Jewish people had a chance to think about whether or not they wanted Jesus or Barabas (a thief, a murderer, and one who incited riots - Mark 15:7, John 18:40). God is always fair and warns us when we are about to make a mistake, if I am in tune with His voice and heed His warnings. We sometimes choose to ignore those warning signals and then complain when we reap the consequences of our decisions. Pilate's warning came from another person, his wife. Judas' warning came directly from Jesus. The Jews were warned by their leadership (Pilate). The Jews also had a chance to lean on their own innate logic, intuition, and experience. Regardless of the source, I have been duly warned. On judgment day, I will be without excuse (Romans 1:20).

Matthew 27:27-31, 38-44. Jesus was the laughing stock of the soldiers, of the religious leaders, of convicted felons, and of those passing by. He was the subject of ridicule and bullying. The soldiers made sport of tormenting Him. The people taunted Him. When we go through similar hazing at school, home or at work, He knows how that feels. Down in verse 54, we see some of those who persecuted Jesus had a revelation He was indeed the Christ, but it was a little too late. They had already done their awful deeds. Perhaps some of them went on to participate in the Day of Pentecost and be saved, but there still would have been consequences for their actions. The Law of the Harvest is in place.

Matthew 27:32. When our trials are just too much to bear, God will place someone in our lives to help us carry the load. It may be the kind word of a stranger. It may be the prayers of an unknown person. It may be the spirit of God speaking peace and hope in our hearts. God never just leaves us out alone. We are *never* alone.

Matthew 27:33. Jesus was crucified at the place of the skull. My death to sin still needs to take place at the skull/mind. The battlefield of my soul takes place in my mind. I have to have a made-up mind. If my focus is on pleasing God, every decision I make will be based upon that focus. I must reign in my thoughts and imaginations (II Corinthians 10:5; I Peter 1:13). My focus is important. If my focus is on being saved, things will be difficult because I will have to split hairs over whether or not each decision I make is a heaven or hell issue. If my focus is on pleasing God, my decisions are easy. When I focus on pleasing God, I become more and more like Him and His ways/thoughts become my ways/thoughts. If something is pleasing to God, I want to do it, even if it is not a salvational issue. Living for God is easy when my focus is on pleasing Him.

Matthew 27:46. This scripture confuses a lot of people. Jesus was both fully man and fully God. Jesus had *never known* what it was like not to have God's presence with Him. God cannot tolerate sin (Exodus 33:3; Revelation 21:27). Therefore, when the sins of mankind were placed upon Jesus, the intimacy and communion between the humanity of Jesus and His deity was severed. For the first time, Jesus felt the condemnation and heaviness which comes with sin. For the first time, Jesus felt what a sinner feels. He felt abandoned, although God's presence was still abiding. It was at this point in His life Jesus could finally relate to humanity on all levels, qualifying Him to be our mediator (Hebrews 4:15; I Timothy 2:5)

Matthew 27:60. Jesus was buried in someone else's tomb. This man had *already* prepared it. He had to hew a place out of a rock. There are so many lessons to learn from this. My primary thought is this man (Joseph) had worked very hard prepping the grave. He actually prepared it for his own burial. When he was chiseling out the rock, he was thinking of his own death. Perhaps he contemplated his life and how he had lived it. Perhaps he did a lot of soul searching during that time. He made a decision to offer his own, personal grave for Jesus to use. He probably didn't think Jesus would be merely borrowing it! He probably thought he was donating his grave. He had a giving heart. How many times do pastors and teachers pour themselves into people and work hard in an area, but don't realize the fruit of their labor? Does it matter? Aren't we working for God and not for our own personal kingdom? Does it matter who gets the credit for what I do? God knows. God will take care of me. God will provide. God will reward ~ maybe not until I get to Heaven, but He will reward. I don't need to worry about that part. I need to keep working, keep chiseling, keep hewing out a place for Him. My husband has resigned the pastorate of two churches as soon as he felt a release from God. Both times, I had a slight "panic" over our finances. "Oh, no! Whatever shall we do?" (Said in my most British accent!) However, I have been around churches long enough and have seen many pastors who stayed at the churches they pastored long past their time. These churches died a slow death because the pastor hung on too long. I admire my husband for being brave enough to following the leading of God's spirit. We've never reaped the fruits of our labor, but others have. I admit, it is hard to see it sometimes, but God has already blessed us enough. Isn't it funny how we view things backwards? We think God should reward our hard work for Him when in actuality, we should work hard for Him to reward HIM for all He's done for us!

Matthew 27:63-64. There's always someone who will attempt to explain the spiritual with the natural. I suspect when the rapture of the church occurs, scientists or politicians will be able to spin a tale to explain it away. I don't intend to be here to find out, though!

Matthew 28:3-4; 12-15. Bribery has always been around, even in church! The grave guards passed out when Jesus came out of the tomb. After they came to and reported on what happened, they were given hush money to twist the facts. Nothing has changed. Don't believe anything you hear and only about half of what you see ... or actually, with the digital age and Photoshop, don't believe much of what you see, either!

Matthew 28:16-17. Some of the 11 remaining disciples still doubted, even after *seeing* Jesus! Not everyone in my family or church is going to be on the same page as each other all of the time. Eventually, these 11 did get in "one mind and in one accord", but that wasn't until they had spent quite some time praying together and taking care of church business (see Acts 1-2). I must be patient when others have a different level of commitment or are at a different place in their walk with God than I am. As long as their *trajectory* is right, they'll get to where they need to be.

God will see to that. God will lead and guide anyone whose trajectory is right. Likewise, there is always someone from whom I can learn. Someone is ahead of me on the path. We need to help each other get to Heaven. "Lord, I believe. Help Thou my unbelief" (Mark 9:24; Luke 1:8-20).

Matthew 28:18-20. This passage is to be compared with the others that record the same event for a full picture of what Jesus said (see Mark 16:15-17; Luke 24:47-49; Acts 1:8). Jesus reiterated the New Testament plan of salvation and healing. By merging all accounts of this same incident, we find Jesus reinforced His previous teachings about (1) repentance, (2) baptism, (3) receiving the Holy Spirit, (4) living a holy, separated life, and (5) healing. His speech that day was His parting words to His disciples. He summarized what He had been teaching them for the past 3 years. They understood *exactly* what He meant; obeyed and taught the same things (See Acts & Epistles). The words, "father, son, Holy Spirit" denote *relationship*. These words are not proper nouns. I cannot cash a check signed by "mother, daughter, aunt". The check must have a proper name, or the bank will not honor it. Likewise, baptism is to be performed in His name. Jesus is the proper name.

MARK

Written to the Romans, who were big on having servants. Theme: Jesus, the servant. As the son of Abraham, Jesus is entitled to the land. As a servant, finesse is not important.

Mark 1:4-8. The New Testament plan of salvation was introduced by John the Baptist. His existence had been foretold in the Old Testament (Isaiah 40:3; Matthew 3:3). John preached (1) confession & repentance. Confession brings realization of sin, but not the power to overcome sin. (2) Baptism. John baptized unto repentance. This is because the ultimate sacrifice (Jesus) had not yet been paid. Baptism is for the remission of sins. This means expungement of the record. Remission goes beyond forgiveness. Remission means the sin is totally erased and done away with. (3) John preached the baptism of the Holy Spirit. Again, Jesus had not yet been glorified, so this baptism was for the future. The Holy Spirit is what gives us the *power* to overcome sin (Acts 1:8).

Mark 1:6. John the Baptist ate off the land. Most translations say he ate locusts. One says grasshoppers. The Wycliffe Bible translates it as honeysuckle. Most scholars believe John, like Samson, was instructed to take the Nazarite vow (Luke 1:15; see also Numbers 6:1-17). At any rate, he was reclusive and poor but had a powerful message.

Mark 1:12-13. The devil often comes right after a spiritual victory or experience. We are not ignorant of his devices (II Corinthians 2:11). We can expect a trial after a victory. The victorious experience gives me the faith to walk through my trial. I know God has just given me a victory. Therefore, He can get me through the next trial.

Mark 1:15. Repentance and faith go hand in hand. They cannot be separated. Faith demands action. Believing the gospel means I will take action. I believe the bridge is sturdy, therefore I travel across the bridge. I believe the gospel is true, therefore I obey it. This is a conscientious decision I make. If I say with my mouth I believe, but I don't obey, then my actions tell God and the rest of the world I really don't believe. Let's go back to the bridge. If I say I believe the bridge is sturdy, but I steadfastly refuse to travel across it, everyone knows I have some hesitation and doubt concerning that bridge. My actions deny my lip service. It really is just a matter of faith! It's that simple. ***It's not rocket science!***

Mark 1:23-24. The demons knew who Jesus was even before He cast them out. Never underestimate the spirit world. The devil is smart. He has the advantage of seeing spiritual matters and being around such a long time that he's had the chance to study human behavior. The devil is really an expert in both spiritual and human matters. He is pretty good at guessing how a scenario will play out. ***However***, he is powerless up against Jesus. He also does not have any power that is not given to him. If I surrender to his temptations, I am giving him power over me. If I have the Holy Spirit, I have the power to overcome and say "no" to those temptations and am surrendering myself to the protection of Jesus. It is one or the other. I can't serve two masters (Matthew 6:24).

Mark 1:32, 34. *All* of the sick were brought to Jesus and *many* were healed. In light of the bigger picture, and for reasons maybe only God knows, not everyone is healed. (See essay entitled "Is God Deaf?" in *It's Not Rocket Science, Volume 1*.)

Mark 1:35. Corporate or community prayer is good, but sometimes I need to separate myself and have some alone time with God. Jesus did that on more than one occasion. It is just like any other relationship. We all love get-togethers with family and friends, but there is a point when a relationship just needs "alone time". If I'm going to develop that "friend of God" relationship, I must spend some time alone with Him. Just singing about friendship doesn't make it real any more than me sitting in McDonald's makes me a hamburger (although I might smell like one)!

Mark 1:44. Isn't it interesting that after Jesus healed the leper, he told him to go and submit to the law of Moses? Jesus came to fulfil the law (Matthew 5:17), but until his resurrection, the ceremonial law was still in place. (The moral law was never abolished.) Jesus himself even obeyed the law.

Mark 1:45. We sing about how the leper just couldn't keep the miracle to himself. We applaud him for testifying of his miraculous healing. However, the truth of the matter is this: he disobeyed Jesus. Because of his disobedience, Jesus' ministry in the city was curtailed. How many people did NOT get their miracle because of the leper's disobedience? I must obey God, even if human wisdom thinks otherwise. There is a bigger picture out there than me and my story.

Mark 2:17. Miracles are an attraction to sinners, but the motive is to get sinners to repent. Miracles attract people so the gospel of salvation can be preached. Miracles are the attraction. Salvation is the message.

Mark 3:5. God gets angry ... especially at stubbornness!

Mark 3:12. Satan knew who Jesus was, but Jesus would not allow Satan to expose Him (yet). Timing is important. I must work with God's timing and not be impatient.

Mark 3:14-15. Jesus ordained the twelve for a specific purpose: (1) to be with him, (2) to tell others, (3) to have power to heal, and (4) to have power over demons. If I spend some time with Him, I have a chance of becoming more and more like Him. The more I am like Him, the other 3 purposes will fall into place. If I concentrate on spending time with Jesus and becoming like Him, I don't have to worry about anything else.

Mark 4:8. There are different levels of spiritual maturity (or fruitfulness). Not everyone is going to be on the same level, and that's ok. The requirement is to be fruitful. He said that in the beginning (Genesis 1:22), again to Noah (Genesis 9:1), and says it to me. There is no quota mentioned, just to be fruitful.

Mark 4:14-20. The main thing I take away from the parable of the sower is this: three-fourths of the seed ultimately did not prosper. Only one-fourth of the seed actually took root and lived. I'm not going to be discouraged when three-fourths of the people I work with backslide. I need to focus on the one-fourth who will live for God. I need to make sure I have prepped *my* soil so that I am part of the 1/4 who thrive. There are 4 types of soil: (1) Wayside ground. These people immediately reject God. (2) Stony ground. These people live for God a little while and then get offended and backslide. Shallow people are easily offended. (3) Thorny ground. These people allow things to push God out of their lives, such as worry, materialism & lusts. (4) Good ground. These people listen and obey. The word of God can grow and flourish in their lives!

Mark 4:20. I need to keep my "soil" prepped. Only when my soil (heart) is properly prepared, can I receive the word of God and it will take root and grow. Jesus told his disciples (in the Garden) to watch and pray "lest ye enter into temptation" (Mark 14:38). I prepare my heart by being on the lookout for evil and by praying. If Peter had been praying, he wouldn't have fallen into temptation and denied

Jesus. If he had been watching, he wouldn't have been caught off guard when they came to arrest Jesus. He wouldn't have had a knee-jerk reaction and sliced off someone's ear!

Mark 4:39. "Peace, be still". God brings peace first, then takes care of the crises. He told Jarius not to be afraid (spoke peace) in Mark 5:36, but his daughter wasn't healed until verse 42. Paul & Silas told the jailer to believe and he would be saved (spoke peace) and, after explaining what they meant, the jailer was baptized (Acts 16:31-33). I don't need to preach the whole entire Bible to people when they are in a crisis situation. I just need to speak peace into their crises. The rest will come in due time, if they have a heart for God.

Mark 5:25-34. Jesus healed the woman with the issue of blood (Mark 5:25-34). Life is in the blood (Genesis 9:4; Leviticus 17:11). Could this be applied to the issues of life? Do I have an "issue of life"? Jesus can heal me. Am I endlessly grieving over the loss of a loved one? Jesus can heal me. Am I stressed over a relationship? Jesus can heal me.

Mark 6:11, 34. In verse 11, Jesus instructed His disciples not to spend the time of day with those who rejected truth, however, in vs 34, we see that Jesus was moved with compassion. What was the difference between the people? In verse 11, the people rejected truth. Truth was presented to them and they rejected it. In verse 34, we find that the religious leaders had not done their job and the people had never been exposed to truth. Therein lies the difference. I've got to stop wasting my time with people who have heard but refuse to obey and focus on those who are hungry for God.

Mark 6:37-43. Jesus performed a miracle with the loaves and fishes, but the disciples had to identify, organize, and deliver it (Mark 6:37-43). Am I doing my part? Is Jesus trying to accomplish something in the church, but am I refusing to deliver it? Is Jesus trying to answer a prayer request of someone, but am I too lazy to do my part? God does the impossible. He does not do the possible. That is my job.

Mark 6:48-49. The disciples were in a storm. Jesus walked on the water and would have passed by, but they cried out. God will not force himself upon me. He knows I need Him, but I must "cry out" and ask for His help and intervention. Failing to cry out to Him when I need Him is (1) pride and (2) results in an unanswered prayer.

Mark 6:51-52. Even Jesus' disciples had bouts of unbelief! In our humanity, sometimes we forget about the miracles in our lives when faced with a present daunting situation. I must remember that Jesus can do the impossible! I must trust Him! In my attempt to have a "present" relationship with God (as opposed to living on past experiences), I must not forget the past! Past experiences, blessings and miracles are a foundation to give me faith for the present and the future. I may not know *how* He will get me through my present situation, but I know He *will*. When I realize this, my stress level is reduced dramatically! Most children don't stress over dinner! A child may not know *what* s/he will eat, but s/he is confident that Mom will come up with something!

Mark 7:3, 7. Vain worship is teaching man's traditions instead of God's doctrine. Some traditions are good practices, sure, but the Pharisees turned them into heaven/hell issues. Traditions of men undermines the commandments of God (Mark 7:8, 13). Defilement comes from within, not from without. Outward appearance and actions are a reflection of the inward man. (Mark 7:15, 21-23). Missionaries can attest to the fact that some things are culturally wrong. That doesn't mean it is wrong in another culture. We must preach the Bible and the Bible alone. Leave cultural protocol to the protocol police and just preach Jesus and the way to salvation!

Mark 7:15, 18-23. What can separate me from the love of God? Nothing but myself. I can take myself out of God's hand! No outside force can. Only my innermost heart can turn God away from me. My sin is what repels God (Romans 8:38-39).

Mark 10:30. Remember English 101? Diagraming sentences is good to know! If we diagram this verse, we find the root message is we will receive blessings in this life accompanied by persecution, as well as the blessing of eternal life. So, why are we surprised and feel abandoned when we face trials?

Mark 12: 16-17. What bears the image of God? I do (Genesis 1:27). All God wants is ME! He wants my heart.

Mark 12:24. These were religious leaders, but they didn't know God's word! Knowing religious traditions is not important and my knowledge won't save me. I've got to know what God says.

Mark 12:25. There is no need for marriage in Heaven because marriage is an example of our relationship with God.

Mark 12:30-31, 33. True holiness is *love* ... Everything else falls into place when I truly love (1) God and (2) my fellow man. True love towards *all* is more desirous to God than sacrifice. To love is to obey (I John 5:3). If I say with my mouth I love God, my actions should back up my statements.

Mark 12:40. Are there "degrees" in hell? I don't want to go and find out, but this scripture makes me wonder if there are.

Mark 12:43. In 1991, a "mite" was valued at 1/400 of $.01. If this mite had been in a bank at 6% interest per annum, it would have been worth (in 1991) $4 septillion, 800 quintillion (or $4 with 20 zeros after it)! She invested that mite in God's bank.

There is no telling what it is worth today and it is still drawing interest! The rich gave some, this lady gave her all and God took notice. I had bacon and eggs this morning for breakfast. The chicken gave some. The pig gave its all. What will I give God?

Mark 13. Ahh, the "end time". So many people worry about whether or not we're living in the end time. The "end time" is not our focus. My focus is on MY, personal "end time". I want to be ready to meet God whenever my time is up. My last breath on this earth is the end time! Having said that, Jesus does give us a few hints. I'm sure every generation has thought theirs was the last. I've heard so many end time preachers over my lifetime and they all have a different interpretation of the scriptures. I think Jesus purposefully left out details so we wouldn't focus on it. Here is what Jesus had to say. Don't take away from it and don't read more into it.
1. There will be a lot of false teachers. Don't let yourself be deceived (vs 5-6, 21-22).
2. Wars and rumors of wars doesn't mean it's the end time (vs 7).
3. Earthquakes in many places, famines & troubles are just the beginning (vs 8).
4. Persecution for standing for truth is common. Expect it (vs 9).
5. Every nation will have a chance to hear (vs 10).
    a. The Gideons have published & distributed the Bible in every language.
    b. As of 2017, Acts 2:38 has been preached to the general assembly of the United Nations, which has representatives from all nations.
6. Families will be torn and turn against each other (vs 12).
7. True Christians will become hated (vs 13).

All of the above are the "norm". Beginning in vs 14, Jesus gives instructions.
8. When the abomination of desolation establishes himself, FLEE ~ "get out of Dodge" ~ and pray (vs. 14-20).

I've got to make sure I am grounded in the Word so that I am not swayed by the "WOW" factor of false prophets (vs 22). I have been duly fore-warned (vs 23).

Mark 13:20 Parallels with Matthew 24:24. False doctrine will be so rampant the "cream of the crop" will be in danger of being swayed. God will come quickly for their sakes.

Mark 13:22. I've got to make sure I am grounded in the word, so I am not swayed by the "wow" factor of false prophets. Remember, even Pharaoh's magicians were able to duplicate Moses' miracles up to a point, albeit by sleight of hand (Exodus 7:22). Satan always has a counterfeit. The only way to spot a counterfeit is to be intimately familiar with, and become an expert of, the real. Experts don't study counterfeits. It would be impossible to know them all. Experts study the real thing. If they spot something that doesn't look like the real thing, they have found a counterfeit! A miracle is to grab someone's attention, thereby drawing them to God. A miracle does not mean God approves of that person's life. A miracle is a result of faith and faith alone. God approves of the obedient, not of those who merely have faith. God can perform miracles. Likewise, God's anointing does not equate God's approval. Saul even prophesied (I Samuel 19), all the while plotting to kill David. Does that mean Saul was in the right? No! It means that Saul was able to yield himself to God when he wanted to. I know people like that. They come to church and can flow in the gifts one minute and go out and pick up their sin where they left off. Remember, a gift is a gift ~ God doesn't take it back. I don't want to be deluded into thinking I'm living right just because I can feel God's presence. Anyone can feel God's presence if they just worship Him a little bit. Feeling all warm and fuzzy when I go to church doesn't mean I'm living right. It merely means that God is responding to my worship and wanting a closer relationship with me. He longs for me to surrender completely to Him.

Mark 13:23. I have been duly warned. There will be no excuses on judgment day. I will not be able to say, "I didn't know ....." or "But, my pastor told me it would be okay to ....."

Mark 13:33. I don't bother too much with those who claim to be able to pinpoint when Jesus is coming back. They don't know. Period.

Mark 13:37. The conclusion of Jesus' dissertation on the end time is this: Live like He is coming back any minute. It is like the military. The military is always prepared for war. War may never take place while a soldier is on duty, but s/he is prepared if it does. As I live my life, I must constantly be on guard. It might not happen in my lifetime, but it just might! "Watch."

Mark 14. The alabaster box story is beautiful. Many sermons and even songs have been written. I don't think this woman knew she was anointing Jesus for His burial. I think she was just so grateful to Jesus and she wanted give Him something in return. This was all she had of value. All God requires of me is that I do what I'm capable of doing and do it to the best of my abilities. God does not require me to replicate what someone else has done. He doesn't require me to do more than I am capable of. If I will surrender my best and all of me to Him, He will be able to take that gift and do something with me.

Mark 14:15. This man was prepared for Jesus's coming. He didn't know when or who all would be there, but he went ahead and prepared for the event. (Being prepared is a recurring theme: remember the 5 wise virgins?) Don't hotels do this? Don't they clean up a room as soon as it is vacated? That prepared room may be vacant for a few days, but if a guest shows up, it is ready! A hotel would not stay in business very long if they waited until the guest came to begin to get a room ready! Why do we (humans) not stay prepared for death? We know it is coming, and yet we behave like we will have time to get right with God! Why do we (Christians) not stay prepared to be used by God? We know God wants to use us to bless others, but we act like we'll have a chance to study God's word for answers before someone needs us! Why do we (self-proclaimed Christians) not stay prepared for emergencies? We know we will need God ASAP to perform a miracle, but we act like we'll have time to repent and get rid of the weights that bog us down before bringing our petitions to God. Wouldn't it be so much better if we just STAYED prayed up and living right? ***It's not rocket science!***

Mark 14:27. *ALL* of us (me included) will be offended at some point by God. I'm ruffling my own feathers, but it is true. I've gotten miffed at God before when bad things happened to me! "Why, God? I've been living for you wholeheartedly! Why did You allow this to happen?" I have to check myself and realize my sin means I will reap what I have sown. When good things happen, it is a sheer blessing from God I don't deserve. Sometimes we start thinking God owes us, when in actuality, we owe Him everything. He doesn't owe us anything. This realization changes my attitude. Instead of a complainer of bad things, I become a praiser over both the good and bad things. Instead of "why me", I wonder how God will bless me THROUGH my trial. I understand God sees the big picture and all things will ultimately work together for my good (Romans 8:28). God is trying His best to get me to heaven! I need to cooperate!.

Mark 14:35. Some battles just have to be fought. If I pray them away, I will still have to fight that battle at a later date. It is best to fight it within the parameters of God's timing because if the timing is off, I just might lose. I had a woman, whom I respected very much, tell me that each of her children had been at the point of death during childhood. She told me she prayed God would, at all costs, spare their lives. She couldn't stand the thought of losing them. God did heal those children. Unfortunately, they grew up and completely turned against the scripture and teachings of their godly parents. This lady, full of sorrow, admitted to me that, "It would have been much easier to have lost them then to sickness, than to lose them like this." My heart aches for her. I wonder how the story would have played out if she had only surrendered their lives to God? He might have spared them anyway, as He did Abraham's son.

Mark 14:36. It is okay to pray what I want as long as I submit my will to God's. I do want God's will, even if His will means that I don't get my way. God has the big picture. I don't. Just as a parent agrees for the doctor to inflict pain upon a child (shots, surgery, etc.) because the parent knows that pain would result in an ultimate good, God knows what is best for me. When I think I know best, it's just my **pride** rising up.

Mark 14:37. Jesus prayed long enough for his disciples to go to sleep three times! He shook them up twice to ask them to stay awake. This tells me the prayer Jesus was praying wasn't a short, "now I lay me down to sleep" kind of prayer. Some prayers are a spiritual fight. Some prayers take agonizing over. Some prayers take time. Jesus was so stressed out that he had hematidrosis. He was so stressed out that his blood vessels constricted and dilated to the extent that blood was pushed out of his sweat glands! That is being stressed out! That situation called for him to pray ~ and pray until He had the victory. It took a while.

Mark 14:38, 40. Why pray? For my own sake. God is omniscient. He knows everything. He doesn't need my declaration to know what is going on in my head. *I need to pray* to receive enough strength so things which should be tempting are not. I know that drinking bleach is bad for me. I trust the medical books and the wisdom of elders on this. I have no need to find out for myself. Drinking bleach is not even an option. As a parent, I conveyed this concept to my children. They trusted me and never drank bleach either! Likewise, sin is specifically spelled out in the Bible. When I educate myself in the Word and in prayer, sin is not an option and ceases to be a source of temptation for me. This ***isn't Rocket Science!*** I wonder how many times I've been prompted to get out of bed and pray, but shook it off because I was too tired? How many difficult situations could I have avoided had I obeyed that "still, small voice"? It makes me sad to think I have let myself (and others) down.

Mark 14:50. This verse might have read differently if they had prayed and not slept in the Garden! Perhaps the stories in my life would read differently if I prayed a bit more. *See notes at Matthew 26.*

Mark 14:56-59. Deuteronomy 17:6; 19:15 strongly emphasized that witnesses MUST agree. These two witnesses couldn't get their stories to agree. Here we see a religious system so skewed it was far from what God had intended. (1) Can I defend my beliefs and doctrines with strong Bible teachings? Have I made a doctrine by taking something out of context to fit what I want to believe? The scripture will *never* contradict itself. Therefore, if there is seemingly a contradiction, I must dig a little deeper to find the real meaning of the passage. (2) Satan is the originator of all lies (John 8:44). He will constantly barrage a child of God with lies, attempting to trip us up. "God will never forgive you" is one of his favorite lies. If Satan can convince me not to repent, he has conquered me. I will not believe Satan's lies! God will forgive me (I John 1:9). God does love me (John 3:16).

Mark 14:68-72. I would have thought the first time the rooster crowed, Peter would have remembered what Jesus had said and that would have been his wake-up call. However, it wasn't until after the second time (and before a third), that Peter realized he had done exactly what Jesus said he would do. We humans can be bullheaded, can't we? I shake my head at people who backslide and wonder how many wake up calls they will need before they actually wake up and get back where they need to be with God. This salvation business is a very serious matter. Some people spend more time thinking about and planning a vacation than they do for eternity! Eternity is a lot longer than vacation time! ***This isn't Rocket Science!***

Mark 14:72. Peter wept. He later became the spokesman for the rest of the disciples. Judas was sorry for his sin, but committed suicide (Matthew 27:3-5). What is the difference? Peter followed through on his sorrow, repented, and corrected his error. It took a little time, but he made things right. Judas didn't. If he had only asked for forgiveness, he would have received it! What a testimony he would have had!

Mark 15:15. Pilate had the chance to be a real leader, but wanted to please the people, so ..... he released a dangerous murderer. This reminds me of King Saul, who was ever wanting to be a people pleaser. God always takes precedent over people. I'd love to be able to please everyone, but that is impossible. I must, however, take care to make sure I please God. Is He really going to allow someone in Heaven He is not pleased with?

Mark 15:34. *See notes at Matthew 27:46.*

Mark 16:1, 9, 12, 14. The women were the first ones at the grave site, and the first ones to tell the good news that Jesus had been resurrected. The women were the first missionaries! The women told the disciples. Women have a knack for being intuitive and sometimes are able to hone in on something. Man would do well to give credence to Woman's intuition. Men have their strengths as well. Man + Woman = a great team, if they will work together and not be in competition with each other.

Mark 16:7. Jesus wanted Peter to know all was forgiven. Jesus knew the condition of Peter's heart.

Mark 16:15-18. This is Mark's version of the events that Matthew recorded in Matthew 28:18-20. What is the difference? Matthew was writing to the Jews who were looking for a King. He was telling them Jesus was *everything* ~ the Father, the Son & the Holy Spirit. Mark wrote to the Romans, who were all about conquering and having servants. Therefore, Mark's emphasis wasn't on the majesty of Jesus, but that Jesus was the ultimate servant, with supernatural powers.

Mark 16:17. The signs follow the believers, not vice versa! As a believer, I carry the power to work miracles with me.

Mark 16:20. Miracles (signs) confirm His word. It is not confirming *my* word, but God's word. This is God's kingdom. I get tired of people flocking to hear (uhm, see) ministers who "operate in the gifts". True, they have yielded themselves to be used by God, but it is GOD who is operating, not any human being. Too many times we treat these ministers as being "special" and by doing so, some of them have gotten to the point they feel special and demand VIP treatment. Pride comes in, to their detriment. If that pride goes unchecked, their ministry begins to deteriorate. God doesn't work well with prideful people.

LUKE

Written with the Greeks in mind. The Greeks were all into the "perfect man". As the son of Man, Jesus was entitled to all of the earth (Luke 19:10).

Luke 1:4. Importance of the *written* word vs the *spoken* word. The spoken word changes in the retelling. The written word sets forth what the speaker wants to say.

Luke 1:15. John was born under the old covenant. The new covenant was not in effect until the Day of Pentecost.

Luke 1:18. Mary and Zacharias both had questions. What was the difference between the two?
- Mary was willing and had faith.
- Zacharias was a crusty, religious man with unbelief.

Luke 1:20. God's timing is not human timing! I need to remember that.

Luke 1:28. The angel called Mary "blessed", however, at the time, I'm sure she felt like it was a curse and not a blessing! What seems to be a difficult trial at the time, just might turn out to be a blessing in disguise. It's a matter of *trusting* that God knows best and *resting* in that thought. **This isn't Rocket Science!**

Luke 1:30, 37; 2:9-11; Matthew 1:18-21. FEAR NOT.
- "Mary, God is going to do a work in you that has never been done before, nor will ever be done again ..... **Fear not** the impossible" (Luke 1:30, 37);
- "Joseph, I know you can't wrap your head around this, but .... **Fear not** the incomprehensible!" (Matthew 1:18-21);
- "Shepherds, all of those prophecies you scratched your head about but yet hoped for are coming to pass .... **Fear not** the supernatural!" (Luke 2:9-11).
- One of the Hebrew words translated as "fear" in the Bible literally means to "result in paralysis". Moses said (1) Fear not; (2) Go forward; Be still; and (4) Be quiet (Exodus 14:13-15). Be fearless! Walk by faith. Don't try to tackle this by yourself. God is in control.

Luke 1:35. Jesus "shall be *called* the Son of God". There's really no other way to describe the dual nature Jesus had. Just because He is "called" a son, doesn't mean He is actually a "son", as in a by-product of God. A human "son" is a by-product of two people. Jesus was fully God and fully human. No one else is like that, therefore, there is no perfect word to describe that entity. Luke just said we're going to CALL Him the son of God. The purpose of this book is not to enter into a huge theological discussion, but to say Jesus is not a by-product of God. He IS

God. My cousin liked to say Jesus is God in work clothes! God put on flesh and came to earth to mix and mingle with us. He forced Himself to be confined to human limitations so He could relate to us. As such, He is able to be an advocate for us. Whereas His spirit (as God) says "BAM, here's the law and that's that", His flesh (as human) says, "Well, humans have limitations, so they need mercy ...."

Luke 1:45. What a contrast! Mary's attitude was to bless the Lord. John's attitude was of skepticism (Luke 1:18). I must be careful as I age, that skepticism and cynicism don't overtake me. I have to work hard to keep that childlike wonder and awe of God's promises. Disappointments in life happen, but I can't let them transfer over to God. God has never disappointed me! God has never gone back on His promise! God has never failed. Blessed be the Lord! I will trust Him and cling to His promises, even if they take a little longer than I initially expected to come to pass.

Luke 1:51. I have to giggle at the wording of this verse: "He hath scattered the proud in the imagination of their hearts." That is exactly what pride is: imagination of the heart, which reflects the *trajectory of the heart*. Other people don't think nearly as highly of a proud person as the proud person thinks of him/herself.

Luke 1:74-75. Perfect love casts out all fear (I John 4:18). How do I serve God? (1) without fear (which means in perfect love) and (2) with holiness, which results in my living in (3) righteousness. Serving God in fear is exactly what the "rich young ruler" did. He was very careful to follow the letter of the law. Unfortunately, he completely missed out on the purpose of the law. The purpose of the law was for Israel to be separated from the rest of the world, and separated unto God. The Jews missed the "separated unto God" memo. They followed the rules without the relationship. The rich young ruler's question was "what do I have to do to make it to Heaven?" Jesus wanted his question to be "How can I get closer to You?" Many people today focus on relationship without the separation. Serving God in LOVE will enable me to live a separated life as is pleasing unto God and enjoy it. When I have perfect love, it is not a burden to live a life separated unto God. I am happy to make that sacrifice.

Luke 1:77. (See also John 3:5; Acts 2:38) The steps of salvation go hand-in-hand. Spiritual knowledge comes when sins are remitted. Remission means the slate is wiped clean. Remission happens upon baptism in the name of Jesus. We see in John 16:13 that the Spirit will guide into truth. The baptism of water & spirit go hand in hand, and can only be effective after I have decided to make a U-Turn and live for God. I cannot expect someone who has not experienced proper, scriptural water & spirit baptism to be in truth or to be on the right, truthful path. They may *feel* the presence of God because God is trying to woo them. However, *feeling* God's presence does not equate God's approval.

Luke 2:1-7. Politicians don't realize the role they play in God's plan (Proverbs 21:1).

God used a tax levy to get Mary & Joseph to the right location for Jesus to be born. Jesus had to be born in Bethlehem to fulfil prophecy.

Luke 2:19. Sometimes it is just best to take Mary's lead and ponder prophecies in the heart. Blabbing them out to everyone didn't work for Joseph back in Genesis, did it?

Luke 2:22-24. Mary & Joseph knew they were caring for the Messiah, but they still obeyed the law (see Lev 12:6-8). Some people think just because God speaks to them or through them they are above the laws of God.

Luke 2:28. It is not enough to have head knowledge of Jesus. I must embrace Him!

Luke 2:44-48. Jesus had been alone for about 4 days. His witnessing style was to listen and then ask questions. We see this over and over in His ministry. He was not "lecturing" the doctors, but listening, asking questions, and then giving his perception and understanding. This is the best style of witnessing.

Luke 2:50-51. Jesus, the almighty God robed in flesh, submitted to his earthly parents! Even *He* obeyed His own law. Who am I to do otherwise?

Luke 2:52. Jesus, like Samuel (I Samuel 2:26), had a period of growth, both physically & mentally.

Luke 3:3. John definitely set the precedent for the purpose and mode of baptism. Baptism is for the remission (doing away with) sins. John baptized by immersion and for repentance, and taught baptism of fire would be forthcoming. He actually set the tone for Acts 2:38. All of the elements of the plan of salvation set forth by Peter are in John's message. John was truly the forerunner.

Luke 3:8-9. Merely saying "sorry" is not enough. John demanded that there should be fruit of repentance: Actions back up talk. In fact, without visible proof (fruit) of repentance, one cannot be saved. There is no generic salvation.

Luke 3:11-18. John preached on what it means to be repentant:
- Brotherly love, benevolence, donations (vs 11).
- Extortion condemned (vs 13).
- No violence, no false accusations, but contentment (vs 14).
- Hope in Jesus (vs 16).
- Judgement will come by fire (a) either by the fire of the Holy Spirit, which will burn the chaff or (b) fire of judgment. Which type of fire is my choice (vs 15-17).
- Many other things (vs 18).

Luke 3:17. Jesus began the separation process of the wheat and chaff. He healed and delivered those who <u>wanted</u> it and <u>believed</u>. In other places, he could not do any works because of their unbelief. The choice is mine, but that very choice creates separation. Jesus gives me the opportunity to see the options and gives me the power or freedom to make the right choice through the Holy Spirit.

Luke 3:23-38. This genealogy is of Mary's side. Matthew's genealogy was on Joseph's side and proved Joseph could not be Jesus' natural father. Jesus got his royal (human) lineage and the right to be a human king from Mary's side, thus satisfying the Israelites' thirst for a king (I Samuel 8:5).

Luke 4. Jesus faced the pressure test. He was pressured into making some wrong choices. Fortunately for all of mankind, he passed the test and made the right choices. This gives me strength that I, too, can make the right choices. If Jesus can, then by His help, I know I can. Israel is a type of Jesus (Exodus 4:22-23). They (1) passed through the water, (2) went into the wilderness, and (3) was tempted. They did not pass their test. Jesus did!

Luke 4:1-9. All temptations fall under one of three categories: (1) lust of the flesh; (2) lust of the eye; and (3) pride of life (I John 2:16). Jesus faced all three of these trials and overcame each.

Luke 4:10. The devil knows the scripture and will quote it to me. He uses it out of context to try and trick me. This is his specialty. I must be knowledgeable enough of the scripture not to be tricked by the devil. Eve didn't know God's word well enough to combat Satan. God never said they couldn't *touch* the tree, only they couldn't eat of it. Once Satan realized Eve wasn't 100% sure of the word, he was confident he could twist it and Eve would just fall for his logic. He was right.

Luke 4:13. Is all going well? The devil has departed for a season. Soak up the word of God because the devil will come back to tempt again!

Luke 4:18-19. Christ's mission is 6-fold and contained all spiritual things. The miracles were merely an attraction, an introduction to what He could do.

Luke 4:24-27. There is a danger in the spiritual becoming commonplace. When God's blessings are taken for granted, I become lukewarm. I must be on-guard against this. The spiritual experience cannot be passed from generation to generation. Each generation must get it for "themselves" or risk becoming calloused. Sometimes a total "outsider" receives more from God than those who have been born and raised in the church. Why? Because those who have been born and raised become "Professional Christians" and live by rote and not by conviction and experience. These people are in danger of losing the truth. (See essay entitled "Christian Parasite" in *It's Not Rocket Science, Volume 1*.)

Luke 4:32. The anointing makes the difference.

Luke 4:34. The devils know who Jesus is! (vs 41).

Luke 5:3-6. I must listen to Jesus and must go deep in His word. These fishermen had failure in the past, but with renewed hope in Jesus, they found victory.

Luke 5:17. A worrisome scripture is Luke 5:17. Some Pharisees and doctors of the law were assembled together to hear Jesus. Verse 17 states that there was enough power of God in their midst to *heal them*. As we read down further, we realize that only a man sick with palsy was healed. How sad. I don't see where any of the Pharisees or lawyers were healed. Perhaps it was because of the ***trajectory of their hearts*** (vs 22). Jesus knows where my heart is. I can go to a buffet where I can have as much food as I can eat. There is usually a huge variety of foods on a buffet too. It is guaranteed that I will find some foods that I thoroughly enjoy and enough food that I do not have to leave hungry. However, if I refuse to go up to the buffet, I will leave even hungrier that I was when I came. The smell of the food will trigger my gastric juices and I will anticipate the comfort of food. When I go to church, God has a buffet spread for me. It is up to me to partake, though. I can leave more spiritually hungry than I was when I came if I don't freely take what I need from God. It's not God's fault when I don't get what I need. One thing is for sure, I won't leave the same. I will leave either full and satisfied or hungrier. If I leave hungrier, I will look for satisfaction in the world. That's how people backslide.

Luke 5:20. My soul is the first priority, not my flesh. In the grand scheme of things, it doesn't matter whether I live 50 years or 100 years. A lifetime of sickness is nothing in light of eternity. My soul must be well. God does care about our infirmities, but God's first priority is my soul. My soul must be my first priority as well. I must be saved!

Luke 5:30. Why could Jesus eat with publicans and sinners? Because of John 3:16!

Luke 5:36-39. These bottles were made of skin, which would get brittle over time. Fermentation would burst them. There is a change when I serve God (II Corinthians 5:17). I can't have both my sinful life and a godly life.

Luke 6:8. Jesus knows our thoughts (Luke 7:39-40; Hebrews 4:12). He knows everyone's weaknesses, even Judas' (John 2:24-25). He sent Judas out to preach too (Matthew 10:1)!

Luke 6:13. Jesus chose 12 out of a larger group of disciples. He even chose Judas, a "tare". Judas had the potential of being a traitor, but wasn't one at this point. Matthew also had a money problem, but overcame His temptation.

Luke 6:24. We all want credit for our hard work. No one likes it when others get the credit. Don't get all bent out of shape, though, when you're the "background" person and are forgotten. Some get their "consolation" (payment in full) here on earth; others get theirs in Heaven. I think the reward in Heaven will be greater than whatever reward or accolades I receive here on earth!

Luke 6:33-38. Giving has nothing to do with assets. It has everything to do with ATTITUDE. Jesus preached this in his "Sermon on the Mount". Let's take a look at Luke's version. We find Jesus' discourse on giving in Luke 6:33-38. The question is: Am I a contributor or a consumer? Am I a giver or a taker?

Luke 6:35. Don't expect anything in return. GIVE, not trade.

Luke 6:36-38. The subject here is mercy, not money (Matthew 6:12). When I show or give mercy, I receive mercy.

Luke 6:40. When he is trained, he shall be like his teacher. Christ in you = the hope of glory (Colossians 1:27). Heaven wants me fully trained!

Luke 6:42. Self-judge. Repent daily as exemplified by the daily sacrifices in the Old Testament.

Luke 6:44. Do I have the Holy Spirit? Do I bear the fruit of the Spirit (Galatians 5:22)?

Luke 6:45-46. Actions speak louder than words. The *trajectory of my heart* is exposed by my mouth (I Corinthians 12:3).

Luke 7:3-4. Jesus interceded for a Gentile!

Luke 7:23. God raises up and pushes down ministries. ***Don't get offended!***

Luke 7:30. It is always my choice whether or not I will accept or reject.

Luke 7:35. We've never truly gotten out of 5th grade!

Luke 8:3. No doubt Herod heard of Jesus' message!

Luke 8:5-11. See notes at Mark 4. The seed is the word of God. The human element is the soil.

Luke 8:18. How do I hear? How do I take and apply the word of God? Do I think I'm not accountable ... that the word is for someone else and not for me? I can deceive myself if I refuse to accept the word's authority in my life.

Luke 8:35. An encounter with Jesus brings modesty. God established modesty in the Garden after mankind sinned. Modesty predates the law of Moses and is still a requirement today.

Luke 8:24-39. Demoniac - see notes at Mark 8:32 & Matthew 8.

Luke 9:13-16. Jesus first empowered them for a miracle. They obeyed him. The actions of the disciples produced the miracle. Jesus, then blessed, broke & gave. The disciples then had to deliver. God acted solo during creation, but He now wants and demands my help and involvement.

Luke 9:20. The people's opinion doesn't matter; mine does! Where do I stand? What do I believe? God wants to know this. Sure, He already knows since He is omnipotent, but He wants me to take a stand and declare it.

Luke 9:32. It's easy to be too "sleepy" that I miss out on God's invitation to greater depths of intimacy with Him. He *looonggs* to have that with me, but I too often spurn that invitation in favor of doing something else. Remember the transfiguration (Luke 9:32)? Remember the Garden of Gethsemane (Luke 22:45)? Remember the 10 virgins (Matthew 25:5)? Sleepiness (laziness) overtook them and they missed out on something really important. True, five of them were prepared and had enough oil, but they were scrambling frantically to meet the bridegroom. At the transfiguration, the disciples completely missed out on the conversation Jesus, Moses & Elijah were having. They could have been involved in that intimate moment. Instead, they were spectators to just the glory, but not the conversation. The three disciples slept through the Garden of Gethsemane experience. Jesus specifically instructed them to watch and pray so they wouldn't fall into temptation (Mark 14:38). There's a reason I shouldn't get "sleepy" (spiritually)! It's for my own good: that I don't fall into temptation. Not too many people deliberately sin. Most of us "fall into" or get tripped because we're sleepy and not really spiritually alert. We've got to maintain our "A" game. This is an eternal issue.

Luke 9:46; 22:24. This passage tells of two separate occasions where there was strife in the "church" over position. I must be happy with whatever position God has placed me in. I can't fight over who gets to sing the solo (or something else). I must do what I do for God and not for my own vain glory. If God really wants me in that position (that someone else has), that's God's problem and He will have to make a way. I will let Him remove the other person (remember Saul & David?). He will do it in His own time. I don't have to jockey for that spot. If I do, God will have to punish me for my wrong doing. Why should I put myself through that stressful process?

Luke 9:49-50. It's good to know the disciples were human beings with human thoughts and feelings just like us! John couldn't understand why someone who was not a disciple could have their prayers answered. Jesus said to just leave them alone. The power is not in the person praying, but in the name which is invoked in prayer (Jesus). Just because a prayer is answered doesn't mean the person praying is right with God. It means the person praying has faith and understands there is power in the name of Jesus.

Luke 9:60-62. Jesus was not being calloused, but was telling him to cut the apron strings. There's <u>always</u> something else to demand my time. I can't allow family, job, etc. to prevent me from doing God's will. I must be involved in kingdom work (ref. Elisha's calling I Kings 19:19-21).

Luke 10:2. A prayer request of Jesus should be a prayer request of mine!

Luke 10:9. Ministry is being involved with the sick: (1) physical (2) mental (3) spiritual.

Luke 10:11. Jesus gave them cause for washing their hands of another person, *with the caveat* they are <u>sure</u> it is a hopeless situation. That is a lot of responsibility. It is best to leave the judging up to God, for He and He alone knows the heart of a person. Sometimes a person really does want God, but pride prevents him from reaching out. God knows how to work on pride and ultimately, that person can be saved. I should never just write someone off, unless I have spent some time in prayer and fasting for them and God has directed me to leave them alone, lest I face judgment as well.

Luke 10:19. The power comes from Jesus a.k.a. the Holy Spirit (Acts 1:8)!

Luke 10:20. The Holy Spirit power enables me to have dominion over the devil, but I must have the right motives! God knows the intent of the heart! The devil can't make anyone backslide. We have power over the devil. If I backslide, it is because I just don't want to live for God.

Luke 10:27. Jesus set forth the foundation of holiness, which is LOVE. (1) love God and (2) love people. Those who do not wish to act, think, or dress the way God wants them to don't love God, no matter what their mouth says. It's that simple. ***It's not Rocket Science.***

Luke 10:29. It is ingrained in human nature to want rebellion validated. The danger of living by the law instead of by love, is that you tend to split hairs over an issue. Not everything is definable as a "heaven or hell" issue. Something in and of itself may not send a person to hell, but is merely a slight step off the correct path. The trajectory of that step, if not corrected, will ultimately take a person to hell, even if that initial step doesn't. A mailbox on the side of a road is not dangerous, but the potential for danger is present. We don't allow a child to play by the mailbox because of the potential of danger. Likewise, there are some things I don't participate in because of the path it will send me down. (See essay entitled, "Playing by the Mailbox" in *It's Not Rocket Science, Volume 1*.)

Luke 10:31-35. The priest and the Levite thought they were doing the Lord's work, but they were doing "church" work and not God's work. There is a difference. (See essay entitled, "Am I A Samaritan?" in *It's Not Rocket Science, Volume 1*.)
Lessons from the Good Samaritan story:
- Attitude of the robbers = I'm taking what is yours.
- Attitude of the religious = I'm keeping my blessings to myself.
- Attitude of the Samaritan = I'll give you what I have.

This parable gives us a portrait of both a sinner and a saint.
- Portrait of a Sinner:
    - Robbed
    - Humiliated
    - Abused/wounded
    - Forsaken
    - Ignored/neglected.
- Portrait of a Saint:
    - Gave of time
    - Inconvenienced
    - Cost money
    - BUT:
- Saved a life, which is LOVE IN ACTION!!

Luke 10:40-42. Martha was consumed with temporal things. She had to feed Jesus + 12 disciples + Lazarus. That is 14 hungry men! Of course, there were lots of chores to be done. There is always a lot to do, but I must make time for Jesus. I must spend time with Jesus. I must choose what my priorities are. Apparently, Martha took Jesus' rebuke to heart and made some changes, for we see a different Martha in John 11:20. (See also essay entitled, "The Lazarus Story", in *It's Not Rocket Science, Volume 1*.)

Luke 11:1. I must be ever learning. A person with a black belt in judo has reached the top, but there is always room to hone those skills and keep at the top of their craft. A person with a white belt still has a way to go. I don't want to get to where I *think* I know everything. The disciples said, "teach us". God will always work with a teachable spirit. Every time I read through the Bible, I want God to pop a new revelation out at me! I want to get to know God more and more fully each day.

Luke 11:2. God's will is being done in Heaven. Let it be done on Earth as well. (See notes at Matthew 6:9-11).

Luke 11:7-9: It was customary for houses to be built on pilings with a door in the middle of the floor. The animals were kept under the houses. The family slept together on the floor. This event required the entire family to be inconvenienced. The animals were awaked. The entire family had to get up and move the bed cushions before the door could be opened. The neighbor was persistent and had shameless boldness. God knows what I need even before I ask (Matthew 6:8), but He wants me to ask. God wants me to become passionate about it. Is my petition something I am passionate about?

Luke 11:24-26. Repentance alone is not enough. I must be filled with the Holy Spirit.

Luke 11:27-28. Those who hear and keep the word of God are more blessed than Mary!

Luke 11:29. The people wanted to be entertained. They were seeking a side-show and not seeking the truth. Nothing has changed. People still wanted to be entertained in church. In actuality, we should be entertaining God!

Luke 11:34. I must guard my eye. Most sins begin with the eye.

Luke 11:42. True, I must obey the outward principles of holy living, but I can't neglect the inward principles of holiness, which is love.

Luke 11:46. Politicians are the same everywhere! They make laws, but exempt themselves. Some preachers are like that too.

Luke 12:2. Secrets are ultimately exposed.

Luke 12:12. The Holy Spirit may not come early, but He'll be on time!

Luke 12:16-31. Lessons from the parable of the Rich Fool.
1. Jesus didn't condemn him for being rich. The problem was
    i. selfishness;
    ii. not giving God credit for the sun/rain
    iii. no thought of the eternal, only temporal.
2. Vs. 23; 31. What are my priorities? Temporal or eternal?
3. Focus of my treasures reveal the *trajectory of my heart.*

Luke 12:48. A busy person is given more responsibility. I have a responsibility to use whatever talents God has given me for His kingdom and not to sit idle. A secondary application of this scripture is someone who knows the truth but fails to obey, will be judged a little harsher than one who sins out of ignorance (I Timothy 1:13).

Luke 12:51-53. Doctrine divides.

Luke 13:3-5. Sin is sin in God's eye ~ no big or little sin. Just sin.

Luke 13:6-9. God is patient and merciful. He doesn't cut me off after each sin!

Luke 13:19-21. (Matthew 13:31). The mustard seed is tiny, but the plant ...
- Grows into a tree.
- Provides shade.
- Provides shelter.
- Greater than all herbs.

Luke 13:25-27. It is possible to sit in the presence of God day in and day out and Him not know me. Just because I sit in church doesn't make me a real Christian. I must develop a relationship with Him.

Luke 13:31. Hypocrites ~ they were the ones who were plotting!

Luke 14:7-11; 22:23. It's always best to take the humble route. If there is friction with another, try to get in the other person's head and figure out how they think. Put the other person first. Then, you'll know what corrective action to take. Apologize for your part in the misunderstanding, disagreement or mistake. I'd much rather God to elevate me than for God to demote me! Putting the other person first is a by-product of love (I Corinthians 13:4-5).

Luke 14:12-13. The choice is mine.
- My fellow man can "pay me back" or
- God can "pay me back".

Luke 14:18. "Make excuse" = really a lie.

Luke 14:26. Put God first before anyone else.

Luke 15:11-32. Lessons from the Prodigal Son.
1. The prodigal son wasn't entitled to his inheritance yet, but the father loved him more than the possessions.
2. The celebration upon the son's return wasn't about the son, but about the father's joy in the son's return.
3. The son was willing to give up being a son, but the father was not willing to give up on being a father.
4. The son realized *all* wrong doing is a sin against God (vs 18; Genesis 39:9).
5. The younger son was:
    4. Immature,
    5. Impatient,
    6. Immoral,
    7. alone, now immobilized (vs 13),

         8. stripped of pride (vs 16),
         9. inspired to mobilization,
         10. had a personal revelation: change or die (vs 17), and
         11. arrogance, now gone (vs 19).
5. The husks were used to fatten swine - contains sugar (vs 16).
6. When I sin, I sin against <u>God</u> and man is my witness of that sin (vs 21).
7. The elder son (vs 29):
    1. had a servant's heart
    2. was stable
    3. was "sinless"
    The above are proper and necessary, BUT he also
    4. was slack about wisdom & understanding,
    5. was aggressive (vs 28), and
    6. was prideful in his righteousness.

Luke 16:1-13. Lessons from the unjust steward:
1. I must always be accountable.
2. I must access my situation.
3. I must take action. God gave him time to fix the problem, but he had to fix it.
4. Did he knock off the bill, or just charge what he really should have to begin with (vs 7)?
5. Trust must be earned, not given. Trust can be measured.
6. Just as he prepared for his future, I need to prepare for my eternal future. The funds I invest in the Kingdom will pay large dividends in Heaven.

Luke 16:15. Have you ever tried to draw a straight line off the previous line drawn? After drawing a series of lines like that, you realize the last line is nowhere near like the original line drawn! In order for the last line to be equal to the first one, you have to measure down from the first and not from the previous one. The plumb-line by which I must measure myself by is God's word, not the opinion of others (II Corinthians 10:12-13). If everyone lives for God based upon the previous generation, after just a few generations, the belief is watered down. In the carnal realm, the third generation statically loses the first generation's wealth, morals, etc. Look through historically wealthy families. The grandfather works hard to create wealth. By the time the grandchildren are adults, that wealth has dwindled. It's the same spiritually. Those who base their religious beliefs and experiences upon the previous generation are far from the relationship God designed us to have with Him. Many church denominations are very far removed from the doctrines of the church Peter established in the book of Acts. I need MY OWN relationship. I need to dig into the word of God and figure out why I believe what I believe. Do I believe it just because Mom (or Pastor) taught me that? Or, do I believe it because it's in the Bible?

Luke 16:27. This was a good prayer, but too late and the wrong time.

Luke 17:1. See essay on Offence in *It's Not Rocket Science, Volume 1*. I must take care not to offend someone.

Luke 17:5. Forgiveness is hard sometimes! I need to have faith God's word and promises on forgiveness are true.

Luke 17:10. Living for God is the base line. It is the least I can do. It is my duty and not a favor to God (Ecclesiastes 12:13). It always amazes me when people act like their participation is doing the church a favor. The opposite is true. The church does us all a favor! I *need* to participate more than the church needs for me to.

Luke 17:14. My action brings God's action.

Luke 17:20-36. The Lord's second coming:
1. Can't be calculated. God's time is not the same as man's (vs 20).
2. I can't dismiss Heaven as being within me such as is taught by the New Agers, Hindus, Yoga, etc. (vs 21).
3. Don't follow after all the prophecy teachers (vs 23).
4. None of these actions are sinful of themselves. It's the business and neglect of Godly things that presents a problem. Do not neglect the spiritual. Do not get caught up in the temporal.
5. Lot's wife clung to her old life (vs 32). The ***trajectory of her heart*** showed through when she looked behind.
6. Lose my life in God (vs 33).

Luke 18:1. I have a choice. I can either pray or be faint (weak, dizzy, unsure, unstable). Verse 7 mentions having a mindset of continual prayer - praying without ceasing (I Thessalonians 5:17). In vs 8, Jesus is indicating and lamenting that there would be few clinging to faith on the earth. Prayer and faith go hand in hand. Without prayer, my faith becomes weak. Look at the disciples. At the last supper, they were all gung-ho about sticking with Jesus. Just *a few hours* later in the Garden, they slept instead of praying. When the soldiers came, they were too weak spiritually to hang around and forsook Jesus ~~ **even though** He had given them fair warning. How many times am I prompted to pray, brush off that unction, only to find myself in a situation I am too weak to handle? We sabotage ourselves when we neglect to pray. I can't blame God for my trials if I'm in one because I was too weak to handle a temptation. God's grace is sufficient (II Corinthians 12:9) to help me overcome my temptations, but I must be in a position to receive His grace.

Luke 18:6. God is our judge and He is just.

Luke 18:7-8. Is God equating prayer with faith? I get the sense that Jesus is a little frustrated looking into the future and seeing how the world would degenerate.

Actually, He will shorten the days so there will be some saved (Matthew 24:22).

Luke 18: 9. There is a huge danger in being self-righteous.

Luke 18:17. A child is (1) obedient, (2) trusting and (3) loving.

Luke 18:18-25. See notes at Matthew 19.

Luke 18:30. Some blessings are given now; others will be given later.

Luke 19: 8. An encounter with Jesus changes me!

Luke 19:10. What was lost? Worshipers. Lucifer once worshiped and then changed his focus of worship from God to himself. Adam did the same. God is seeking worshipers (John 4:23) who will worship Him.

Luke 19:42. Everyone has "their day". I don't want to miss my day! I want to seize the opportunity to serve God while I can.

Luke 19:44. God reveals secrets to His friends, so why didn't they know? They had a lack of intimacy. (See essay entitled "Me 'N' You Stick Together like Glue" in *It's Not Rocket Science, Volume 1*.) God wants intimacy with me.

Luke 20:18. Fall on Jesus. Be broken so He can rebuild. When Jesus falls on me, there is destruction. When I fall on Him, He can make me whole again.

Luke 20:25. The image of Caesar was on the money. The image of God is on a man (Genesis 1:27)! I am to give myself to God!

Luke 20:45-47. There're always the fakes (21:8). Beware of philosophy. The scribes could quote the scriptures and talk about it, but they didn't *know* it by experience.

Luke 21:2. Widow's mite. See notes at Mark 12:41.

Luke 21:14. Make up your mind! The mind must be made up *before* a trial. A made up mind sets the ***trajectory of the heart!***

Luke 21:19. By patience and perseverance, the snail reached the ark!

Luke 21:34. Worldliness
1. Surfeiting = excessiveness, especially in eating & drinking
2. Drunkenness
3. Temporal things (cares of life)

This is very similar to the sin of Sodom (Ezekiel 16:49-50). Our natural, human inclination is to over eat, over drink and over spend on temporal things. When we do so, we become lazy and our focus is on the next "thrill" and not on God. We see this in every aspect of all societies, regardless of culture. One generation works hard and suffers for the betterment of the next. The second generation has learned that work ethic, but because of affluence, overindulges their children. The third generation doesn't know the meaning of hard work and doesn't appreciate the family's wealth. The third generation is lazy and demanding. The same can be said for spiritual things. Each generation must learn how to work, both physically and spiritually. The warning is clear in vs 35 that worldliness would be a snare to many. Material things are not wrong, per se, but moderation is the key (Philippians 4:5).

Luke 22:3. Judas wasn't a traitor yet. Although as God, Jesus knew Judas would betray Him, Jesus was long-suffering. Jesus didn't cut Judas off just to spare the eleven. He was still kind and merciful to Judas till the end.

Luke 22:21. Even though God's plan had to be accomplished, Judas didn't have to be the one to betray Jesus. That was Judas' choice and he would have consequences. Sometimes Christians fail to pray for their politicians, country, etc., using the excuse that "we're in the last days and it is prophesied in the Bible." True, the world will deteriorate until God can't stand it anymore, BUT all of that doesn't have to happen on my shift!

Luke 22:24. Don't let "church politics" throw you off. Jesus had to deal with it in His disciples (Luke 22:24). Humans are humans and self-elevation is part of the (carnal) human mind set. I can't worry or stress about others. I can only make sure I'm not the carnal one. Let God deal with the others.

Luke 22:26. Take the humble route and let God elevate you.

Luke 22:31. Warning to Peter. Satan asked for his soul, BUT Jesus has prayed for him. Satan is demanding my soul. Peter made it and I can too! Jesus is rooting for me.

Luke 22:32. Even after 3 years of walking and talking with Jesus, Peter was not 100% sold out. It is possible to sit on a church pew day in and day out and not be converted. It is possible to witness signs and wonders and not be converted. It is possible to go out and preach the gospel and have power in the Spirit (as Peter did Matthew 10:1, 5), and not be converted. Once Peter became 100% committed, he received power after the Holy Spirit came upon him (Acts 1:8; 2:38). Up until Peter was converted, he buckled under the pressure of temptation. After his conversion, the Holy Spirit gave him power to overcome temptations and to even stand tall in times of persecution.

Luke 22:40; 46. Why pray? So, I don't fall into temptation. Good reason. There is a huge danger in being lazy and not having a prayer life. There are always a million other things to be done in lieu of praying. I can't afford to fall for that trap. If Satan can't get me to out and out sin, he will try to get me to be spiritually lazy. If my prayer life is not up to par, I will sin on my own, without Satan's help! Here in south Louisiana, most people "leg" their crepe myrtles. Crepe Myrtles are naturally a bush. By legging them, they can be made into a tree with just a few trunks. Since the natural inclination is to be a bush, shoots grow up from the roots. Those shoots need to be cut back once a season in order to maintain the leggy look. Likewise, my natural, human inclination is to sin. I have a sinful nature. My prayer life cuts off the carnal shoots that are always breaking out from the roots. If I neglect to keep those shoots trimmed, I will revert back to my sinful, bushy state.

Luke 22:43. These 3 disciples slept through a supernatural experience. Will I?

Luke 22:62. Saying "sorry" is not the same as repentance. Godly sorrow brings about a change, a repentance. Being "sorry I got caught" ultimately brings death. Judas and Peter were both "sorry", but one had an attitude of repentance and the other didn't (Matthew 27:3-5; II Corinthians 7:10).

Luke 23:8. Even Herod had a chance. Unfortunately, all he wanted was a side-show. We will *all* be without excuse on Judgment Day. I don't know how everyone will have a witness and a chance to be saved, but God is just and fair. He'll make sure we all have a chance.

Luke 23:12. An encounter with Jesus produces friendships, even for the wrong reason! Isn't it interesting that backsliders clump together? I suppose they help each other justify their actions.

Luke 23:14. Pilate and Herod both knew the accusations against Jesus were false. Some individuals in the mob may have been manipulated by the religious leaders, but Pilate and Herod <u>knew</u> Jesus was innocent and yet, submitted to the mob mentality (vs 23).

Luke 23:34. *Forgiveness* personified by Jesus.
   1.   His injuries killed him, but still He forgave.
   2.   Forgiveness comes before resurrection power.
   3.   Forgiveness did not change His suffering, but changed the world forever!
If Jesus was able to forgive through all that He went though, how can I not? How can I stand before Jesus on Judgment Day and say, "But .....?"

Luke 24: 10. Women were the first to see Jesus after His resurrection. Peter went to check out their story, but didn't see Jesus (vs 12, 24) until much later (vs 36).

Luke 24:29. After Jesus' resurrection, He walked and talked with two disciples (not two of the 11) as they were walking to Emmaus. He would have kept on going down the road had they not constrained Him to stay. It wasn't until after they constrained Him that He revealed himself and their eyes were opened. How many times have I had a visitation of the spirit of God, but didn't "constrain" Him and He just went on? How many times have I missed out on a special experience; a revelation? How many times have I been unaware I was entertaining an angel (Hebrews 13:2)? I don't want to miss those opportunities. Lord, help me to be sensitive to You!

Luke 24:39. It's personal. Living for God *is not Rocket Science*, but it is Personal. Jesus said "handle me and see". It is one thing to partake of a meal, but it is quite another thing to prepare the meal. When I "handle" the food, I have a vested interest in it. I'm concerned that it tastes good. I want to make sure I have handled it correctly. When we had special speakers at the church we pastored, we would ask church members to prepare a dish for the evening meal. This connected them to the evangelist. They had a vested interest in his sermon because they had handled his nourishment. When I touch Jesus, I become more than a bystander. I become vested in Him. When I touch Jesus, virtue is passed to me (Luke 6:19). When I touch the lives of others, that virtue from Jesus shines through me to them. I may be the only "Jesus" they experience. Do I have enough in me to cause people to want to know Jesus more, or does my so-called "Christianity" repel them?

Luke 24:44-45. The disciples were "slow" in "connecting the dots". Jesus explained and connected the Old Testament to its fulfillment. Jesus spent some time with them explaining how things fit perfectly together. We see evidence of this in the epistles. The disciples taught what Jesus had revealed to them during the private teaching times.

Luke 24:47. Jesus instituted the Acts 2:38 message, and the gospel going to the Gentiles.

Luke 24:49. There was one more test of obedience and faith for the disciples. Who of the disciples would go to Jerusalem and just wait until???? Do I have that kind of blind faith? If God tells me something, will I not get impatient, but have the faith to wait until????

JOHN
Written to ALL people who would believe. Written much later than the other gospels, possibly to correct false doctrine concerning the Godhead. Theme: Jesus, the son of God, is entitled to all things!

John 1:1, 14. "Logos" is the Greek word used for "word" in this passage. It means, "the thought behind the thing", or the "expression". The body form of Jesus was thought of way back when God planned humanity. God, because He is omniscient, knows everything. Therefore, He knew mankind would sin and would need a redeemer. He planned out the body He would want to dwell in here on earth. That thought was from the beginning, but was fulfilled in Jesus (vs 14).

John 1:12-13. To those who received Him, He gave the *right* to become His child. We are not sons of God by blood, flesh, or will of man, but by the spirit.

John 1:17. The law proved man cannot live without sinning. Jesus fulfilled the law. He paid the price for sin. It is by His grace I have the opportunity to apply His sinless state to my life through the new birth experience.

John 1:18. A spirit cannot be seen. God *had* to come in flesh in order to be seen.

John 1:23. Those who knew the scripture, knew John the Baptist was the forerunner of the Messiah (vs 41). God always lets His people know what is going to happen. There are no surprises. This is why everyone will be speechless on Judgment Day. We know. We are without excuse.

John 1:29. John is referencing JHVH Jireh (the Lord provides). He is declaring that God has provided the sacrifice.

John 1:31-33. The scripture does not say a literal dove came down and perched on Jesus' head. It says that the Spirit came down *in the manner of a dove*. A dove glides down gently, unlike an eagle who dive bombs his prey. This was a sign to John. It was the confirmation that John needed. The Bible doesn't say anyone else saw this. John's spiritual eyes were opened and He saw the anointing fall gently, like a dove.

John 2:4-7. It wasn't on the schedule for Jesus to start His ministry until later, but He submitted to parental authority and performed a miracle anyway. On the surface, it appears Jesus was rude and publicly rebuked his mother. This interpretation would be contrary to other Biblical teachings. I think Jesus' question to His mother was more along the lines of, "What does this temporal problem have to do with my spiritual ministry" than a harsh word to her. He honored His mother anyway and submitted to parental authority. I imagine He chuckled a bit as he performed that miracle. Being rude to her would be a conflict of a Biblical principal. The Bible does not contradict itself. When there appears to be a contradiction, dig a little deeper and find the meaning. Perhaps this is what is meant by the words, "Seek and ye shall find". I need to ask God to "open my eyes and ears" so I understand what is really happening underneath the seemingly contradictions.

John 2:24-25. Judas & Matthew both had "money" issues. Matthew was a tax collector. Tax collectors were known to charge a little extra and keep the extra for themselves. Jesus knew this. He knew the potential for the good and the bad in both of them. He gave both men plenty of opportunities to make the right choices. Matthew did. Judas didn't. Even though Jesus knew of Judas' weakness, He still gave Judas a chance (3 years) to overcome that weakness. Jesus allowed Judas to be in charge of the group's money, even though He knew Judas was a thief (John 12:6). Judas should have resisted temptation and said, "No, let Andrew keep the money." Judas carried around his temptation with him all of the time. I need to stay away from my temptations. First of all, I need to pinpoint my weaknesses. It's time for me to take a deep look into the mirror and be honest with myself. I can't avoid all temptation and still live on this earth; however, I CAN avoid dwelling on it. If I dwell on my temptation, I will have plenty of opportunities to return to it (Hebrews 11:15). If I dwell on sinful thoughts, God will not hear me (Psalm 66:18).

John 3:3. Our spiritual eyes are not opened until we experience the new birth. It is pointless to debate scripture with someone who hasn't experienced the new birth. They just won't "get it". Lead them to the Holy Spirit by being so excited that they want it too. Then, their understanding will be opened and the Holy Spirit will lead and guide them into all truth (John 16:13). It would behoove me to remember this as well. When I don't understand something either in the Bible or something that is happening in my life, I need to renew myself in the Holy Spirit and God will give me some understanding.

John 3:8. Just as the wind cannot be seen, the Spirit cannot be seen. The evidence is in the sound and the affects. Every place receiving the Holy Spirit is recorded in the book of Acts. They spoke in tongues and lives were changed. If someone's life does not change when they receive the Holy Spirit, then they have consciously quenched the Spirit.

John 3:16. Soul winning is a one-on-one job. One of the most quoted scriptures is John 3:16. This was spoken to ONE person, Nicodemus. Another famous scripture is the one where Jesus revealed to ONE person, the woman at the well, He was the Messiah (John 4:26). One-on-one is not nearly as glamorous as preaching to the masses, but that's where the job gets done. As a result of that one-on-one encounter, a whole city had a witness (John 4:29-30; 39-42).

John 3:21. It is not enough to "hear", but I must also "DO". When I "do" the truth, I come into the light. Jesus is the light (John 8:12; 9:5). I am not saved by my works, but works are a by-product of my salvation.

John 3:30. John's attitude was amazing. His attitude was this: "we're on the same team. However, God sees fit to use me is fine (vs 27). I don't have to be in the spotlight. In fact, I need to hold the spotlight pointed toward Jesus!" I wish more preachers

& saints had that attitude!

John 4:6-28. Thoughts on the Samaritan Woman's story.
- Most ladies went early in the morning to gather enough water for the day. This woman was an outcast, so went when there would be no one to bully her or gossip about her. Jesus knew when she would be there.
- How many men does it take to go get lunch? *All* of them? Yes, because Jesus had to get their prejudices out of the way.
- The greatest and most effective witnessing is done one-on-one. We all like to preach to the masses and them receive the Holy Spirit, but discipleship is one-on-one.
- vs.23-24. "spirit and truth". This refers to the human spirit: enthusiasm, spirited worship.
- vs. 28. This woman left *all* for God (ref. Elisha I Kings 19:21). An encounter with Jesus causes me to break from my past and leave it behind.

John 4:37. This is God's church. I can't be picky as to which role I play ~ whether I sow or reap. (I Corinthians 3:6-7). Don't worry so much about what "job" you have in the church. One sows and another reaps. One plants and one waters, but God is the one who gives the increase (I Corinthians 3:6-7). It's not MY kingdom, but GOD's kingdom. I don't like to refer to a church as "Bro. Richard's church". It's not the pastor's church. It's God's church. Remember that. I do what I do for God and not for the people, the pastor, or anyone else. When I give, I give to God. If there is a misuse of funds, God will deal with the culprit.

John 4:50. Faith requires action. If I believe the Word, I will DO the Word.

John 5:6. I must have the desire to be made whole. Jesus is ready. Am I? Am I content with the familiar or do I want a change? I once offered a friend a job. His response? "No, I don't want to jeopardize my government benefits." As sad as that is in the natural, it is sadder to have that attitude in spiritual matters.

John 5:8. Faith demands action. My actions will always reflect my belief, regardless of what my mouth says. This man obeyed, even though his actions went against the teachings of the Pharisees (vs 10).

John 5:14. Sin will take you farther than you ever intended to go: Backsliders, beware. Once someone knows truth and walks away from it, things go downhill. One sin gives birth to another. It is difficult to break out of the cycle of sin. It is vicious.

John 5:18. The Jews clearly understood Jesus' claim He was God. They were so positive this was His claim, they plotted to kill Him!

John 5:26. Jesus is qualified to judge because: He is God and as a man, He became sin.

John 5:37. No man can see the Father, which is a spirit, except by the incarnation of that spirit, Jesus.

John 6:6-7. God sometimes asks us questions to prove us. Being God, He knows what to do. He doesn't need my advice. Being God, He also knows what I am thinking, so He doesn't need to ask for His own sake. He asks so I will bring my thoughts together, form an opinion, and verbalize it. I found myself using this same technique in raising my children. Teachers use this in the classroom. God asks questions for *my sake*, not His. I need to determine what I can "bring to the table". God will take care of the rest. If I give my all, He will give His all. There is no miracle without my effort and my involvement. Creation was the only time God performed a miracle without some involvement by man. Man was then charged with maintaining creation.

John 6:9-13. Jesus will only do the impossible. He's not going to do that which I can do. Jesus is not a magic wand to wave around. The boy had to give up his lunch (willing), Jesus had to bless it (able), and the disciples had to distribute it (action). If I am willing to surrender to Him, He will bless me. Then, I have to get up and get moving - do something about His blessing. God doesn't bless me so I can hoard the blessings. He blesses me to be a blessing to others. I must be a conduit of God's blessings to others.

John 6:29. Are you trying to do the "Lord's work"? Look no further. Believe on Him. That's a deep subject. Believing (true believing) requires action. If I really believe, really believe, I will obey.

John 6:30. People are always looking for "a sign". God had already given a sign at Jesus' baptism (John 1:33; 12:30). Don't search after signs. The rainbow is a sign (Genesis 9:13). There are signs in nature (Genesis 1:14; Luke 21:25). There are already plenty of signs. We don't need any more signs. Seek after a relationship with God. Then, you don't have to run around trying to interpret a sign: you'll have direct communication with Him and you will know. People flock to hear prophecy preachers, hoping to hear from God. Why don't we just go straight to God? Trying to hear from God vicariously through someone else is the lazy way and is subject to the interpretation of the human messenger. *Example 1:* Monique was dying with cancer and many, many tongues and interpretation went forth declaring she would live to see her grandchildren. There was a whole lot of whooping and rejoicing that God would heal her. That's NOT what God said. He said she would see her grandchildren. She did. Two grandsons were born in October. She died the following January. Unfortunately, the human messengers read more into God's statement than what He actually said. When I get a word from God, I must be very careful that I don't add to it and embellish it with my own emotions. If I tell someone something incorrect, I will damage their faith. When people tell you a word is from God and it doesn't happen like they said, don't lose faith in God. HE'S not the one who messed up. The human messenger obviously didn't interpret something right. *Example 2:* Mitchell told a couple who already had a handicapped child the next child would be in perfect health. That's all he said. The lady was pregnant at the time and that child died in the womb. She got pregnant again and that child is in perfect health. The people around her thought God meant the child in the womb would be perfect. Not so. God meant the next child who was born would be perfect. God was preparing her to have faith for another pregnancy. He knew the child in the womb would die and He wanted her to have faith for another pregnancy. Have faith in God. He doesn't get things wrong.

John 6:48-63. Jesus is the bread of life. Internalize Him. The Jews, of course, were thinking cannibalism, but He was talking spiritually. If I can be more like Jesus, if I will allow Him to reproduce Himself in me, if I can internalize Him, all will be well.

John 6:69. In the early 1980s, I taught in a Christian school. In going through disciplinary training sessions, I learned that five well placed swats to alternating sides of the "glutimous maximus" was within legal parameters and did not constitute abuse. We were told when defendants used the Biblical "spare the rod, spoil the child" defense in court proceedings, the court tried to determine whether or not Biblical principals were a preference or a conviction to the Defendant. That determination most often was the deciding factor in a guilty or non-guilty verdict as to child abuse. Peter had such conviction when he blurted out that Jesus was the Christ (the Messiah). It was an "ah-hah" moment for Peter. He said, "we believe and ARE SURE that thou art that Christ..." Peter was convinced. It was a conviction he carried to his grave. My question today is a little bit cliché, but I'll use it anyway. If you were arrested for being a Christian, would there be enough evidence to convict you? (Bear in mind, the word "Christian" is an adjective meaning "Christ-like" and is not a noun or label I wear.)

John 7:5. Jesus was rejected by His family members. He knows what rejection feels like, even the pain of rejection by loved ones.

John 7:6-8. It is true that anytime is the time for repentance, but there is a specific time in God's time table for my ministry to begin, end, etc. Patience is truly a virtue. Jesus told His disciples "my time is not YET come" (vs. 8). Sometimes we just have to bide our time. While I am in that "holding pattern", just circling the airport (so to speak), let me make the preparations. Let me put my table in its upright position, fasten my seatbelt and stow away my belongings. Let me mature and get my act together. Let me study the scriptures. Let me prepare, for as soon as God takes me out of the holding pattern, I will have to hit ground running.

John 7:24. Jesus told us to "judge righteous judgment" (John 7:24). We must be very careful when we judge, for with the same judgment we dispense on others, we shall be judged ourselves by God (Matthew 7:1-2). I must show mercy. If I judge, I must be righteous. That's pretty hard, since my righteousness is as filthy rags (Isaiah 64:6). As a leader, I may be forced to make a judgment call. I really need to pray about that and let God lead me into making the right decision. I need to be careful I don't judge based only on what I see. This is another scripture that seemingly contradicts the scriptures that tell us not to judge! Judging (passing of a sentence) is God's business. However, judging (making a judgment call) is a Christian's business. I must learn to differentiate between the two.

John 7:31. There were people who believed, but still didn't think He was the Messiah. Believing requires a follow-through action. It is possible to believe the Bible, but if I don't obey it, my belief that the Bible is true is not going to save me. I'm not going to lose weight because I believe eating only salads will give me the desired result. I've got to actually *eat* only salads. Mere belief won't shave off those pounds.

John 7:38. Don't dam the river! If I have the Holy Spirit, I have rivers of living water springing up from my innermost being. I can't afford to let the cares of life dam it up. Our hurts, our disappointments, our confusion, our loneliness, etc. can all dam up the Holy Spirit. If I don't let the spirit of God flow freely, I become stagnant. Look at the Dead Sea. It is "dead" because it doesn't flow. Plenty of water flows INTO it, but there is no outlet. The result is water evaporates and leaves behind so many minerals, you can actually SIT in the water! The rocks from the Dead Sea have a terrible taste from the minerals they have absorbed. (Yes, I've licked them.) NOTHING can live in those waters. I have met many a Christian, who at one time, was filled to overflowing with the Holy Spirit, but for some reason, the flow has been dammed ~ and they are damned. Just because someone faithfully sits on a pew and outwardly looks the part doesn't mean they are saved. The river has got to be kept flowing. That requires lots of maintenance. I've got to keep the debris out (and the pesky little critters!). *[PS: Oh, yeah, and God will separate the wheat from the tares. That's HIS job (Matthew 13:30), not mine. I'm not to judge anyone else's flow but mine, and mine alone.]*

John 7:39-40. The Holy Spirit could not come because Jesus had not yet ascended. One God, different manifestations.

John 7:42. If they had bothered to investigate the facts, they would have known Jesus had been born in Bethlehem and was merely raised in Galilee. People, by and large, believe what is told to them and don't investigate the facts. Look at the posts on social media! Look at all of the rumors that go out in printed form! Many people don't bother to see if their pastor is preaching the truth. They just blindly believe that he/she is. Perhaps this is why Jesus said, "Seek and ye shall find." I've got to dig and seek out truth.

John 8:3-11. Under the Old Testament, both parties in an adulterous situation were to be stoned, not just the woman (Leviticus 20:10; Deuteronomy 22:22). The actual witnesses to the adultery were to stone the guilty. Under Roman law, murder was not allowed. The Jews here were only trying to trick Jesus, however He was able to deflect that trick and, in vs 11, offers emotional peace. Judgment knelt down and wrote something in the sand which caused the men to drop their stones and leave. Mercy stood up and forgave the woman of her sins. Mercy and judgment meet together (Psalm 85:10) because of Calvary.

John 8:33-36. Bondage. Ha! Ha! I've heard people say how God has delivered them from the bondage of holy living. Bah-Humbug! I have freedom *because* I keep God's commandments (Psalm 119:44-45). The Holy Spirit gives me the freedom to **do what is right**. Without the Holy Spirit, I can't help but sin. I was born in sin (Psalm 51:5). When Adam and Eve sinned in the Garden, sin entered into the human DNA. Different people have a different propensity to sin in different ways. Some have a tendency to develop addictive behavior; for others, lying is second nature. The Jews told Jesus they had never been in bondage (John 8:33). I suppose they forgot about Egypt, Babylon and wait, they were under Roman rule at the time! Talk about being in denial! They were flat-out lying to themselves. SIN is the bondage (vs 34). The law of the Old Testament proved how it was impossible for mankind to live sinless. Even when the sin was spelled out in great detail, they couldn't help themselves! Jesus breaks me free from sin (vs 36). The book of Romans deals with the freedom the Holy Spirit brings. The Holy Spirit does not give me license to do what my fleshly desires want, but the freedom, liberty and power to do the right thing. There are certain "decrees to keep" (Acts 16:4) that the apostles delivered to the church. Living for God means I live a separated life. That's more than lip service. Someone should be able to tell I live for God without me opening my mouth. I need to be careful that I don't misuse my freedom to fulfil the desires of my flesh (Galatians 5:13). Through the power of the Holy Spirit, I now have the freedom to actually do the right thing and not sin!

John 8:39. What are the works of Abraham? (1) Serving God. (2) Being in close communication with God. (3) Obeying God.

John 8:44. The devil is a liar and cannot tell the truth. When someone "prophesies" something or "hears from God" and it is contradictory to God's word, that person is not of God. The devil really wants people to worship him, however, there is a certain segment of the human population that wants to believe in God. If the devil can pervert the truth *just a little*, he knows he can lead these people down the path to hell. That's what he did in the Garden. He didn't expect Eve to fall down and worship him! He knew Eve had a relationship with God. Satan perverted the truth a little and took Eve down an intellectual path that lead her to sin. Be careful about these intellectual and/or philosophical paths (Colossians 2:8). I can eventually justify everything. A nun once told Michelle her daughter, Andrea, was in heaven after committing suicide, because God knew Andrea wasn't thinking right when she took her own life! Andrea didn't just wake up one morning and decide to kill herself. Her state of mind was a progression which could have been avoided had she dealt with her problems by bringing them to God. I personally knew Andrea. Her state of mind was brought on by jealousy and not by a chemical imbalance or medications. [On a side note: I do think medications can cause otherwise godly people to have a twisted mind. God is the judge. I'm glad God knows the ***trajectory of the heart***. I'm glad I'm not God and I don't have to make those judgment calls!] Remember our earlier discussion about the wise man building his house upon the rock and the foolish man building his house upon the sand (Matthew 7:24-27)? I ask you, what is sand? Sand is ground up particles of rock. The foolish man also built upon rock, but upon particles of it. All religions of the world have some grains of truth in them. The Buddhists teach materialism does not bring peace. True! The Scientologists teach that you must take responsibility for your own actions. True! Some Christian groups believe the essentiality of water baptism so much, they will baptize an infant by sprinkling! True, baptism is essential (their application is not Biblical, though). I need to make sure I don't just take out particles of truth out of the Bible and discard the truths I don't particularly want to follow. When the trials and storms come, I want my house to be anchored on the rock. A trajectory that is only 1% off will still miss the mark just as a trajectory that is 100% off. The devil doesn't care how little my trajectory is off. He is vindictive and wants to hurt God as much as he can by throwing me off course.

John 8:52. When God talks about "death", He is most often talking about a spiritual death, not physical. Jesus usually spoke of a physical death as being "asleep". A spiritual death is final; a physical one is not.

John 8:59. The Jews knew *exactly* what Jesus was saying. They wanted to kill Jesus because He was claiming to be God. This was blasphemous to them. They could not conceive of different manifestations of God, even though God had appeared in different forms throughout their history (burning bush, cloud by night, etc.)

John 9:7. God does His part, but I must do my part to receive. The Blind man didn't see or know what was happening (probably a good thing). He obeyed BEFORE he received. In John 20:21, we find Jesus is "sent". The word "Siloam" means "sent". By sending the man to wash in the Pool of Siloam, Jesus symbolically sent the blind man to himself.

John 9:24-39. Who made the Pharisees God? I must be very careful when I judge lest I miss the truth. In fact, I need to leave the judging to God. Whomever He allows in Heaven is fine with me! The purpose of miracles, signs and wonders are to bring people closer to God, not to be a side-show. This blind man had a **personal**

experience and the Pharisees could not take that away from him. Once the Pharisees realized that, they began to harass the blind man. Their persecution just made him more adamant about the miracle. Once he took a stand against the Pharisees, Jesus revealed Himself to the blind man. This points back to the scripture which says, "Seek and ye shall find" (Jeremiah 29:13; Matthew 7:7; Luke 11:9). When I take a break from the hustle of my activities, and search out truths in the scripture, God will reveal Himself to me. I can't accept just what the religious status quo says. I've got to search out the truth!

John 10:7, 9. Jesus said He was the "door." Just as there was only one door to the Tabernacle, there is only one door into Heaven. The implication in this passage is Jesus was the gateway into Heaven, or everlasting life. Judas kissed the door to Heaven on his way to hell. I don't want to be guilty of the same. Judas had a part in Jesus' ministry (Acts 1:16-17). Wow. What a shame he never repented. What a testimony he could have had concerning God's grace & mercy!

John 10:10. One sheet of paper is very easy to tear, but not 30 sheets stacked together. Satan sometimes works on us one "sheet" at a time. He wears us down. If we don't tear the sheets one at a time as they come, we get trapped and can't tear them collectively. Satan's purpose is to steal, kill, and destroy (John 10:10). Something that is stolen, can possibly be recovered. Since Jesus is the resurrection, something that is killed can be revived through Him. However, something that is destroyed is done over a process of time and can never be regained. Babies aren't born to rape and murder. They go through some process whereby they are slowly turned into that monster. The rapist and murderer may be able to repent and even be saved, but the lives they have affected can never be restored to the pre-victim state. Jason is in prison today for murder. At age 12, he was called to preach! Somehow from age 12 to age 40ish, he turned into someone who could callously kill and not even be sorry for it. He has zero remorse. He's been to church services in prison, but says he "can't feel God at all". He has been destroyed over the process of time. He had plenty of opportunities to get back to God before this deed and even since he's been in prison. He has a praying mother and many other family members. Before this crime, he would pop in to church every so often and have lengthy discussions with the pastor and an uncle of mine, and cry and cry ~ but never made the commitment to live for God. So sad. God would forgive him if he repented, but he sees no need for repentance. He has allowed too many "sheets" (life circumstances) to pile up in his life. He can't see how to tear them up.

John 10:29. This scripture is sometimes misunderstood to mean that once someone is saved, they will always be saved. Not so. This scripture is stating that no person other than *myself* can sever my relationship with God. I can, by turning away.

John 10: 30-39. The Jews understood Jesus was claiming to be God Himself. They understood this so well, they wanted to kill Him for making that claim! Too bad modern people don't understand this!

John 11. Synopsis of the Lazarus Story.
- As God, Jesus knew Lazarus was sick. He cared because as God, Lazarus was His child and as man, Lazarus was His friend.
- Jesus did not intervene until He was asked.
- The power to heal is not based upon the pray-er (an unknown person, vs 3), but based upon the power of God's love.
- Why did Jesus stall (vs 6)? Did Jesus realize His human nature needed to submit to His spiritual nature? Here was an opportunity for pride to get in the way. Jesus had to allow the Spirit to control his human nature. As a human, of course, he wanted to rush and heal Lazarus, but that would have prevented a greater miracle of raising Lazarus from the dead.
- Truth is sometimes misunderstood (vs 12-13).
- Revelation results in becoming a witness (vs 27-28).
- Martha was there at the scene, taking care of business. Mary was at home, perhaps wallowing in sorrow. She seems to be the more emotional of the two.
- Martha brought Mary to Jesus and Mary brought many others. Had Martha not called for Mary, all of those with Mary would not have witnessed the miracle. I may not be the one who brings the multitude, but I will have a part in all of those brought to Jesus by someone whom I've witnessed to (vs 45).
- The miracle of Lazarus only happened with the cooperation of humans! Lazarus had to be loosed! If not, he would have suffocated and died again. It is up to me to help people get loosed from their baggage.
- Even in the face of a miracle, there will be the group who is worried about politics (vs 48)! If God could raise Lazarus from the dead, why couldn't He take care of the nation? Humph.

John 12:4-6. Jesus knew Judas had a weakness for money, but gave him the chance to overcome by allowing him to be the treasurer for the group.

John 12:8. Jesus said, "The poor always ye have with you". I think "poor" is a state of mind. I've seen many people who were not wealthy monetarily, but considered themselves very rich. I've seen others who had a little jingle in their pockets but are always bellyaching about one calamity or another. One time I gave someone an opportunity to get a good job, with the potential to make a very nice living for his family. He declined because it would jeopardize his government benefits. "Poor" is a mentality.

John 12:16. The disciples didn't realize they were living in the fulfillment of prophecy until after Jesus was resurrected. After Jesus was glorified, it dawned on them they had just witnessed scripture unfolding before their very eyes. How cool is that? Imagine reading in Isaiah about the Messiah and thinking, "Hey, I was there! I saw that happen!!" They were actually helping prophecy to be fulfilled! It amazes me that today (2014), I see and hear things on the news that makes me think that I, too, am seeing prophecy being fulfilled. As a little girl, I couldn't think how "Christian" America could become one of those nations in the book of Revelation. I thought that there were enough people who really knew the Bible in the USA, that even though they might not obey the scriptures and be saved, they would recognize the antichrist and not bow. In the few short years of my lifetime, I see how the things in Revelation are being slipped into our society. People (even self-proclaimed Christians) vote with their pocketbooks and not with their beliefs. This proves the *trajectory of their hearts*. With the onslaught of the computer age, it is easy to see how everyone will be tracked and watched and how a computer chip in the hand would make life so much easier. It is my understanding that 3 sets of 6 numbers would assign the whole human race an identity number. Just think: With such a computer chip no debit card needed, medical information and history could be scanned by EMS, there would be immediate access to your data on the "cloud", no passport needed, food & drug allergies could be scanned, identity theft would be virtually impossible, and petty theft would be slashed ~ after all, who is going bring a severed hand to the cash register? Sounds amazing, doesn't it? Yep! Whoever is still living on this earth when this becomes mandatory will welcome it in. The recent NSA revelations showed us how our every movement is tracked. Drones are used by our military now. I heard an interview concerning drone technology. They are capable of making a drone with a camera the size of a mosquito. The only problem is the battery life is too limited. Once they figure out how to overcome that technical problem, how easy would it be to send a camera down the chimney of someone they wish to track (such as a Christian)? I think the only way of surviving those times will be for people to live off the electrical grid, live purely off the land (no job), living as they did back in the stone age. I'm better off living for God NOW and making the Rapture! If I'm not strong enough to live for God now, what makes me think I'll have the strength to live for Him during the reign of the antichrist?

John 12:25. Jesus is not talking about having suicidal thoughts here. The key phrase in this verse is *"in this world"*. If I love life *in this world* so much I refuse to live for God, I will eventually lose my life and not be saved. If I realize this world is not my home and I put my focus on my heavenly home, when my life here on earth is over, I'll have a place in Heaven!

John 12:26. Give God control of what you have and He will bless you with what He has. I believe I'll get the best of that trade-off!

John 12:27. In His humanity, Jesus dreaded this dying process, but in His spirit, He knew this was the purpose of His existence in human form (the body). Jesus accomplished His mission (John 17:4). What has God put me on this earth to do for Him? When my cousin, Tommy, was shot and killed in a hunting accident, we were all, naturally, upset. At a prayer meeting that night, there was tongues and interpretation which said, "Don't cry for Tommy. He accomplished what I put him on this earth to do and I have brought him home. Once you've completed your assignment, I will come and get you too." God said something very similar at the gravesite service of another family member. Through tongues and interpretation, God told the surviving spouse that she still had a work to do. Doors of ministry began opening for her and she has been teaching many Bible studies and bringing many souls to God. We all have a specific purpose. Makes you think differently about things, doesn't it?

John 12:28-30. The Jews kept asking for a sign, but they had plenty.
- Virgin birth,
- Angels appearing to shepherds & wise men,
- Baptism of Jesus,
- Miracles,
- Fulfillment of prophecies, and
- This incident.

I have had plenty of signs pointing to the truth. What is my excuse?

John 12:38-40 quotes Isaiah's prophecy how God blinded their eyes. It sounds a little harsh until you keep reading. I wish verses 42-43 came before verses 28-40. Many of the religious rulers actually believed on Jesus but were afraid they would be excommunicated by the others if they admitted their belief. They valued their position in the "church" more than they valued a relationship with God. Their spiritual blindness came as a result of their rejection of Jesus. If I don't have a love for the truth, God will send a strong delusion that I would believe a lie and be damned (II Thessalonians 2:10-12).

John 12:48. The Word is the standard of judgment. It does not matter what anyone else says. I will not be judged by the criteria set by anyone except what God set forth in His word. In fact, those who add or take away are cursed (Galatians 1:8). It is easy, through philosophy, to twist scriptures to say what I want them to say. Attorneys do this all of the time. Arguing and winning a case is an art form. If an attorney is appointed to defend a criminal, s/he must do so without regard for the truth, or he could be disciplined or sued for failing to defend. I worked for an attorney who was assigned to defend a man who told him, "Yeah, I had drugs in my hotel room, but what they found wasn't my drugs. They never found my drugs." My boss hated having to defend that man, but he legally had to. That man walked free even though he was guilty of the charge. There won't be any of that kind of thing happening on judgment day. I will either line up with God's word, or I won't. Plain and simple. No questions. No arguments. No defense. It's that simple. *It's not rocket science.*

John 13:1, 34-35. Jesus loves us. He loves us to our dying day. He grieves when I refuse to repent. God doesn't send anyone to hell. If I go, it will be because I sent myself there. He is merciful and gives me plenty of chances to repent and live right. Because He loves, I must love. God is Love (I John 4:8). If I don't love, I don't have God. If I don't love my fellow brother/sister, I am renouncing my brotherhood with Christ.

John 13:2. Judas had to have entertained the devil's suggestion. I can't prevent the devil from putting something in my mind, but I can prevent myself from dwelling on it and taking action. It is when the seed is allowed to germinate that it becomes sin. (James 1:15)

John 13:5-10. The whole foot-washing process is a humbling process. The very act of washing someone's feet serves to humble me. I need that ever so often.

John 13:5, 11-12. How many "assets" do you need to have to pray for those who hate you? Only the love of God! What will I do with what I have (Luke 6:27-28)? Love caused Jesus to wash even Judas' feet. That's love!

John 13:16-17. People are searching for happiness. Jesus gave us the key. Happiness comes from service to others. Help people. (That's not to be confused with letting them take advantage of you, though!) Selfish people are not happy people.

John 13:21. Knowing one of His friends was about to betray Him hurt. Jesus knows what it is like to be betrayed by someone close to Him.

John 13:36. Jesus knew Simon would ultimately follow Him fully. Jesus knew Simon would deny him, but since the *trajectory of his heart* was right, Simon would overcome the hurdle and, once he received the power of the Holy Spirit (in Acts), would be strong and never deny him again. Judas betrayed. Peter denied. There is a difference.

John 14:1, 16, 18. Trouble? What trouble? Troubles come from:
- Reaping what I have sown
- No convictions
- Cursed earth
- Don't know the truth
- Misunderstandings

Nevertheless, Jesus prays for me and promises to be with me.

John 14:3. God spent 6 days creating the earth. So far, He has spent 2,000+ years preparing Heaven!

John 14:6. Jesus is referencing Psalm 43:3. He is claiming to be the fulfillment of David's prayer to Jehovah. John 16:13 tells us the Holy Spirit would lead into truth. The scriptures are not contradictory. There is only one God!

John 14:12. Jesus said we would do greater works than He did. Now, what is greater than raising someone from the dead, opening blinded eyes, or healing lepers? Why, praying someone through to the Holy Spirit, of course! The miracles we read Jesus doing were temporal miracles. The indwelling of the spirit of God in a human being (salvation) is eternal. That is the greater thing. The Holy Spirit baptism was only available after Jesus' ascension because Jesus couldn't be on earth and fill people with His spirit at the same time. If I get cancer, sure, I want you to pray for my healing, but the truth of the matter is that my healing is temporal. My healing will only give me a few more years of life on this earth. Along with praying for my healing, please pray that I make sure my soul is right with God. That is the greater thing.

John 14:15, 21, 23. If I love God, I will keep His commandments. ***It's not Rocket Science.*** This isn't complicated. I don't know why we hold a double standard. If there are rules at my job and I don't keep them, I get fired. If I am to be at work by 8:30 and I consistently show up when I am good and ready, I will get fired. If there are uniforms at work and I refuse to wear them, I get fired. No one even questions work rules. Why do we think we can live for God our own way and think God will be fine with our rebellion? Regardless of how many "I love yous" come out of my mouth, my actions reveal the *trajectory of my heart*. God has promised permanent residency with me IF I obey Him! It doesn't get any simpler than that. It doesn't get any better than that!

John 14:27. The world does have some pleasure (Hebrews 11:25; Job 20:5), but it is not lasting peace. When my natural world crumbles, God gives inner peace and gives me the power to face the difficult days. Christians who stand in the midst of severe persecution are human just like I am. They have the same fears I do. What enables them to stand is the peace and the power of God. God gives me grace and His grace is sufficient (James 4:6; II Corinthians 12:9; I Peter 5:5).

John 15. Watch the "ifs". So many of God's promises are contingent upon me. IF I ... God will .... Many times, I hear preachers spout off God's promises but fail to teach the contingencies. People get discouraged when they don't receive what the preacher said God promised. John 15 is full of "ifs". Everything boils down to loving God 100%. If I love God 100%, I will blindly obey and I will automatically love my fellow man and treat everyone right. Then,
1. vs 5-8. I will bear MUCH fruit (fruit of the spirit see Galatians 5:22-23).
2. vs. 10. I will be consumed by love.
3. vs. 12. Do I have a hard time loving others? I need to check my obedience-odometer! Loving others is not an option. I can be correct in what I say, but say things in a hateful manner. That should not be. I must love others (Ephesians 4:15-16).

4. vs. 14. I am a friend of Jesus ONLY IF I keep His commandments.
   5. vs. 15. God reveals things to His friends.
   6. vs 15. I am chosen to:
      a. bear fruit
      b. disciple the fruit so it remains
      c. receive my petitions
   7. vs 17. Love is once again, COMMANDED.

John15:18-19. When the world treats me badly, they really are doing that to God (Matthew 25:40, 45). There was a man in our church who walked out in the middle of my husband's sermon almost every service. My husband would get so angry! One day, the man walked out and slammed the door behind him. My husband's blood boiled and, *while he was preaching*, the Holy Spirit spoke to him and said, "What are you so upset over? He didn't walk out on you, he walked out on Me!" That man was under conviction and was storming out to get away from God. Sometimes we think someone hates us, but they are really rejecting God. God knows the heart, remember? He knows when someone is mad at Him and is just taking it out on us! An unsaved spouse, child, or friend gets mean when they are under conviction. Don't take it so personally (although it is hard not to). Pray for them. Pray they will turn towards God. He is trying to woo them. Showing them love will help God draw them in. If I show meanness back, not only am I sinning, but I am pushing them away from God. I don't want to be the reason (excuse) of someone not serving God. This is one more reason for me to have the Holy Spirit; so He would be a comfort to me in the difficult times of persecution! Instead of getting a chip on my shoulder, I need to change my attitude and realize God is on my side!

John 16:1-2. Don't be offended when persecuted (Luke 17:1). Sometimes, those who persecute you think they're doing God a favor and do it in the name of religion. Remember Saul, aka Paul? He sincerely thought he was doing the right thing. Because the ***trajectory of his heart*** was God-ward, God revealed to Saul he was doing wrong. Saul humbled himself and became Paul. The fact that I have the Holy Spirit means people will feel convicted around me. The Holy Spirit convicts. I don't have to say anything (John 16:7-8). When people receive that conviction, they will turn to God and the Spirit will guide them into all truth (John 16:13), but if they don't receive that conviction and rebel, they will most likely take it out on me. Remember, when someone is hateful to you *without cause*, they're probably under conviction of some sort (if you have the Holy Spirit).

John 16:7,13. The body form of God (Jesus) had to go away so He could come and dwell in us in spirit form. The Spirit will guide me into all truth, if I will listen and obey.

John 16:14. Is someone of God? Do they glorify God? If someone doesn't glorify God, s/he is not of God. See also John 17:5. Everything, from the blade of grass, to the bird that soars, to me, was made to glorify God.

John 16:16-19. Just remember that God is timeless. "A little while" to God may be a lifetime (or more) to me!

John 16:20-22. IT WILL BE WORTH IT ALL. The trials and hardships I go through in this life will fade. Not only will the memory of my trials fade as time goes on, they will be nothing in light of eternity. A mother who gives birth with much pain, declares she will never do that again. However, after a few years, she is willing to do so because the memory of that pain has faded somewhat and the joy of a new child outweighs the pain. When we get to Heaven, our trials will seem so small ~ if we even remember them.

John 16:23, 26. People often misuse this scripture. I must keep it in context. Jesus has been talking about His second coming in the preceding verses. Verse 23 starts off "in that day". The name of Jesus isn't a magic wand to waive around for instant results. He is not broadcasting this discourse to the world. He is talking to His close friends, His disciples. These are people who obey Him and whom He considers His friends (John 15:15). I can't be disobedient to God, fling out His name in prayer, and then get mad when He doesn't do what I want!!

John 16:33.
- Jesus conquered the world. He wasn't born in sin like I was because He did not have a natural father. He faced temptation, but He didn't succumb to sin. Therefore, I am able to overcome and climb out of the world if I have His spirit dwelling in me.
- Having troubles and tribulations in this life is a given (I Peter 5:9). Remember that little song, "Every promise in the Book is mine"? Oh yeah, this verse is also a promise!! Having troubles doesn't mean God is against me. It merely means I live in a sinful world. Trials are a given. Rather than be surprised when they come, I take comfort in the knowledge Jesus overcame and so shall I!!

John 17:1. Jesus prayed for himself (John 17:1), for the 12 disciples to have unity (John 17:6-19), and for all future believers (that means you and me) (John 17:20)! When He was on the cross, I was on His mind. I'm not going to allow myself to crucify Him over and over by sinning (Hebrews 6:6). I am not going to let the crucifixion of Jesus be in vain. How can I say I "love God" and continue in my sins? It is my opinion intentional sinning is the most grievous to God. How can anyone claiming to be a Christian intentionally sin?

John 17:15. Living for God does not give me immunity from the world, but POWER to overcome! I am going to have the same trials and temptations whether or not I live for God. Why wouldn't I want the power to overcome all of those things? Why wouldn't I want God to help me be victorious over my trials?

John 17:17. Part of Jesus' prayer was that I would be set apart by truth. He went on to clarify "truth". Truth is the word of God. *It's not Rocket Science.* I've got to know what the word of God is. Commentaries and religious books are nice, but they are some human's *interpretation* of God's word. What does the Word say? That is truth.

John 17:20. Jesus validated the disciples' ministry and their preaching. He acknowledged people would come to God through the word of His disciples. Without their word and writings, I would not have any knowledge of God. Jesus gave an introduction and laid the *foundation* of Christian living. In the epistles, the disciples built upon that foundation and applied those principles to everyday life. I can't ignore the teachings of the disciples.

John 18:2. Judas knew exactly where to find Jesus. He knew the place. It was familiar. He had been there many times with Jesus and accurately predicted where Jesus would go. How sad to know where to find Jesus, but to betray Him instead of embracing Him. People don't realize when they backslide, they are really betraying Jesus. Backslidden people don't realize when they call on a believer to pray with no intentions of turning their lives around and living for God themselves, they are slapping Jesus in the face.

John 18:10. Had Peter prayed in the garden instead of slept, he would have been better prepared for this emergency situation. He drew a sword on impulse. What would my response be in an emergency situation? Will I rely on my human, natural abilities, or will I call upon the name of the Lord? My response will show my spiritual condition. I want to be in a place where I trust God totally.

John 18:11. Sometimes, those we love try to talk us out of doing a particular something for God. They mean well, but if God has specifically directed you and you are absolutely sure of His voice, go for it! Jesus rejected Peter's attempts to talk Him out of going to Calvary. My father was called as a missionary to Korea. Several calamities happened prior to us going, and a preacher-friend said, "Maybe God is telling you NOT to go." My parents had had a most definite experience with their calling in an all-night prayer meeting at the house a few years prior to that time. My dad replied, "Brother, God only has to tell me ONE time what to do!" Sounds like Paul, huh? He knew he would be arrested in Jerusalem, but he also knew God told him to go. His church buddies tried to dissuade him, but he chose to obey God (Acts 21:11-14). It's okay to be challenged, though. It helps your church friends understand you really did hear from God.

John 18:15. Who is the "other disciple known to the high priest"? Perhaps it was John. He seems to refer to himself in the third person format. John also called himself the "disciple that Jesus loved". Now, Jesus loved them all, but John personalized his relationship with Jesus so much, John felt Jesus loved him more. Perhaps he felt this way because he loved Jesus more. He was the only one who stuck it out with Jesus. It was John whom Jesus asked to care for His mother (John 19:26-27). I've always thought it was interesting none of His siblings were there. My daughters each claim they are my favorite ... and, they are! Both of them!

John 18:38. Pilate asked Jesus the question, "What is truth", but didn't bother to wait for the answer. He missed his opportunity to find out. What a shame! If I'm going to ask God a question, I need to have enough patience and consideration to wait for the answer! My strength comes when I wait on God (Isaiah 40:31).

John 19:26-27. Sometimes a "church" family is closer than a "physical" family. Mary had other children besides Jesus, but her "church family" took her in. Jesus, as the eldest son, made sure His mother would be looked after. Good to know He cares for the details! He cares about my details, too. John was one of the "sons of thunder" (Mark 3:17). His father as, at least, mentally abusive. He had likely picked up on some of those traits. We also know John was vying for a position in the kingdom of God. John wasn't particularly liked by the other disciples (Mark 10:41). John was rough around the edges. He needed the mother of Jesus' to help him. She did a good job, for we see John wrote more about the love of God than anyone else!

John 20:1. Women are important to God. Again, here we see that it was a woman who was the first to carry the gospel (good news). Mary (a woman) was the first to know of the Messiah's imminent birth. Now, Mary Magdalene was the first to know of Jesus' resurrection!

John 20:9. How did the disciples "not know" the scripture? They had the Old Testament prophecies. They also had heard Jesus tell of his death, burial & resurrection. However, they didn't put it all together for a complete understanding. This type of understanding of scripture only comes when I dwell on the word of God. God will reveal meanings to me when I study and meditate upon His word. He will open up my understanding. He will guide me into all truth (John 16:13).

John 20:11-12. Mary stood outside of the tomb, looked inside and saw the two angels, positioned just like the angels on the mercy seat in the tabernacle. Peter and John had also peered into the tomb (vs 6-8), but did not see the angels. Perhaps it is because they looked and left. Mary, on the other hand, stayed and wept. The angels spoke to her and told her what had happened. I need to stop the hustle and bustle of everyday life and spend time in the presence of God! That's when revelation comes.

John 20:17. I don't think Jesus was telling Mary not to touch Him, per se. I think He was telling her not to cling to Him and hold Him back because He had to ascend into Heaven.

John 20:22. Although Jesus breathed upon them and said "Receive ye the Holy Spirit", they didn't actually receive the Holy Spirit until Acts 2. Why? Because He had to ascend in to Heaven in order to return in Spirit form. There is only one God (Deuteronomy 6:4), but multiple manifestations.

John 20:23. Peter was given the authority in Matthew 16:19 to lead the group and established the salvation plan in Acts 2:38. The other disciples stood with him as he proclaimed it for the first time. Peter just didn't dream up a plan of salvation. Jesus had already been instilling it in His disciples (Matthew 28:18-20; Mark 16:16-18; Luke 24:47). In fact, John the Baptist also spoke of it (Matthew 3:11; Mark 1:4-8). The Old Testament was also a blueprint for the plan of salvation. Peter just put it all together in a concise format.

John 21:3. Peter felt unworthy and couldn't forgive himself, so he went back to what he knew: his old ways. He was apparently a natural born leader, for six others followed him.

John 21:4-8. How sad that Jesus was right there and the disciples didn't know it was Him! Jesus is always standing by, waiting for me to recognize Him and ready to come to my assistance once I do. At the time of His crucifixion, they (except for John) all abandoned Him (backslid). They went fishing and Jesus went to meet them. Most of the time, Jesus got IN the boat with His disciples. This time, though, He did not walk on water or otherwise get in their boat. He stayed on the shore and called out to them. John was the first who realized it was Jesus, but it was Peter who jumped out of the boat and swam ashore. The others came to the shore on the boat. A backslider knows the way back. Jesus will lead them from the shore. He will guide them, but they have to take the first step to get out of their mess and start back. Jesus will meet them where they are. The prodigal's father did not go chasing after his son. His son had to "come to his senses" first. He already knew the way back. He just had to make the move. The father was always on the lookout and waiting for him, but the wayward son had to take the steps necessary to get back (Luke 15:11-32) A backslider knows the way. Someone who was never saved does not.

John 21:15-17. Jesus made Peter decide if he (Peter) loved Him (Jesus) more than his (Peter's) passion for fishing. Fishing was comfortable. Fishing was what he knew. Fishing was his source of income. Fishing was a competitor of Jesus. Jesus, being God, knew what was in Peter's heart, but Peter didn't know what was buried deep in his own heart. Jesus had to question Peter multiple times. He was wanting Peter to realize this was a serious matter and was a life-changing point. Did Peter just go on a three-year sabbatical from his (fishing) job, or was he willing to continue down the path of being a fisher-of-men? The question is: Do I love Jesus more than any other passion?

John 21:18-22. Jesus revealed to Peter which manner he (Peter) would die. Perhaps there was a little jealousy going on because Peter then asked Jesus how John would die. (People often are jealous of others when they are embarrassed. Peter had denied Jesus, but John had stuck it out with Jesus at the cross.) Jesus told Peter that John's future was none of Peter's business. This is personal. God's will for *me* is personal. I need to know His plan for my life and not worry about others' lives. Someone else may have a more glamorous work for God, but I have to stay the course and do the work God has planned for *me*. God is just and fair. I do what I do for Him and not for the glamor and reward.

John 21:25. The biographical writings about Jesus only touch on the highlights of Jesus' ministry. They do not, and cannot, contain everything single thing Jesus imparted and taught to them, just as no one can write down all of the life lessons imparted by a parent. The subsequent books of the New Testament tell how the disciples applied the things taught by Jesus into their everyday lives. To say the four Gospels are all one needs to read because they quote Jesus, is to miss out on important applications.

ACTS
Historical record of the birth of the church.

Peter's "keys". In Acts, Peter (having received the keys to the kingdom per Matthew 16:19), established 6 things:
1. the oneness of God (Acts 2:36);
2. initial salvation (Acts 2:38);
3. universality of salvation (Acts 2:39);
4. holiness (Acts 2:40);
5. healing (Acts 3:6-8); and
6. specifically opened up the door to the Gentiles (Acts 8:14-15).

This was not something he just made up on the spot. The other 11 disciples were standing there with him in agreement (Acts 2:14). Early in His ministry, Jesus established the availability of healing and the fact He was God. Prior to His ascension, He "opened up their understanding" concerning the scriptures. We see in Luke 24:44-49, Jesus taught all of the elements of Acts 2:38. Jesus established initial salvation and the universality of it. Peter merely preached what Jesus said to preach and the other disciples backed Peter up. People have all kinds of different ideas on what it takes to be saved. I want to go to the same Heaven Jesus and His disciples are! Therefore, I am going to believe and obey what they preached.

Acts 1:1-3. Some key words in this passage jump out at me, which tell me the forty days after Jesus' resurrection was boot camp! Jesus put it all together for them, helped them to understand, and helped them to tie the Old Testament together with what would become the New Testament. The epistles are a result of this 40-day instruction period. The key words are:
- "Both do and teach",
- "Given commandments",
- "Forty days", and
- "speaking of the things pertaining to the kingdom of God".

Acts 1:7. It is not for us to understand all things in life, BUT ... verse 8 ... you shall receive power. When the time comes, if I am full of the Holy Spirit, I will have the necessary power. The "when" of things is not any of my business. That is God's business. My business is to receive the Holy Spirit. God isn't going to explain every single thing to me. I wouldn't even understand it. What I do know is whatever life will bring my way, the Holy Spirit will give me the power to overcome.

Acts 1:12-26. About 120 out of the 500 who received the instruction to go to Jerusalem actually obeyed. Well, maybe more went, but got tired of waiting and left. That is a 24% retention record: less than 1/4! Good to know that Jesus' mother and siblings were a part of that group! At any rate, Peter lead them in exhortation and in taking care of business. Don't stress over how many are in your church. God is in charge of the numbers. All I'm in charge of is being a witness by watering and planting the seed (I Corinthians 3:6).

Acts 1:8. The Holy Spirit does not give me immunity to sin and its consequences, but it gives me the power to overcome sin. That's why I need the Holy Spirit. Many churches no longer teach the necessity of receiving the Holy Spirit. I just know I have to have that power! God gives us the Holy Spirit because He can't trust us to live right without it!

Acts 1:24. The first thing the early church did when faced with a decision, was to pray. Is that the first thing I do? Do I consult with others first or do I go to God? Doesn't God know best? The speculation of my friends is no match to God's wisdom. Whether it is deciding on a job, or deciding on a new pastor, I must enter into a season of prayer first.

Acts 2:3-4. Something visible appeared at the first infilling of the Holy Spirit. It appeared to be fire that sat on each individual. Unlike the speaking of tongues, we don't read of this phenomenon happening again with any other instance of people receiving the Holy Spirit. Why? This refers to a similar incident recorded in

Numbers 9:15. This was a sign to the Jews. They knew the significance of the appearance of fire. On the day the tabernacle was first raised in the wilderness, the appearance of fire settled upon the tabernacle. The Jews knew the symbol of fire indicated the presence of God. During the day, the tabernacle was covered with a cloud. At night, that cloud looked like fire! On the Day of Pentecost, those who were observing the 120 praying, heard them speaking in tongues and saw the appearance of fire on them, immediately knew something supernatural from God was transpiring.

Acts 2:21. Salvation is not a one-time thing. Salvation is a process. Peter said, "whosoever called on the name of the Lord, SHALL BE saved" ~ not "is" saved, but "shall be". Believing is the very first step of a process, which was more fully defined in Acts 2:38-40. Don't forget verse 40. Peter had a lot of things to say which are not recorded. His final words, however, was "save yourselves from this untoward generation". In other words, live a separated life!

Acts 2:33-34. Is Jesus "by" the right hand of God or "sitting"? Other scriptures say "standing". Scripture cannot contradict itself. When there seems to be a discrepancy, it's time to dig deeper and find its meaning. The "right hand of God" is a figure of speech denoting power (Psalm 110:1; Acts 7:56).

Acts 2:38. "Repent" means to change your mind, or to return to your right mind. "Remission" means to expunge the record and comes only by the shedding of blood and applied by baptism (Hebrews 9:22). Remission is deeper than forgiveness. I can forgive someone for robbing me, but that doesn't do away with the crime. A court of law, upon hearing all of the evidence, would convict a thief, no matter how many times I declared forgiveness. God serves in two different roles: As my father, He forgives, but as the Judge, He must judge according to the evidence. God forgives when I repent, however, the evidence against me (my sins) is still on my record. In the aftermath of Hurricane Katrina in 2005, flood waters destroyed many forensic labs and evidence lockers. When it came time for those incarcerated to stand trial, there was no evidence, and they were allowed to walk free. When I am baptized in Jesus' name, His blood is applied to my "rap" sheet, and the evidence against me is destroyed! When my trial in Heaven takes place, there will be no evidence against me and I will be admitted into Heaven! I would much rather my sins go before me and get expunged than to follow up to judgment after me. At that point, I would have no remedy for my sins (I Timothy 5:24). I have to make sure my sins are expunged from my record NOW.

Acts 3:1. The Jews, and consequently the early church, had a "hour of prayer" set aside when they physically went to a specified location to pray. I must have a devoted time of prayer. Sure, I keep an attitude of prayer at all times, but that does not take the place of getting down and praying. When I pray while driving, or while doing any other activity, my focus is divided. In many societies, distance and transportation prohibit a daily visit to the church house to pray, but I still must spend time in focused prayer, one-on-one with God. Corporate prayer is necessary as well. I find strength in the prayers of others.

Acts 3:2. I wonder how many times Jesus had passed by the gate Beautiful at the synagogue and had seen the lame man! How many times did Jesus pass that man by? Who knows, but apparently it wasn't the right time for his healing until Peter and John went in Acts 3:1-8. It's really hard to grasp the concept of God's timing, because He is timeless and we are confined to a 24/7 clock. One of the most profound truths came to my husband, seemingly on the spur of the moment. His father (my father-in-law) was nearing the end of his life and was lamenting he had made a promise to God thirty years prior and had not fulfilled that promise. He felt God had rejected him. The Holy Spirit truly does inspire when needed! My husband blurted out since God was timeless, if he (his father) would turn to serve God now, he would be fulfilling that promise. To God, it was as if that promise had been just made yesterday instead of thirty years prior! That statement gave my father-in-law the hope and faith he needed to be baptized!

Acts 3:7. Peter had to step out on faith and take action. God will do His part, but I must also do mine. God honors my faith.

Acts 3:8-9. Everyone loves miracles. Just remember miracles are an attraction, but not the main event. Miracles should be merely a stepping stone to bring people to salvation. This passage is a fulfillment of Isaiah 35:6. Peter used the Gate Beautiful healing as an opportunity to draw a crowd to preach to! He then preached salvation (Acts 3:19) to them.

Acts 3:12. Too often, people (preachers) accept the praise heaped on to them by others. All of the glory belongs to God. Remember, one good car wreck, one good stroke, one good airborne virus can render me helpless. God will not share His glory with another. As a matter of fact, the first commandment addresses this issue (Exodus 20:3-5). Whatever I am, it is because of the goodness and mercy of God, and not because of anything I am.

Acts 3:19-20. Peter revisits his sermon of Acts 2:38 and demands repentance, baptism, and receiving the Spirit. Jesus is the Holy Spirit.

Acts 3:24. The office of "prophet" has not ended. Unfortunately, there are false prophets as well. How do I know the difference? (1) I must be full of the Holy Spirit so I can discern who has a word from God. (2) A true prophet will *never* contradict the word of God.

Acts 3:25. God does not go back on His promises, even if the human does. He promised Abraham He would bless Abraham's descendants (Genesis 17; 18:18). The Jews didn't keep their side of the bargain, but God did/does. Peter reiterates the promise the whole world would be blessed by them.

Acts 4:8. I have been blessed not to have experienced too much persecution for my faith. Sometimes I wonder if I could hold up like those have throughout history. I have concluded that God will give me strength and boldness in the time of need.

Acts 4:11-12. The counsel knew Peter was quoting scripture (Psalm 118:22; 54:1)!

Acts 4:24, 29. Prayer starts with worship. Before you ask, worship. God isn't always going to deliver me from my trials and tribulations. The early church had already been told by Jesus they would face hard times. There was no point for them to ask for deliverance from persecutions. That would be asking amiss. They asked God to give them the strength to withstand (Acts 4:29-31). They actually rejoiced in the trial (Acts 5:41)!

Acts 4:32-33. Unity is a powerful force, regardless of the cause. When people unify, they encourage and empower each other and things (both great and evil) are accomplished. This natural phenomenon is even more powerful when joined in unity with God!

Acts 4:34-35. The idea of selling out and pooling resources together was not a commandment from God. Giving is a by-product of blessing. The people were so overwhelmed with the presence of God, they gave. Sacrificial giving is great as long as the *trajectory of the heart* is right. Sacrificial giving to bring glory and attention to oneself results in the sin of Ananias and Sapphira.

Acts 5:1-10. Lying is plain wrong. The sin of Ananias and Sapphira wasn't that they kept a portion of what they sold for themselves, but that they lied about it. There was no commandment for them to sell out and donate all to the church. God struck them dead for lying. Lying is a big deal to God. Now, what lie is worth going to hell over? Our American culture encourages us to lie. Employers ask us to lie if they don't want to talk on the phone. Magazine articles tell us that it is okay and even good to lie to spare someone's feelings. However, the ends do not justify the means. The Bibles doesn't differentiate between "white" lies and "bad" lies.

Acts 5:11. "Fear" in this verse means a somberness. Their concept of the church began to be formed. The seriousness of living for God began to set in. The word of God is for daily living and not just occasional observance.

Acts 5:12-16. As they stayed unified and prayed up, miracles abounded. Jesus' words of Mark 16 came to pass.

Acts 5:17-18. As always, when there is a move of God, the devil rises up. Don't be surprised when, after a spiritual victory, we come under attack. The devil is NOT happy and will try his best to thwart what God has done for, in and through me. Remember, after every victory, Satan tries to slip in. He did it to Jesus (after His baptism, Matthew 4:1). We're not ignorant of Satan's devices (II Corinthians 2:11). It is to be expected that Satan will work hard to take away the spiritual ground gained this past week. PREPARE your mind (I Peter 1:13). Remember: God has already proven Himself to you. Remember: God has already given you the victory. Remember: withstand the poisonous darts of the wicked (Ephesians 6:16). Remember: the antidote to those poisonous darts is JESUS! Remember: just stand (Ephesians 6:13).

Acts 5:29. Again as in Acts 2, Peter is the spokesman and the other apostles stood by him and backed him up.

Acts 5:32. The Holy Spirit is given to those who OBEY God! Do I want the Holy Spirit? I've got to be obedient to the word of God. If I truly believe God's word, I will obey, for God's word plainly states those who don't obey will not be saved.

Acts 5:33. These people were convicted by Peter's sermon. Unlike those in Acts 2, however, they refused to draw closer to God. An encounter with the Almighty changes me. I will either draw closer to God, or be repelled from God. I will never be the same. When I am a witness, either by word or deed, and those I encounter reject that witness, I can expect them to turn on me. *It's not rocket science.* They are really not rejecting me, per se, but they are rejecting God, and things take a turn for the worse (Matthew 25:40; 45). I shouldn't be surprised when this happens.

Acts 5:38-39. Sometimes when I hear a prophecy from someone, I take Mary's lead and "ponder it" in my heart (Luke 2:19). Then, I take the attitude of Gamaliel: if it is of God, I'd better leave it alone. If it is not of God, it will fizzle and not come to pass. If it never comes to pass, I shrug my shoulders and know they missed the mark. I don't ever want to get offended. God doesn't make mistakes. Humans do. Even spiritual humans. The best of humans are merely humans, at best. Turning my back on God because a fellow human made a mistake hurts no one but myself. God will have a church with or without me.

Acts 5:41. The apostles were humans just like me, so I am certain they did not enjoy being beaten. However, they decided to rejoice in their trial. They were grateful God thought of them enough to allow them that trial. God had confidence they would not bow to the pressure put on them to cease preaching. God knew *the trajectory of their hearts*, just like He knew Job's. God trusted them with His word and they didn't disappoint Him. What Satan tried to use as a means to dig at God backfired on him and the apostles were empowered to keep on preaching! My trial can be turned around and used *against* Satan. What Satan means for evil, God can turn it around, use it for good, and foil Satan's plan (Genesis 50:20).

Acts 6:1. There's always going to be murmuring and complaining in the church, sometimes it is even racially motivated! Different cultures have different customs. It's not that one is right and the other is wrong: there are just different ways of looking at things. Don't get caught up in that. Pray about it and let God deal with it. Preach the word (Acts 6:4). Feeling that I have a superior culture shows **pride** in my life. I have dealt with 5 distinct cultures in my life: (a) Caucasian-American; (b) African-American; (c) Korean; (d) Hispanic and (f) French. Believe me, when I say different cultures have different customs. Something considered friendly in one is considered very rude in another. Jokes that are hysterically funny in one don't even make sense in another. A play on words NEVER translates into another language well. I have found some things in other cultures that I prefer over my own and vice versa. It is natural for me to prefer my culture because that is what I am the most familiar with. However, it would be wrong for me to demean or discount another culture and to feel the other culture is inferior in some way. Love conquers cultural differences.

Acts 6:2-4. I must beware of spending so much time with the mundane, daily tasks of living that I neglect the spiritual. Daily tasks must be accomplished, but not at the expense of my spiritual life. Ministers: be extra careful. Delegate as much as you can to trusted members of the congregation and devote yourself to taking care of the spiritual needs of the congregants and community.

Acts 6:7. For the first time, we see many priests became believers. Could it be because the apostles were devoting themselves solely to the task of soul winning and discipleship? Winning a religious leader takes time.

Acts 6:11. People can be bought to tell a lie. Truth will ultimately prevail, but might not in this life. Usually when people trump up charges against another, it is because of jealousy.

Acts 7:6. God will judge evil. Always. He will judge us as individuals and as a nation. I should pray for my nation, that it would adopt godly principles. God has been known to use both nature and other nations (war) to chastise.

Acts 7:10. What better way to pray, than to pray the scripture! Pray God's own words back to Him. "Lord, I pray for favor and wisdom in the sight of my employer & coworkers!"

Acts 7:25. Moses assumed his kindred would accept him and realize as the next-in-line for Pharaoh-ship, he could deliver them from slavery and even give them a military escort them back to their land. Unfortunately, people get jealous over the success of another. Don't assume someone is a friend, even if they are family or attend the same church. Friendship must stand the test of time.

Acts 7:35. Forty years after they had refused Moses, God sent him back to deliver them. They had endured 40 more years of slavery. All was not lost, though. Moses needed to come off his high horse a little bit. He had been raised as a prince and became a shepherd. This experience of being a shepherd gave him the understanding and patience to lead people. We are like sheep (Isaiah 53:6). Moses spend 40 years getting the best education in the world. It took God 40 years to get Egypt out of him and humble him enough to lead God's people. We do need to be educated, but then we need to get over it and remember we are to be servants to each other.

Acts 7:39. The Israelites (as a whole) were physically headed to the promised land, but *the trajectory of their hearts* was pointed back to Egypt. People can attend church faithfully and be involved, but have their trajectory wrong. I must constantly examine myself and correct my trajectory when needed. I don't want to get off course. When my eyes get on the world and my trajectory gets off, I will have the opportunity to backslide (Hebrews 11:15).

Acts 7:41-42. One of the first red flags of a wrong trajectory is taking credit for things accomplished. The Israelites made a golden calf out of jewelry, which was quite a feat. They had learned the art of working with metals as slaves and now they did it for themselves. No doubt the calf was beautiful. They worshiped their own creation. By doing so, they took credit for their escape from Egypt. Once that happened, God turned away from them and even allowed them to go as far as to worship astrology. I must be careful not to take credit for the blessings of God in my life. One stroke or one car wreck can devastate me, my finances, my abilities, my mind, etc.

Acts 7:48. God's dwelling place is in my heart via the infilling of the Holy Spirit.

Acts 7:51-52. Stephen accused the Jews of resisting the Holy Spirit. He went on to specify they resisted the Holy Spirit by not keeping the law. When I resist the Word of God, I am quenching the Holy Spirit. If I find a scripture that I think is too hard for me to follow, I am quenching the Spirit. Of course, God's commandments are too hard to follow on my own! That's why I need the Holy Spirit ... to be able to live righteously! "Quench not the spirit" (I Thessalonians 5:19).

Acts 7:54. Conviction brings about a change. I will either repent or I will resist. If I repent, God can mold me, use me, and work with me as the potter does a good piece of clay. If I refuse to repent, I will still change. I will change for the worse. I will resent the conviction and become hardened. God can't work with a hardened heart. An encounter with Jesus changes me one way other another. I am never the same. The question is: Will I be pliable in His hands or hardened to be cast out?

It's my choice. The same sun which melts a candle, hardens the clay. The difference is the material. What material is in my heart?

Acts 7:59. Stephen point blank declares Jesus to be the name of God. *It's not rocket science!*

Acts 8:1, 4-6. No one likes persecution, but something good can come out of it. Persecution caused the early church to scatter and spread the gospel. We humans tend to cluster with those who share similar beliefs, customs, etc. The early church was beginning to fellowship with each other. God wanted them to "go into all the world and teach".

Acts 8:9, 18, 20-21. There is always a charlatan. There is a fake. Not everyone who "believes" will be saved. Simon believed (vs 18), but he wanted salvation *his* way, not God's way. He wanted to be in charge and he wanted the power for his own benefit. It all boils down to the *trajectory of the heart*. A true believer will obey. I call people like Simon a Christian tourist! A Christian parasite might be a better term. (See essay entitled "Christian Parasite" in *It's Not Rocket Science, Volume 1*.) Peter rebuked Simon. People misinterpret Acts 16:31 to mean that a mere verbal claim of belief equals salvation. Not so. More on that later.

Acts 8:22. Not every sin is a visible action. There are sins of the heart. I must make sure the *trajectory of my heart* is always on course. I want my heart, my actions, and my thoughts to be pleasing to God.

Acts 8:26. The Lord will go out of His way to help a searching soul. The Lord uses people to help people. If I feel like God is making me take a detour in life, perhaps it is to answer someone's prayer. Why did God not allow my father to die by his stroke? Why did God allow him to linger seven long years? He steadily witnessed to all of his nurses and aides in the nursing home. They had a witness!

Acts 8:35. Good evangelism: Philip began at the point the man was. He began at the point of understanding and then expounded upon the scripture. There is no need to preach Genesis to Revelation to someone. Begin where they are and lead them to a better understanding.

Acts 8:36-37. The pre-requisite for baptism is belief. This is why infant baptism is not effective. Infant baptism is based upon a measure of belief by the parents, not the person being baptized.

Acts 9:1. Saul was a terrorist. He was on a mission to rid the country of Christians. Sound familiar? It is good to pray for those being persecuted, but it is also right to pray for those perpetrating the persecution to have an experience like Saul. Some terrorists are just evil, true, but others sincerely think they are doing the right thing.

Can I pray for them? Just think of how they could change their world if they had an encounter with God like Saul did in this chapter!

Acts 9:5. Even though Saul was hurting the church, the ***trajectory of his heart*** was right in that his desire was to please God and he was teachable. God can work with a teachable spirit. Saul just didn't know Jesus was God. The Greek word for "Lord" in this text is "Kyrios", or Supreme One. The word "pricks" means ox goad. To hit against that which is pushing you forward is pointless and ends badly.

Acts 9:7. Not everyone around me will have the same experience. We pastored a lady who went to a conference, learned a lot, and was changed. She came back and immediately wanted to make everyone change as well. Unfortunately, she was unable to communicate her passion and a spirit of superiority got a hold of her. She decided she couldn't pray in the prayer room with everyone else. She needed to be "free" to pray as she wished and went into a classroom to pray. This spirit festered a bit and was passed on to her best friend. They all left and went to another church. Of course, the problem was *their own spirit*. After flipping to several churches, not all of them are serving God today. If God has taught me something, the best way I can convey that passion is to live it, not dictate it. God knows another's heart and God will lead us all from level to level.

Acts 9:9. Saul was blind for three days before God sent Ananias to pray for his healing. God will sometimes let me "stew" in my calamity. Perhaps this is to give me the opportunity to meditate on my own condition and plow up my heart so it is teachable. Perhaps it is to humble me. So many times, we turn to our friends for their advice when we should be turning to God. Doesn't He have all the answers? I am not suggesting that we never seek the advice of godly counselors, but we should turn to God first and God should be included in the counseling session. A counseling session should never turn into a gossip session.

Acts 9:10. Who was Ananias? This is the only mention of a preacher by the name of Ananais in the Bible. He is not mentioned after this passage. He may have thought he was not important, but he trained one of the most important preachers in the Bible (Paul). Whatever Paul's ministry was, Ananais had a part in it. It doesn't matter how many people know my name. I just need to do my part for the kingdom of God. Ananais had reservations, for he had heard of this guy, Saul. However, he obeyed God and because of his obedience, a great missionary was won to the Lord.

Acts 9:11-16. God is okay with talking to friends. He is okay with my questioning Him. Ananais was very worried about going to pray for Saul and wondered if he had heard God's instructions correctly. God didn't take offense. He patiently explained the situation to Ananais. God reveals things to His friends (John 15:15). What if Ananais had called up his church buddies instead? They probably would have advised him NOT to go to Saul. I want to make sure I hear from God! God is our counselor (Isaiah 9:6). Friends (and professionals) always do have advice, and sometimes it is good advice. However, God is the master Counselor. Why don't I just go to Him? I guess we don't because it takes a little more work. Talking with other humans is easier. I need to turn to Him in times of crises.

Acts 9:16. God reveals things to His friends (John 15:15). God assured Ananias He would reveal unto Paul the suffering Paul would endure for the gospel's sake. We always reap what we sow. Paul persecuted Christians. He reaped that persecution back.

Acts 9:19, 23; Galatians 1:18. Paul studied in Damascus for about three years. Who were these people who mentored and discipled him? They may be unnamed in the Scripture, but God knows their names and they have a huge part in Paul's ministry. This reminds me of my little, quiet, unassuming maternal grandmother. She witnessed to her neighbor, who in turn, witnessed to her son's friend, who became the author of a well-known Bible study. My grandmother has a little part in all of the souls who have been and will be won through that Bible study. It is not who plants, or who waters that is so important. God gives the increase (I Corinthians 3:6)!!

Acts 9:24, 29. My personality doesn't change when I get the Holy Spirit. God works within the parameters of my personality. Saul's personality didn't change when his name was changed to Paul. He was just as recklessly zealous FOR Jesus as he was AGAINST Jesus. He was almost killed twice in just Acts 9! Peter's impetuous personality may have been the key to his obedience to minister to Cornelius. A pondering man may have "talked" his way out of this assignment because it went against traditional Jewish theology (Acts 10). My own mother is independent, tenacious and always gets to the bottom of a problem. That made her great as a missionary, but it sure is difficult to deal with now that she has Alzheimer's!! God uses all kinds of personalities. I shouldn't judge someone because they don't worship or witness the way I do. God can use each style of personality. If I won a million dollars, I would not scream and jump up and down and run around in circles. I would be excited, but would not express that emotion in a hugely demonstrative way. I would probably just say, "thank you" and go hug a family member and cry thinking of how that would alleviate my financial stress level! People are different and react differently. God uses all personality types.

Acts 9:31. After Saul's persecution of the church ceased, they had peace and rest for a while! Whew! Don't you know they were glad to be able to go about without fear of being killed!

Acts 9:43. With all of the excitement going on in the book of Acts, it is easy to overlook the numerous times the scriptures tell of teaching time. After the huge miracle of Dorcas being raised from the dead, Peter stayed in Joppa "many days". Miracles are a great tool to attract people to God. However, it is not about the miracles, signs and wonders. It is about bringing people to the point of living for God and ultimately being saved. It does no good to introduce people to the wonders of God without teaching them how to live for God.

Acts 10.
1. There are many sincere, good people in this world, yet unsaved. Cornelius
    a. was devout,
    b. respected God,
    c. lead his household to live for God to the best of his knowledge,
    d. gave to charity,
    e. had a mind to pray,
    f. was fair,
    g. had a good reputation, and
    h. was teachable (Acts 10:2, 22, 33).
2. No matter how good we are or how devoted we are to charitable work, we still need to be saved according to scripture (Acts 10:44, 48;)! If the *trajectory of the heart* is pointed in the right direction, God will take great pains to reveal truth to us! How long had Cornelius prayed for direction? The scriptures indicate he had prayed enough for there to be a memorial built before God (Acts 10:4)! One interpretation of the Hebrew word for "memorial" means "gnawing upon". That means a lot of prayers to me! He didn't get an immediate answer to his gnawing prayers. He had **to do something**. He had to (1) send for Peter, (2) listen to Peter, and (3) do what Peter told him to do (Acts 10:5-6). It's not enough to listen to the word of God being preached. Some other action will be required. We are not saved by our works, but our faith will produce works. Faith and works go hand in hand (James 2:18, 20, 26).
3. God had to really work on Peter to get him to go to preach to a Gentile! Peter argued with God and God patiently worked with him until Peter was willing to obey. If I'm proud of my walk with God and my holiness, I am a Pharisee. We all have the potential to be proud and self-righteous. True holiness is on the inside. "Outside" actions are all that is visible to others. God looks on the inside to determine whether my "outside" comes from inner holiness or from pride. This gospel is for ALL of mankind, not just for those *I think* are interested.
4. Peter had an unnamed support team (vs 23)
5. Cornelius had quite a group gathered. For what? He was expecting something from God, but didn't know what to expect.
6. Peter admitted his prejudice. God had to correct him and give him a revelation. It is okay to admit it when I am wrong. I must also realize that just because I'm saved, doesn't mean I am 100% correct in all that I do. Peter was the head of the church and yet had a tinge of racial prejudices that God had to work out of him (vs 28, 34, Galatians 3:28).

7. Cornelius had been a devout man, but at this juncture, he fasted four days (vs 30) until his answer came. He gathered his friends and was open to hear what God had to say through Peter (vs 33).
8. While Peter was preaching how remission would come with obedience, Cornelius, his family and friends were so hungry for God that they received the Holy Spirit (vs 43-44). Those with Peter were now convinced the Gentiles could also be a part of the church. Baptism was not an option (vs 48).
9. Peter didn't just leave Cornelius to figure things out by himself after he had received the Holy Spirit and was baptized in Jesus' name. They stayed "certain days" (vs 48) to teach and disciple him and his household.

Acts 11:2, 18. Any human endeavor is flawed. Unfortunately, this means the church is not going to be perfect. There was strife when Peter opened the door of salvation to the Gentiles. Peter was called in before the "church board". Even though Peter was the head of the church, he was still accountable to the other ministers. Paul and Barnabas had a knock-down-drag-out fight over an issue of holiness standards (Acts 15:1-2, 7). Don't let church politics throw you off. That is no reason to quit serving God. Serve God for your own soul's salvation.

Acts 11:19, 25-26. The persecuted believers were dispersed. Many settled in Antioch. Isn't it interesting to note their pastor, Barnabas, hunted down Saul, the very man who had persecuted them and had their family members killed, and brought Saul to Antioch? For a whole year Saul & Barnabas taught. At this point, the believers began to be called Christians. Why? Could it be because they finally *forgave* Saul? This brings up a question: Am I a Christian? Incidentally, they also began to call him Paul instead of Saul (Acts 13:9).

Acts 11:23, 26. The people in Antioch were discipled for a year! Teaching is so valuable.

Acts 11:29-30. The church is to take care of physical needs as well as the spiritual ones.

Acts 12:1. This Herod is the grandson of Herod the Great who tried to kill Jesus. He is the nephew of the Herod who killed John the Baptist.

Acts 12. Much has been preached about Peter's miraculous release from prison. God is in control. Whatever situation I may find myself in, God has allowed it and thus, He will either (1) get me out of it or (2) take care of me through it. His grace is sufficient (II Corinthians 12:9).

Acts 12:20-23. Herod was on the warpath, but flattery appealed to his pride. God doesn't do well with prideful people, though. How many diseases are allowed to humble us? Any natural talents I have come from God and can be removed quickly!

Acts 13:1. I am constantly amazed at the number of people I meet who have some sort of Apostolic background or influence. Even Herod had a relative who was a Christian. Herod's foster or half-brother was a spirit filled leader in the church. Perhaps he had witnessed to Herod. No one will have an excuse on Judgment Day (Romans 1:20; 2:1). We can plead ignorance, but we will have no excuse. I think when we stand trial before God, there will be proof of the opportunities we had to turn the ***trajectory of our hearts*** towards Him (Revelation 20:12). If someone rejected those opportunities, he/she will be speechless when God pronounces judgment. There will be no defense.

Acts 13:2-3. I am amazed when I hear people tell of a vision they had of themselves ministering to thousands! Ahh, that might have been a vision, but it certainly wasn't from God! Ministering is not a glorious role. It is servitude to God. Ministering comes with denying oneself. Preaching and ministering are two different things. Preaching is delivering a religious speech. Ministering is imparting something of oneself. It's hard and takes something out of you (Mark 5:30). Preaching to the masses is a good introduction to the gospel, but ministering to the individual is what it takes to disciple someone.

Acts 13:10. God's judgment will, in one way or another, be upon those who withstand or try to interfere with a hungry soul.

Acts 13:18. The wording of this verse in the King James Version makes me laugh! I've never thought about God suffering through my manners! Seriously, though, God suffers through my doubts, my failures, my fears, and my shortcomings. He waits patiently, hoping I will get my act together and just trust Him! How much better would it be if I just did things His way the first time? (Everyone who has dealt with a toddler should give me a rousing "amen"!)

Acts 13:27. Even though the Pharisees knew the law backwards and forwards, they didn't know God. I must not only know the word of God, but I must have an understanding. I must know the author. When I personally know the author of a book, I have a clearer understanding of the background and the impetus of the book. Universities have entire courses dedicated to getting to know certain authors in order to grasp the concepts of their works. Likewise, I must have an intimate relationship with God in order to completely understand and love His word. Because the Pharisees didn't know God, they inadvertently fulfilled prophecies to their own detriment!

Acts13:34. What are the "sure mercies of David"? I note every time David repented, God forgave and bailed him out. I must repent daily of known sins and even of sins committed unknowingly (Psalm 139:23-24). I want my thoughts, my actions, and my heart to be pure.

Acts 13:42-44. The Jews didn't care too much for Paul's sermon, but the Gentiles who heard were hungry for more. There must have been a lot of talking at home and at the workplace, because when the next Sabbath day came around, almost the entire city came to hear!

Acts 13:46. God is a gentleman. He will not stay when He is not welcomed!

Acts 13:51. I can't waste time with people who don't want to hear. There are many who are hungry for God. There is a point when it is just time to move on!

Acts 14. People are such worshippers! Unfortunately, we (humans) have a tendency to worship each other. Look at all of the gossip magazines and reality TV shows out there. There is no end to "celebrity" news! Even news magazines and newspapers have gossip sections! We may not literally offer sacrifices to each other as in Acts 14:13, but we worship each other still the same. I don't know how a true Christian can accept all of the accolades afforded to celebrities. It feeds in to our egos, but God is not pleased. There are too many scriptures that talk about God not sharing His glory with anyone else to list here. We must have the same attitude as Paul & Barnabas in Acts 14:14-18. They deflected all glory and honor to God. Those in leadership, especially, take heed lest you fall (I Corinthians 10:12)! Don't ever think, "It couldn't happen to me." That's **pride** talking! I am subject to failure just as anyone else. I need God! I am nothing without God. Was someone blessed during a sermon I preached? That was God. God gave me the inspiration and gave me the ability to formulate that inspiration into words. God made the connection with their lives!

Acts 14:13. People are so fickle. The very people who wanted to worship Paul & Barnabas as gods turned on a dime (by the influence of others) and stoned Paul almost to death (Acts 14:19)! When people heap on the praises, be wary. Don't let it go to your head. The very people who were so kind and courteous to Paul (& crew) when they crashed into Malta first decided Paul was a murderer and then a god (Acts 28:4, 6). I must remember this when people heap the compliments and praise on me. Those same people will turn on a dime if I do something they don't like. {{sigh}} I used to dread Mother's Day at the church. It seemed like every year, the person designated to shower me with accolades would be the very one to stab me in the back just a few months later.

Acts 15:1, 7. There was a great dissension and debate over an issue ~ a holiness issue! Not much has changed, has it? Finally, Peter took a stand and James backed him up (vs 13-14).

Acts 15:20, 29. James' advice concerning the Gentiles was that they abstain (1) from idol worship, (2) sexual sins, and (3) eating of blood (Leviticus 17:11, 14). In other words, the church leaders agreed that the keeping of the Jewish *ceremonial* law was not necessary for salvation. (See also discussion on the Ceremonial Law vs. Moral Law in *It's Not Rocket Science, Volume 3*.)

Acts 15:33-34. It is not enough to just bring people to the point of salvation. Time must be taken to properly teach and disciple them. It does no good to have a whirlwind revival without teaching time. In fact, people are worse off if they've come to salvation and don't continue on the journey (Matthew 23:15, Luke 11:26; John 5:14).

Acts 15:39. Sometimes, God uses contention for the good. Paul & Barnabas had a falling out over John Mark. Their fight was so great, they split up into two missions' teams! They had to get over their bad feelings, but God used this split to further the kingdom. I see churches get so big they no longer focus on outreach but on maintaining themselves. Although maintenance is very important, it must not be at the expense of outreach. In my observation, churches who are in maintenance mode, get proud of themselves ... they have the "best" music, the "best" children's church, etc. This **pride** ultimately gives way to contention and strife and a church split is in the making. A church split is not always a bad thing. God sometimes will get us out of our comfort zones so we can get more kingdom work accomplished. (Understand that attitudes, etc., have to be in check.) PS: Paul obviously did get over his bad attitude towards John Mark because he specifically asked for him in II Timothy 4:11.

Acts 16:1, 4. Paul took the time to mentor Timothy. Elders need to mentor young people. Before the baton is passed, the next generation must have the baton firmly in its grasp (Titus 2:4)! As they traveled, they taught the people in the churches matters of holiness. There are "decrees to keep". There are things we must to do to maintain a separation unto God. Holiness is not decrees or laws to be kept out of duty, but holiness is being separated unto God. That means I am conscious of doing things which please God. I am setting myself apart. Just as an engaged person sets him/herself apart from the dating pack and concentrates solely on his/her fiancé, I am to separate myself unto God. This comes with certain "decrees" which help me maintain that separation. With these decrees, the churches were established in the faith (vs 5). It is not enough to come to salvation. I must be established. If I am established, the winds of false doctrine won't sway or uproot me.

Acts 16:12. There was teaching time in Philippi!

Acts 16:16-17. The spirit world recognized Paul & his entourage. Does it know me?

Acts 16:31. Many sermons have been preached about Paul and Silas being in jail. This scripture is often taken out of context and used to preach the doctrine that a mere declaration of belief in God guarantees salvation. Scripture never contradicts scripture. I know James 2:19 tells me the devil even believes (and trembles, which is more than some people do!). Therefore, this scripture cannot mean mere belief equates salvation. The jailer was about to commit suicide. Paul stopped him and delivered an opening statement: Believe. Previously, the jailer believed in Caesar and other Roman gods. A basic belief in Jesus must come first, then salvation steps follow. Verse 32 shows us the jailer & his household was taught more than a mere "belief".

Act 16:37. Paul must have been sensitive to the Spirit by *not* playing the "Roman card" earlier. He could have spared himself (and Silas) from being beaten had he revealed their Roman citizenship earlier. However, by not doing so, the jailer was witnessed to! Help me Lord to (1) be that sensitive and (2) have the courage to go through whatever trial I must to win a soul!

Acts 17:2. Apparently, Paul had a habit of going to the synagogue and talking scriptures with the religious leaders for a length of time. From this dialog, many Greeks and a lot of influential women were won! Different styles of witnessing are effective with different type of people. There is no set formula to win a soul.

Acts 17:9. It looks like Jason & friend had to post bail to get out of trumped up charges by jealous Jews!

Acts 17:11. Those in Thessalonica searched the scriptures to find out what truth was. Question: Do I conform to the scripture or do I try to conform the scripture to me? Am I like what is *already* written in the scripture? Do I have to cut, paste and twist the scripture around to mean what I want it to mean? There were quite a few influential people who were diligently searching the scriptures (vs 12).

Acts 17:21. Fads are nothing new! Athens lead the pack when it came to following fads. They wanted to know what is the latest in everything, even religion. Paul, of course, was determined to seize the opportunity to tell them of Jesus.

Acts 17:23. Paul began at their level of experience with God. When I witness, instead of lecturing, I need to find out where people are, how much they know, what their experience is with God, and *then* build upon their own foundation.

Acts 17:27. God is never far away. A lot has been said about "chasing" God, "seeking" God, etc. God is not playing a hide-and-go-seek game with humanity. However, He stays just off the well beaten path so I must consciously take the time to stop and learn of Him. He is always close by, waiting for me to want to hear from Him. Am I serious enough about salvation to allow Him to speak to me? Or, am I too busy with the cares of this life? Am I too busy working FOR Him that I neglect to be WITH Him?

Acts 17:28. Education is important. God can use baptized brains! Paul is a prime example of that. His learning gave him the opportunity to speak with the very philosophical and educated Greeks. Peter, the uneducated fisherman, would have never had that opportunity. Educated people need salvation too! Paul was able to quote their own poets and reason with them. God is no respecter of persons. He can use both the educated and the uneducated.

Acts 17:30-31. Prior to the time of the written word of God, it was difficult for people to have full knowledge of His word. God is a fair and just judge. I have the word of God and am without excuse.

Acts 17:32-34. Paul didn't have a 100% retention rate, either! I can't worry about those who refuse to accept truth. My job is to sow the seed and disciple (water) the seed that begins to germinate (I Corinthians 3:6). I cannot take offence when someone won't believe and obey.

Acts 18:2. Aquila and Priscilla were refugees!

Acts 18:3. Paul had a trade. He had the means to make money to support himself. Through his work, he was a witness to Aquila. Although Paul was a preacher, it doesn't take a preacher to win a soul. Anyone can be a witness on the job. Even though I might not be a preacher, I need to study and know the scriptures so I can be the key witness someone needs to take them to the next level.

Acts 18:6. Find your niche. Paul finally realized he got too fed up and frustrated with the Jews to effectively minister to them. He decided to primarily work among the Gentiles. God has a tailor-made spot for you in His kingdom. Find where you belong. It may take some time.

Acts 18:9-10. Paul was human. He had human feelings. Apparently, he was dreading the possibility of being beaten (both mentally and physically). God was kind enough to give him a vision that all would be well for a season.

Acts 18:11, 18, 23. Paul took the time to teach and disciple. It's not about the blow and go revival. Those are good to attract people, but it is the teaching time which establishes, roots, and grounds people in truth.

Acts 18:24-26. Apollos preached what he knew. He had a measure of truth, but not all. Aquila and Priscilla recognized that and took the time to teach him. They didn't condemn him and they didn't publicly challenge him. They were wise and expounding upon his existing knowledge. They built upon the fountain he already had.

Acts 18:28. Apparently Apollos had great results, but remember, he was a result of the teaching of Aquila and Priscilla. They weren't preachers, but their witness was powerful and they will have a part in Apollos' ministry.

Acts 19:1-6. Witnessing to "believers" is somewhat difficult because they believe they are already "saved". The key to witnessing to them is to meet them at their level of experience with God and take them to the next level. Paul did not condemn them, but expounded on the truth they had received. It is building upon small faith, step by step.

Acts 19:9-10. Paul taught in the training center (Bible College) for about two years.

Acts 19:13. There are always going to be spiritual vagabonds, even within Christianity. They call themselves Christians, but stray away from the Bible (II Timothy 3:5). I must be able to identify them (I Thessalonians 5:12) and stay away from them. I must not allow myself to be deceived by them.

Acts 19:15-16. Does Satan know me? Is he worried about me? If I don't have power with God, Satan can easily overcome me.

Acts 19:18. My true belief in God results in my repentance. My repentance results taking corrective actions. We are not saved by our works, but our works do reveal our inner condition (Acts 26:20) Faith without works is dead (James 2:20, 26).

Acts 19:19. Sometimes, I have to burn bridges with the past. If my friends, job, even family, pull me away from God, I need to keep my distance or even burn the bridge. It's a hard decision sometimes, but necessary. My soul is at stake. Stephanie is very much in false doctrine and delusion. Her children have elected not to allow the grandchildren to be around her too much. It breaks her heart, but I can understand the stance of her children. They don't want *their* children to be convinced by grandma that the Bible doesn't mean what it says. It is hard on Stephanie to be estranged from her children and grandchildren, but I think it is very hard on her children as well.

Acts 19:26-27. Sometimes, living for God affects my economic wellbeing. Am I willing to change my actions and live for God? Can I trust God will open up another door for me? Do I trust God enough to have confidence He will take care of my economics? I'm not just talking about a drug dealer changing careers. What about falsifying documents so I can get on Medicaid and food stamps? What about working in a country illegally? This area can get tricky! Sometimes the rules of our own government (USA) makes it more profitable to lie. I must obey God first and foremost.

Acts 19:29, 32. People are so fickle. The people here gathered together and developed a mob mentality. They didn't even know why they had gathered! They just went along with the flow.

Acts 19:35-41. The town clerk was the peacemaker and brought some sanity into the mob. He suggested cooler minds prevail and if there was a problem, fight it out in the court system and not with fists. God sometimes uses non-Christians to bring peace and to make a way. It is good to know people in position who will lend a kind hand when the church needs it!

Acts 20:3. Paul took some time to disciple the believers in Greece.

Acts 20:23, 25. God reveals things to His friends (John 15:15). God revealed to Paul he would endure physical hardships in the future and that Paul would not see these people again. God didn't give Paul specifics as to when and how, but He did let Paul know what was ahead. I need to take these little nuggets from God and pray for myself. When I get to those hard spots God revealed to me, I shouldn't be surprised nor should I get discouraged. He knows what I am going through and what I will go through. His grace is sufficient. He will provide.

Acts 20:29-30. There is deception from "outside" the church and then there's deception from "within" the church. Understand that. Not everyone who attends church is right. This is why I need to know what the scriptures really say for myself. Some people are "wolves in sheep's clothing" (Matthew 7:15) and I can't be swayed by their "philosophy and vain deceit" (Colossians 2:8).

Acts 21:3-4. Transform setbacks into opportunities. Paul took a delay in his trip to connect with others and both teach and receive from them.

Acts 21:4, 11. In verse 4, Paul was warned by the Spirit not to go to Jerusalem. In verse 11, he was told what would happen if he went anyway. I'm not sure I understand why he insisted on going. Perhaps Paul just wanted to go "home". We know he had a deep love for his fellow countrymen and wanted them all saved (Romans 9:3). At any rate, he was not forbidden by the Spirit to go. He was warned of the consequences of his decision to go. He went into that trial willingly and knowingly. God reveals things to his friends (John 15:15). God also gives us freedom to make some decisions. Perhaps this wasn't the wisest decision. Perhaps Paul could have lived longer had he not gone to Jerusalem. Nevertheless, God honored Paul's decision. He was a witness to the political leadership (Felix, Festus), and a blessing to generations to come through his epistle written in jail.

Acts 21:20-27. Church leadership isn't infallible. Human reasoning sometimes prevails. The Jewish Christians still wanted to keep the ceremonial law of Moses, even if the Gentiles didn't adhere. They had a double standard. Church leadership wanted to appease the Jewish Christians. Paul was obedient and complied with the demands of the church elders, but it all backfired. The whole city got in an uproar (vs 31), Paul was beaten (vs 32), accusations were made (vs 34), and the soldiers had to rescue Paul from the mob (vs 35).

Acts 22. A personal testimony is undisputable. No one can argue with *my* testimony. *My* testimony is powerful!

Acts 22:9. The scripture always interprets itself. Paul says those who were with him on the road to Damascus didn't hear the voice. Acts 9:7 says they heard the voice. Is the Bible contradicting itself? No! That is *never* the case. In Bible language, "hear" most often means "understand". They heard a sound with their ears, but they didn't hear with understanding. I want to hear and understand His voice!

Acts 22:25. Paul played the Roman card! I don't blame him. He had been through enough persecution for the day. He didn't need another beating.

Acts 23:5. This is hard, but we have to still honor leadership even if they're in sin. David honored King Saul. Paul was ordered to be slapped by Ananias and Paul prayed God's wrath on him. Paul's attitude changed when he was told he had just prayed against the high priest.

Acts 23:7-10. Politics again. There is always partisan divide. Paul was able to wiggle out of trouble by just getting the Pharisees and Sadducees riled up against each other! Here is how to remember the difference: The Pharisees believed in the resurrection. The Sadducees didn't (vs 8), which is why they were "sad, you see"?

Acts 23:11. I'm so glad in the midst of a hot trial, even if it may be self-imposed, God shows up to assure me that He is still there!

Acts 23:19. Did God use a child in this case to persuade the chief to rescue Paul from the Jews?

Acts 24:1. Lobbyists were used back in Biblical times! Some people are just gifted orators, and can be powerfully persuasive. I must measure my beliefs against the Bible and not against the reasoning of a great orator.

Acts 24:2-9. Flattery appeals to our human egos. Kudos to Tertullus for beginning his accusations against Paul with a line of flattery to Felix. I must not allow my ego to impair my judgment. Ego is pride and pride are displeasing to God.

Acts 24:10-21. Paul keep his cool. He denied the charges and demanded strict proof. He stated his personal policy (vs 16) was not to offend God, and to avoid offending his fellow man, if possible.

Acts 24:22-27. God gives chance upon chance. There really won't be an excuse on judgment day. Felix already had heard of Jesus before Paul ever appeared before him. Then, he and his wife listened to what Paul had to say. He was convicted, but the ***trajectory of his heart*** was wrong. He wanted a bribe to loose Paul. Two years passed with Paul still in Felix' care. He had plenty of chances to yield to his conviction and be saved.

Acts 25:7. Sometimes people bring accusations they cannot prove. Unfortunately, damage is still done. Life isn't fair. These things happen. More often or not, my accusers are either jealous of my success, or feel threatened. In this case, it was probably both. Both of these are a result of pride. Some may have been jealous of Paul's travels and success. These Jews felt their belief system was threatened. They were so entrenched with the tradition of their teachings they didn't stop to really examine the scriptures to realize that Jesus was, indeed, the Messiah. Some of them may have even studied with Saul/Paul in their youth. Some of them may have been with Saul when he was persecuting the Christians.

Acts 25:9. Once again, we have a weak politician, trying to please the people! Remember Pilate? Festus could have put an end to things by declaring Paul's innocence, but he forced Paul to make the decision: go back to Jerusalem and be tried by the Jews, or go to Caesar's court. Oh, for politicians who would have a backbone and do the right thing! Politicians are people pleasers and not God pleasers. Felix passed the buck to Festus and Festus sought the counsel of King Agrippa (vs14). Neither of them was willing to make the right decision. They all wanted to pass the buck.

Acts 26. Once again, Paul is given an audience with leadership and what does he do? He gives his testimony! My testimony is powerful. No one can deny it or take it away from me.

Acts 26:20. We are saved by the grace of God and not by our good works, however, when I repent of my sins, there will be a change in my actions/works. I have doubts about anyone's salvation if their life is not changed after coming to Christ. My works reveal the ***trajectory of my heart.***

Acts 26:24. I've used a line from this scripture in jest many, many times! "Much learning doth make thee mad!" Whereas it was not true in Paul's case (vs 25), it is true in some cases. Some of the most learned people are the farthest from God. Why is that, I wonder? People who believe science has an answer for everything overlook one tiny, but important, fact. God is the author of science! God put the laws of science in place! The very reason the universe works like a fine-tuned machine is because God created it perfectly. Since God is the creator, He (and He alone) knows how, and is allowed, to break those laws when He so pleases.

Acts 26:26. Paul reminded the king that God didn't pull a fast one on the Jews. The coming of the Messiah had been foretold for *years*. It was no secret. They just *chose* to believe the scriptures they wanted to believe and ignore the rest. Hmm. Sounds like people today, doesn't it?

Acts 26:28. Oh if King Agrippa had only put aside his political ambitions and allowed God to melt his heart! Think about this: Whatever age you are, add 50-75 years. What matters? Position in society? Monetary wealth? Regardless of my desires and dreams in this life, ***living for God is all that matters***. I must keep eternity in view so that the ***trajectory of my heart*** does not get off course. NOTHING ELSE MATTERS. Sure, I want to be liked. Sure, I want to have a little jingle in my pocket. However, soon this life will all be over and none of that will matter. Living for God will.

Acts 27:1. I find it interesting and comforting that Dr. Luke & other friends were able to get on the same ship as Prisoner Paul. God knows how to take care of me regardless of the situation I find myself in.

Acts 27:3. Paul found favor in the eyes of a centurion charged with escorting him to Rome. In the midst of a yearlong trial which would ultimately end in his death, God gave Paul a bright spot. God allowed Paul to have fellowship with his friends. God's grace is sufficient. Whatever I'm going through, His grace is sufficient to help me bear my burden (II Corinthians 12:9). If I really sit down and analyze my situation, I can see His hand in my life and I can honestly say, "All is well".

Acts 27:10. God warned of the dangerous sailing conditions ahead. If they had listened, they would not have had such a huge financial loss. God will bless others through me. I am the salt of the earth (Matthew 5:13). Christians are the preserving factor. The Christian presence on this earth holds back God's judgment of evil. The entire world is blessed because of the presence of Christians. Every nation who turns to some form of godliness, is blessed. Their economy improves and discrimination of others is diminished.

Acts 27:21. Sometimes I have to let people make their own mistakes and wait until they are ready for me to help them pick up the pieces. It's hard to sit by and watch them self-destruct, but when they won't listen, that's all I can do. I need to be willing to step up and help them, though, when they are ready. I can't say, "Oops, too bad. You should have listened to me!"

Acts 27:30-31. Some of the sailors pretended to cast down anchors, when they were really planning their escape! Paul admonished them that though they may get out of the ship, they would not be out of the storm and would perish. Leaving church (ship) because of a trial (storm) doesn't solve any problems. In fact, it makes it worse. The trial will still be raging, but I will not have the protection of the family of God.

Acts 27:33-34. There is a time to fast, but there is also a time to eat. The physical body needs strength and nourishment. Fasts need to be planned wisely, not rashly.

Acts 28. Paul endured the storm and shipwreck because OTHERS wouldn't listen. He reaped what THEY sowed. Sometimes it is like that. Paul lost all of his earthly possessions along with them in the storm. So did Dr. Luke and the other friends of Paul who were on that ship. People were cursing, his jailers wanted to kill him, and Paul got bit by a snake! Just because I'm a child of God doesn't mean I will be immune to the woes of life. Life can beat us up pretty badly sometimes. In the midst of it all, God provided for them all. There were 276 people to feed (vs 7), but the islanders were hospitable. God performed miracles (vs 8-9) and gave the islanders 3 months of teaching time so they could get grounded in the truth! In the grand scheme of things, the souls saved were worth the possessions lost in the storm. I certainly don't want to go through a trial, but what if my trial would result in souls being saved? Would it be worth going through? Yes. It would.

Acts 28:23. Paul took the initiative, sought out the Jewish leaders, and taught them of Jesus. Leaders lead others. Winning a leader to Jesus will open up the door for many others to be saved. Paul used all of his prison time as teaching time. I don't ever want to be incarcerated, but if I am, will I spread the Gospel as I fight for my innocence?

The book of Acts has no formal ending such as the other books. The acts of the apostles continue and are still on-going until Jesus comes!

ROMANS
Written to the church already established in Rome. Themes: The plea of salvation ~ practical instructions ~ Christian duties.

Romans. The book of Romans was written to people in Rome **who were already Christians**. These people had already been introduced to Jesus and the plan of salvation. Paul tried to establish them and teach them how to live on a daily basis as a Christ-like person. The disciples originally thought Jesus was coming back immediately to establish His kingdom on earth. They sold all and pooled their assets together (Acts 2:44; 4:32). As time went on, and persecutions set in, they began to realize that God's timetable isn't the same as theirs. The church leaders had been evangelizing: just trying to get the plan of salvation out. Now they realized they needed to establish people for the long haul. When we read the books *after* Acts, we need to remember they were written to people who had *already* obeyed the initial plan of salvation. The epistles give instructions on how to live for God, not how to get initial salvation.

Key Verse: Romans 1:17 *"The just shall live by faith."*
Chapter 1-3: Theme: The just (one who is in correct legal standing with God).
Chapter 3-5: Theme: By faith,
Chapter 6-16: Theme: Shall live.
Chapter 6: Theme: Overcome Sin. New Birth is reiterated.
Chapter 7: Theme: Walking after Flesh means Empowered to Fail.
Chapter 8:1-13. Theme: Walking after Spirit means Empowered to Succeed.
Chapter 8: 14-27. Theme: Sufferings & Glory.
Chapter 8:28-39. Theme: God's Love.

Paul's Writings. To understand Paul's writings, I have to remember he was trained as a religious lawyer. Some people really love to go by the "book". Have you met anyone who sees everything as black or white, with no grey areas? They get all bent out of shape if the rigid rules aren't followed. I get the impression Paul had that type of personality. He also seems to have a little sarcasm going on. A lot of his writings are sarcastic, rhetorical questions. He then replies to his own question by giving a discourse to prove his point. Sometimes he says the same thing in various formats. His writings contain many parenthetical phrases. It takes a little concentration to find the root sentence. Perhaps this is why we learned how to diagram a sentence in English class ~~ so we could understand Paul's writings!!! Romans is one of Paul's letters. For an in-depth study, read David Bernard's book dissecting Paul's letter to the Romans. The Bible does NOT state if we say we believe, we are just. That is what a lot of people say, but that's not what the Bible says. The Bible says the ones who are in correct legal standing before God (the just) live by believing on the word of God. If I truly believe the word of God, I will do what it says and will obey the word of God. My obedience puts me in a correct legal standing before God.

Romans 1-3:20. Paul spends a good deal of time establishing the fact we cannot be saved by ourselves ... BUT he gives us HOPE in **Romans 3:21**! God has a way to make man right before Him.

Romans 1:1-4. What is the gospel of God? Jesus = flesh + spirit.

Romans 1:5. Faith and obedience go hand in hand. They cannot be separated (15:18; 16:26). A verbal declaration of faith doesn't mean I have faith any more than squawking around like a chicken makes me a chicken. My obedience proves my faith.

Romans 1:7. Here we have a science lesson! Cause & effect. Because of grace, I have peace. Paul often uses a standard word which is translated in the King James version as "and". In modern times, we consider "and" to mean "in addition to". However, a more correct modern translation is "even", which denotes a deeper meaning. In this verse, Paul is saying God is the Creator ~ hey, He is *even* our personal savior! Paul underscores the fact the almighty, majestic God can be known on an intimate level!

Romans 1:9-10. Paul practiced intercessory prayer for others. He asked God to grant him to go for a visit, but predicated that request upon the will of God. This is very important. So many times, I pray a prayer of my wishes, based upon my understanding of a situation, but what if that isn't the best for me? Do I trust God enough if He deems my solution to be detrimental to me and denies my petition, I will be happy with His answer? Every single prayer I pray must be with the caveat of God's will. I must not cop an attitude when I don't get my way. I must TRUST God!

Romans 1:14. Contrary to popular public opinion, we all have a responsibility to others. Love demands that of us (I Corinthians 13).

Romans 1:17. People often quote the scripture "The just shall live by faith" (Habakkuk 2:4; Galatians 3:11; Hebrews 10:38) and interpret it to mean if you just believe (have faith), you will be just. They are misreading those scriptures. My faith does not make me just. If I am a "just" person, I will let my faith rule. What, then, does the word "just" mean? "Just" (in a scriptural context) means "one who is in correct legal standing with God". Ahhh! This would require me to obey the word of God, wouldn't it? If I believe (have faith), I will love. If I love, I will obey (I John 5:1-3). Obedience and faith cannot be separated (Romans 1:5; 16:26). ***This isn't rocket science!*** My faith in God will cause me to take action and obey His word. It's that simple.

Romans 1:18-20. Tucked in verse 18 is the phrase, "who hold the truth in unrighteousness". This is someone who knows the truth, but their *trajectory is off*. As I study God's word and pray, my understanding is opened more and more as God reveals next steps to me (Luke 24:45). Verse 17 states the righteousness of God is revealed. Verse 19 tells us God shows and manifests His righteousness to us. We have been given the instructions and power to obey those instructions! There is no excuse *not* to be obedient. God has revealed His righteousness through (1) nature (Psalm 19:1-4), through (2) the Bible, and through (3) preaching. We can plead innocence, but there will be **no excuse**.

Romans 1:21-25. These people knew God, **but**
- didn't glorify Him,
- weren't thankful, and
- dwelt on vain things

- so ...

How can God feel anything but anger when we insist on living life on our own terms? If I don't act upon the truth I have received, I will lose it. God allows many diseases and other calamities because man has ignored God's laws. He allows me to reap what I have sowed (vs 24, 26, 28). The end result of ignoring truth is committing sexual sins (Ezekiel 16:49-50). God deals with me until He finally no longer restrains me. Sometimes, I hear people talk about how free they are since they quit adhering to godly principles. Of course, they are free, God is no longer restraining them! They are no longer struggling between right and wrong. God is no longer dealing with their conscious.

Romans 1:25-32. Idolatry is anything that comes before God. Humanism is an ancient philosophy teaching pleasing oneself is of utmost importance. Thus, humanism becomes an idol. I can make an idol out of my own desires. Idolatry leads to uncleanliness. Humanism leads to vile affections. These vile affections lead to being not being "mindful" of God, which leads to being a reprobate. Some people live in sin, but retain a knowledge of God. There's hope for them. Those who reject that knowledge of God will become reprobates (Romans 1:28; Isaiah 66:4; II Thessalonians 2:10-11). Sin is a progression. One sin leads to another. I'm on dangerous ground when I take pleasure in the sins of others (Romans 1:32). I worry about some of the movies Christians enjoy. Do we take pleasure in the sins of others? By doing so, are we participating in their sin? God hates iniquity. He can't even look at it. It is repulsive to Him (Habakkuk 1:13). Because of the attitudes in verse 21, God just let the people go their natural course, which is progressively more and more vile. (Vocabulary in this passage: debate means strife; malignity means evil minded; without natural affection means heartless; implacable means unforgiving).

Romans 2:1. When a sentence begins with "Therefore", we need to pause and determine what it is there for! Because God has been explicit about sin and consequences in both nature and His word (Romans 1:32), we will have no excuse on judgment day.

Romans 2:3. Practice what you preach (2:21-23)!

Romans 2:6. God's mercy (lack of immediate judgment) is to lead us to repentance, not a free ticket to keep sinning! Ultimately, judgment will come. God gives us multiple opportunities to repent (vs 5) and will judge each of us according to our actions! There's that pesky little word again, "actions". Notice God doesn't judge according to what I proclaim via my mouth! I can proclaim I love God all day long, but if my actions don't back up my claims, it is just hot air. God will judge according to what I do.

Romans 2:8-13. It is not going to be anything nice for the disobedient. God is not going to dish out blessing or curses based upon my pedigree, but upon my own actions. My obedience to God will exonerate me.

Romans 2:15. No one has been able to live by their conscience alone. We all override our conscience from time to time. This is why I need the Holy Spirit! The Holy Spirit does not give me immunity to sin and its consequences, but it gives me the power to overcome sin and to live righteously. It gives me the power to say "no" to my fleshly desires.

Romans 2:16. God honors the boundaries set by the ministry. Moses drew the line somewhere on the mountain to mark its beginning. Those who crossed the line Moses drew would be punished by God (Exodus 19:12-13). It was Joshua, not God, who told the people not to speak while marching around Jericho (Joshua 6:10). Preachers need to beware not to abuse this. *It is a serious responsibility and not a ministerial privilege.* I've seen preachers demand things of the congregation that are way beyond scripture. God promised He wouldn't put on more than we can bear, but I've seen preachers put on more than their congregations can bear! I find preachers who constantly harp on a particular thing have a temptation themselves in that particular area. I knew of one preacher who would not allow members of his congregation to wear the color red. His temptation was blingy things. He liked flashy and ostentatious apparel. He transferred his own personal convictions to his congregation. There are some items that are a personal conviction. There are some things which may be wrong for ME to do, but not necessarily wrong for someone else (Philippians 2:12). As a leader, I need to be careful I don't require of others that which is expedient for me. On the other hand, I've seen preachers who allowed what the Bible does not allow. As a member of a congregation, I must make sure my pastor is well grounded in the word of God and at least sets forth the same boundaries God does (1 Thessalonians 5:12). I can't use the excuse of "pastor didn't teach me" on Judgment Day (Romans 14:12). I will be judged by the word of God and not by my pastor (although he/she will have to give an account for me: Hebrews 13:17).

Romans 2:18-29. From time to time, we hear of a preacher who has fallen into sin. This is very sad for two reasons. First of all, the person's soul is at stake. Secondly, this publicity damages Christianity in general. It undermines Christianity. Those who admire or respect this person, not only lose respect for that person, but in many instances, become disillusioned with God. I cannot predicate my relationship with God on anyone else. If someone I admire falls into sin, why should I quit serving God? I serve God for my *own* soul's benefit. Paul warns us of hypocrisy. Hypocrisy is when my inside doesn't match my outside. Religious works alone are not acceptable. My sin always has a negative impact on others. I think sometimes these preachers sin a "little sin" and when God doesn't strike them immediately with judgment, they get a little smug and think they are okay with God. At first, they feel conviction, but with each "little sin", they feel conviction less and less and the "little sin" grows to "big sin". They get exposed and most of the time and cop an attitude. Alexandria was arrested by legal authorities for committing a sin (which was also against the law). When she was disciplined by the church, her response was, "After all I've done for this church, they are going to set me down and not allow me on the platform?" That shows PRIDE on her part. She still calls himself a "Christian", but she no longer obeys the Bible. I'm on her email list and from time to time, she sends out inspirational messages. It makes me so sad. She has deceived himself and she is continually deceiving others. I just don't understand how someone can ignore these scriptures. *IT'S NOT ROCKET SCIENCE*. Obey the Bible and all will be fine!

Romans 3:1-2. What is the advantage of being a Jew? The word of God was originally given to the Jews!

Romans 3:3-4. Just because someone doesn't believe the Bible, doesn't mean they won't stand before God and be judged by the Bible. The Bible is absolute truth. Period.

Romans 3:5-8. Paul's attorney mind kicks in full gear here. He asks a question and then makes an argument against it. In this passage, he is discussing why the theory of the ends justifying the means is incorrect.

Romans 3:10-18. We are all (Jews & Gentiles both) sinners. Our sinful nature causes us to:
- Not want to seek God out (Psalm 14:3),
- Not to do good (Psalm 5:9),
- Sin with lips (lie, gossip, slander, curse, bitter words),
- Sin by actions (Proverbs 1:16),
- Spiral into destruction,
- Fight and have discord, and
- Not have respect for God.

Romans 3:19-29. Why was the Old Testament law given? To show humanity how sinful it is, of course! A pure white rag shows how dirty a dingy rag is! You don't realize how dingy or faded a shirt has gotten over time until you compare it to its original state. Romans 3:19 tells us the law shows how sinful I am, even with all of my goodness. Verse 20 leads us down the path of utter hopelessness UNTIL we get to verses 21-22, which lets us know righteousness is by faith in Jesus! There is remission of sins through the blood of Jesus which is applied to my life by baptism in Jesus' name (Acts 2:38; Hebrews 10:4-5)! Remember, faith demands obedience! Lest we get back into the hopeless of the law, we have the Holy Spirit which **changes** our hearts. There's a lot of talk in the Bible about circumcision, which was a physical act. The New Testament makes it very clear the circumcision of the Old Testament was a type and shadow of the circumcision of the heart (Romans 2:29). My carnal nature has to be cut away so bacteria (sin) can't fester in my heart. Romans chapter 3 establishes the fact we are ALL sinners (vs 23; I Kings 8:46, Psalm 14:3) *BUT* through Jesus, our propitiation (vs 25. defined as a removal of wrath by an offering), we are justified (vs.28. definition: declared to be righteous, opposite of condemned). When God's rules are dictated, they are impossible to follow. When God's rules are in my heart, they become a part of my very fiber, and they are easy to follow. *IT'S NOT ROCKET SCIENCE!* It's a matter of the *trajectory of my heart!*

Romans 3:30-31. The law is now established in my heart (II Corinthians 3:2-3; Jeremiah 31:33; Galatians 3:19).

Romans 4. In Romans chapter 4, Paul is arguing with the Jews over circumcision. Circumcision was their identity. Apparently, over time the Jews had decided circumcision came first. Not so, Abraham was justified by this faith (vs 5). His circumcision was an outward sign of his covenant relationship with God and that obedient work caused God not to charge (impute) him with crimes. Abraham's good works was something like being on probation. His crimes of sin were still on his record, but he was out on good behavior. Those crimes still have to be paid for, however, and the wages of sin is spiritual death (Romans 6:23). [Jesus paid the price for Abraham's sin, and mine, on the cross. (I Peter 3:18; Hebrews 10:10)] My outward holiness or separation is a sign of my relationship with God, *BUT* if my inside doesn't match up with my outside, then my holiness is just vain works. I don't clean up to get God, I get God to clean up (Romans 4:9-11).

Romans 4:13-17. The Jews assumed since they were born Jewish (Abraham's descendants), they had a free pass into Heaven. Not so. I can't ride on my parents' coattails. I've got to get salvation for myself. Abraham's spiritual descendants are those who live by faith (Romans 4:13; Galatians 3:7, 29). The law exposes and makes me aware of my sin. Grace is the unmerited favor of God. I don't deserve His grace. I've done nothing to warrant His grace. When a baby is newly born, that child has done nothing to deserve the parent's love. In fact, up to that point, the child has been nothing but trouble for the mother, at least! Internal beatings, nausea, sleeplessness, heaviness, and excruciating pain in childbirth, all come to mind. The child deserves to be charged with assault and battery! However, when that child is born, the mother has nothing but love and forgiveness in her heart. That's grace. Over time, the child will respond to Mom's love and will pick a flower for her, pat her shoulder, or do some other good deed deserving of Mom's love, but at birth, Mom's love towards that child is unmerited grace. Grace does not mean I can get away with sin. Grace does not mean I can do wrong and get by. Grace merely means I don't deserve any favorable attention from God, but He gives it to me anyway. People use grace as a "get out of jail free card", but that simply isn't true. Paul mocked that attitude in Romans 6:15. God's grace will give me ample opportunities to make things right, but there will be a reckoning on judgment day.

Romans 4:18-21. The faith of Abraham is herein defined. In a nutshell, Abraham fully believed God was able to do that which He had promised (vs 21). Faith is a peaceful knowledge God has everything in control and has my best interests at heart. Faith is stepping out on nothing and landing on something. Faith is a calming assurance even if I don't know my way, God does. As long as I hold God's hand, I will stay on the right path.

Romans 4.22. Because of THAT faith, God imputed (ascribed) unto Abraham, righteousness!

Romans 4:23-25. If I have the same kind of blind, obedient faith as Abraham, I, too, will have righteousness ascribed to me by God! There is hope! Without God, it would be impossible to make myself clean enough to get into God's presence. By applying the sacrifice of Jesus to my life, God assigns righteousness to me. YAY! This is not to be taken lightly. I must take care not to abuse the word of God and assume because I can't live right on my own, I might as well sin because God will understand and forgive anyway. NO! The whole point of Romans is to show us how desperately we need to stay full of the Holy Spirit so we don't sin.

Romans 5:1. The result of justification (being made legally right before God) is peace. I don't have to look over my shoulder and be jumpy worrying whether or not I'm going to get arrested. Why? Because I'm not a criminal. I don't break the laws of the land. I have perfect peace and confidence. I have no problem walking into a police station or meeting a police officer at any function. When my sins are remitted (expunged) through baptism in Jesus' name (Acts 2:38), I have peace knowing that I have no sins on my "rap sheet" in Heaven. The Holy Spirit redirects the ***trajectory of my heart*** toward the love of God. Love enables me to live a holy life. We are commanded to love (Mark 12:31). God's pure love is only possible through the infilling of the Holy Spirit (vs 5). I need to receive the Holy Spirit! It is a priority, not an option. When I hear Christian ministers say the Holy Spirit is a good thing to have, I scratch my head and wonder why anyone *wouldn't want* the Holy Spirit. Receiving the Holy Spirit does require a little effort on my part. I really have to get in my heart and dig all of the sin out. That requires some unpleasant soul searching. Perhaps that's why many Christians don't take that step. I just know that I must have the Holy Spirit. Without it, I can't love the way God requires me to love.

Romans 5:2-4. Trials are a good thing. They are very unpleasant and even hard. However, God allows these things to happen to teach me. Trials teach me patience, which is the first step toward greater things. (See also essay entitled, "Troubles and Trials: Escape Route" in *It's Not Rocket Science, Volume 1*.)

Romans 5:8. Many people die for a good cause. Many people (think military people) die for something they love (their nation, their values, their friends, etc.). Jesus died for a BAD cause ... ME! He willingly died for me while I was still a sinner. He had no guarantee I would take advantage of His sacrifice. He just did it *so I would have the opportunity to* take advantage of His sacrifice and become reconciled to God (Romans 5:10; II Corinthians 5:18-19). This is what sets Him apart from any other martyr. Adam & Eve enjoyed a pure relationship with God. They voluntarily severed that relationship for all mankind (Romans 5:12). The death of Jesus makes it possible for me to have that relationship restored. I have to take advantage of it, though, and apply the death, burial & resurrection of Jesus to my life. Otherwise, His sacrifice is of no use to me. How do I do that? I identify with the death of Jesus by becoming dead to my carnal self (repentance Romans 6:6-7). I identify with the burial of Jesus by being baptized in His name (Romans 6:4; Colossians 2:12). I identify with the resurrection of Jesus by receiving the Holy Spirit (Romans 8:11).

Romans 6. The subject of Romans chapter 6 is: OVERCOME SIN! We can make it! The Holy Spirit gives me the power to be free from the control of sin (vs 7). I now have a choice. We will either serve one or another (Romans 6:16-18), and that choice is made when I yield to either my carnal wants or my spiritual needs. Without the Holy Spirit, I can't overcome the demands of my carnal (sinful) nature. It's hard to live for God when I don't have the power to say no to myself. Paul breaks this thought down further in the next 2 chapters.

Romans 6:3-6. The concise initial plan of salvation set forth by Peter in Acts 2:38 is reiterated and expounded upon here. My repentance (being dead to sin) identifies with Jesus on the cross (vs 6). My baptism (in Jesus' name) identifies with the burial of Jesus (vs 4). My receiving the Holy Spirit (newness of life) corresponds with Jesus' resurrection (vs 4).

Romans 6:15. I don't see how people overlook this verse. Many people read a little bit of Romans, throw up their hands and say, "Well, I'm human! I can't help but sin!" That is only semi-true. Without the Holy Spirit, it is true, but WITH the Holy Spirit, I can live an overcoming life. It is a choice. Who am I going to yield myself to: my carnal nature or God's nature? I'm going to serve one or the other (vs 18). There's not a "get out of hell free card". If God was going to just shrug off my sin and allow me into heaven, why go through the whole agony of the cross? What's the point in even attempting to live for God if there was no consequence of sin?

Romans 6:19, 22. I must live a separated life from the world. Can people spot me as being a Christians? Is there anything that sets me apart? What? Holiness is being separated unto God. Just as an engaged person separates him/herself and refuses to date anyone other than his/her future spouse, so must I be separated unto God and refuse to "date" sin. Holiness is inward, but there is also visible fruit. What is it? It is important enough I study to understand exactly how God wants me to look and act.

Romans 6:23. *Everything* has a price tag. I either pay now and play later or I can play now and pay later. I can either enjoy the pleasures of sin for a while and then face the consequences of spiritual death, or I can deny my carnal self now and enjoy eternal life (Ezekiel 18:4, 21). It's a choice. ***It's not Rocket Science.***

Romans 7. Walking after the flesh means I automatically WILL sin. Walking after the flesh gives me no choice but to sin. If I give in to my carnal desires, I am empowering myself to fail. My natural man doesn't hate sin. I intend to do good and live right, but in my flesh, I don't have the power to do right all of the time (Romans 7:18). Paul gives a marital example to illustrate this point: A woman is bound in marriage to her husband as long as he is alive. Once he is dead, she is free to remarry. Likewise, we are bound to carnality as long as carnality is alive. If I repent (make a U-turn), I kill my carnal nature and that frees me to "marry" Jesus and take on His spiritual nature. Because we are not yet redeemed, we will have temptations. We will have to battle the temptation to return to the carnal nature. Even Abraham would have had the opportunity to go back had he been so inclined (Hebrews 11:15). The battle is all in the mind (Romans 7:23). I absolutely cannot please God if I feed my carnal nature (Romans 8:8). I don't know what part of that scripture people don't understand. It's pretty simple to me. ***IT'S NOT ROCKET SCIENCE!***

Romans 7:4. My life will bear the fruit of my allegiance. Do I bring forth fruit unto God or unto my carnal self (Romans 6:22)?

Romans 7:7. I would not even know what sin was had the law not been given. The Old Testament proved humanity could not live by a set of rules and regulations. It proved without the power to overcome sin, human nature will progressively degenerate and be sinful.

Romans 7:8. Sin ultimately leads to all manner of "concupiscence", which means "strong desire, especially sexual" (according to Merriam-Webster). Why do we see more and more sexual sins in the news? Because other sins have gone unchecked.

Romans 7:14-20. The natural man doesn't hate sin. My carnal nature is ever present. I intend to do good, but in my flesh, I don't have the power to do right all of the time. This is why I need the Holy Spirit! This is why I need to keep the Holy Spirit stirred up (II Timothy 1:6). It is not enough to receive the Holy Spirit and go my way. My carnal nature will overpower the Holy Spirit and rule again. I must keep my heart clean so the Holy Spirit can rule and lead me. Keeping my heart clean demands I constantly check and correct myself. Just as a driver must diligently watch the road and make minor corrections as the car hits bumps and curves, I must be vigilant with my soul. I must examine myself daily and repent for any impure thoughts, words or deeds. I repent for any unintentional or unknowing sins (Psalm 139:23-24). Not making those minor corrections will result in a huge problem with my *trajectory*. I may not be able to recover. If a driver fails to immediately correct the trajectory of a vehicle after hitting a pothole, it may be too late to avoid hitting the light pole! Stay on guard!

Romans 7:23. This is war! Let us run the race before us and never give up (Hebrews 12:1). The word "race" is from the Greek "agon", from which we get the word "agony". The Christian race is not a nice jog, but a rather demanding and grueling race. It takes a lot of effort to finish strong. The "agony" is getting the mind under control. Once my mind is made up, it's only a matter of following through. The purpose of basic training in the military is to psyche the troops into believing in the team. Once the bullets start flying, the soldiers go in auto-pilot mode. They do what they were trained (psyched) into doing. They don't even have to think about it. My mind is the battleground. My basic training is getting strength from corporate (church) worship, studying the word of God, praying, fasting, etc. If I wait until a spiritual battle to get training, I'll be shooting blanks all over the place and never hitting a target. I'll be on the defensive, trying and hoping I don't get hit. I need a made-up mind and a plan of action BEFORE the battle ever begins. It's that simple. ***This isn't Rocket Science!***

Romans 7:24. Side note: "body of this death" mentioned in Romans 7:24 could be referring to Virgil's *Aeneid, Book VII*, originally published around 19 B.C whereby a criminal had to carry a corpse chained to his back until he died a slow death himself from the decaying body he was carrying. (YUCK) Whether or not that was an actual custom of the time or a literary statement is questionable. At any rate, Paul is talking about packing around sin in my life. If I let sin linger in my life, it will slowly begin decaying the rest of me. Sin is a progression. One sin gives birth to another sin, my sin gets progressively worse (John 5:14; II Timothy 2:16). Things that are considered very MILD by today's (secular) standards, were horribly sinful just 50 years ago. Some of the music which shook the mainstream society 50 years ago is considered "elevator music" today! Satan is happy with a slow death. Never forget that his job is to kill, steal & destroy (John 10:10). He doesn't care how long that process is, as long as it takes place. How easier it is to cut off the little sprigs of carnality that come up in my life before they get so big I have to get a chain saw after them!

Romans 8 gives the antithesis of Chapter 7. ***If we walk after the Spirit, we are empowered to succeed!*** This is what the Holy Spirit does for us. It (1) justifies us, (2) gives eternal life, (3) gives peace, (4) gives power over sin, and (5) gives resurrection power - power to break the laws of nature (Romans 8:1-13). I want to ask the question once again. Why wouldn't anyone want that? The attitude is not, "Do I have to have the Holy Spirit to be saved?", but rather, "I can't make it on my own. I've got to have the Holy Spirit. How can I get it?" Romans 8:9 & 14 clearly state that without the Holy Spirit, I am not His, and verse 11 tells me I can't get to Heaven without it. I don't know what part of these scriptures people don't understand. It's pretty simple to me. *IT'S NOT ROCKET SCIENCE!*

Romans 8:1. If I walk after the Spirit, I have no judgment against me (condemnation). A lot of people misuse this scripture and say nothing is wrong if I believe in Jesus. We see this especially during Mardi Gras time here in south Louisiana. Party Hearty is the rule of the day. The idea behind Mardi Gras is to sin all you possibly can because on Ash Wednesday, you can go through the rituals of purification and everything is fine. This is false. This verse says if my *daily* life is pleasing to the Spirit of God, I won't feel the condemnation associated with a sinful life. If I feel condemnation, it is time for me to do a soul search and dig out my sin! There is a danger of ignoring the conviction I feel. If I don't dig out my sin, my heart will become calloused and I will no longer feel the conviction power of the Holy Spirit I Timothy 4:2). This verse only applies if I am walking after the Spirit and not after my flesh.

Romans 8:1-13. Walking after the Spirit gives me:
- Justification (right legal standing before God),
- Eternal Life,
- Peace,
- Power over Sin, and
- Power for Resurrection.

Romans 8:22. Earthquakes, wildfires, tornadoes, tsunamis, hurricanes, global warming, etc., is creation groaning and travailing in pain together. Creation itself is tired and longs for the day when it will be free from the curse mankind has put on it (Romans 8:21). Creation itself wants "peace on earth". Why am I nonchalant and go about my merry way? It's time to look up ~ redemption is drawing close (Luke 21:28). Nature itself is teaching us and showing us God is about to wrap things up. Nature is begging us (mankind) to wake up and come to our senses before it is too late.

Romans 8:26. My sufferings on this earth pale in comparison to Heaven. I need to keep my eyes focused on the eternal goal. Temporal goals change over time. Temporal goals may not even be attainable. Temporal goals are good to make, but my focus has to be on eternity. The Spirit knows the gushings of my heart (Romans 8:26-KJV says "groanings") and helps me in my weakness. This is another reason why I need the Holy Spirit ~ to help me know how to pray! Sometimes problems are so great and so insurmountable I just say, "God, I don't even know what to pray for or how to pray, but You do and I am asking You to take care of this situation!" God knows the ***trajectory of my heart*** and if my heart desires to do His will, God will make intercession for me (Romans 8:27)! Because God put on flesh and came to earth in the form of Jesus, He knows how we feel. Jesus experienced everything, trials, heartaches & triumphs, that all humans face. Because of that experience, Jesus (flesh nature) can make intercession for us to His spirit (God) (vs 34).

Romans 8:28. Separated, most of the components of a cake are disgusting to eat. Who wants a bowl of flour? How about eating a teaspoon of salt by itself? Does drinking eight ounces of oil sound appetizing? I think I would get so sick if I had to eat these separately. However, when it is all put together, how glorious that piece of cake is! Such is life. Our trials and sufferings are very dark and difficult at times. When we are going through a trial, we are so focused on the present that it is hard to see the big picture. This is where my faith has to kick in. I have faith God knows what He is doing. I have faith God has my best interests at heart. I have faith God will be with me. I have faith I will be victorious if I stay on course with God. When I look back on the victorious side of the trial, I see how *all* things have been blended together to make a beautiful thing. All things are not good, but I have the promise if (if, if, if) I love God and live according to HIS (not my) purpose, all of the components in my life will blend together for my good. I don't like trials, but what if the trial I am going through is to extract a hidden thing in me which prevents me from living for God? What if my trial is what would cause me to examine my salvation and make sure I am in good standing with God? What if my trial is to help someone else be saved? Ultimately, wouldn't my trial be a good thing? I trust God knows what I need to make it to Heaven.

Romans 8:28-29. God has a concrete plan. God's plan cannot fail. God's plan is predestined to succeed. The question is whether I choose to go along with God's plan or choose to make my own plan! There is a school of thought which teaches certain people are predestined for heaven or hell and no one can change their ultimate destination. It teaches good works could gain a nicer spot in hell, but if you are slated to go to hell, that's where you will go. This is NOT what the scripture is saying. That would contradict other scriptures which talk about God's desire for *all* people to attain salvation (Matthew 18:14; II Peter 3:9). Scripture cannot contradict scripture. What is this verse saying? It is saying God's plan is predestined to succeed. (Now, in God's *foreknowledge*, He already knows the path I will choose. That path, though, is my choice, and not His.) I need to make sure I am a part of God's plan. God's choice between Esau and Jacob was based upon His foreknowledge of which way each child would go (Romans 9:12). He chose Jacob, not because Jacob was such a good person, but because God knew the *trajectory of Jacob's heart* was pointed in the right direction. Esau's trajectory, however, was toward the profane (Hebrews 12:16). God's plan is predestined to succeed! I will succeed ONLY if I continue in the faith and stay in God's plan (Colossians 1:23).

Romans 8:34. It is nice to know Jesus is interceding for me. On the surface, this sounds like Jesus is praying to God, and so they are two separate beings. That theology would contradict other scriptures, so it must be rejected. God, being a spirit without the ability to sin, could never know how it feels to be tempted. God, being a spirit, could never know how it feels to be exhausted, starving, hurting, etc. God put on "work clothes". God put on flesh and came to earth in the form of a man. This flesh part of Him (son of God, Jesus) was able to be tempted in every way that I am (Hebrews 4:15). This flesh overcame all those temptations and overcame sin. This is why Jesus could die on the cross for me. When I struggle and even fail, the flesh aspect of Jesus reminds His spirit of what it was like to be vulnerable and tempted. He remembers the difficulties of being in a fleshly vessel and intercedes so the judgment I deserve is stayed and I obtain enough mercy to repent.

Romans 8:37-39. Nothing, except me and my own disobedience, can separate me from God. No amount of trials, persecutions or attacks from Satan can drive a wedge between God and me. God will build a hedge around me and will protect me (Isaiah 59:19; Psalm 34:7, 17). I, however, have the power to separate myself from God. When I disobey God, I repel Him (Exodus 33:3; Psalm 5:4-6). I push Him away. I tell Him I'm not interested. He honors my request and respects the wedge I have put between us. He will not cross over that wedge until I remove it (by repentance and obedience).

Romans 9:3. I don't know I can say what Paul said when he stated he wished he could go to hell for his family. Hell is a horrible place and eternity is for a long time! I think at this point, he was so burdened for his family that he didn't think this one through! The fact is, I can't have a proxy. I will stand before God for myself. Likewise, I can't be a proxy for someone else. We each must face the consequences of our own choices.

Romans 9:6-8. Just being a descendent of Abraham was not enough to be considered the chosen nation. Abraham's children *through Isaac* were the ones chosen. However, they are children merely by virtue of the flesh. Children of the spirit are those who have the same faith as Abraham. Gentiles who believe are also considered Abraham's children by adoption. I'm glad adoption is an option for me!

Romans 9:12. God's choice is based upon man's action. God, in His foreknowledge, *knew* which way each child would go. Esau's *trajectory* was toward the profane (Hebrews 12:16).

Romans 9:17. Pharaoh could have repented. The same sun that melts a candle, hardens a brick. Had the *trajectory of Pharaoh's heart* been pointed God-ward, he could have been very instrumental in a vast number of people becoming believers.

Romans 9:21-22. God is in control of all things. God uses men and women to accomplish His purpose. Pharaoh, Babylon, Hitler, etc., are all examples of people God used to chastise the Israelites. (They, in turn, received chastisement for being evil.) God endures a lot of evil before He shows His wrath. I believe God allowed the USA to become a world power for two reasons: to be a friend to Israel and to finance world missions. Woe unto America if it fails in those areas! God will no longer have a use for the USA. (This is just my opinion.)

Romans 9:27-28. Even though God wants all of mankind to be saved, not many actually will, because not many really desire to live for God. It's not because God is mean. People misinterpret God's love for a ticket into Heaven. God's love respects the choices I make. "Many are called, but few are chosen" (Matthew 22:14). The chosen ones are the ones whose ***trajectory of heart*** is right. He calls out those who are willing and He works with them unto salvation (Revelation 22:17). I want my heart to be right! So few are actually on the right path that God will make a "short work" and finish it up. Be ready!

Romans 9:31-32. Israel sought salvation by their works. We can't earn salvation. Salvation comes by complete faith in God. Faith will produce works pleasing to God, but those works don't save me. My faith and obedience do. Which comes first, faith or works? Faith does. Good works are a by-product of my life of faith. I need to be careful I don't mix up the order of those. Many denominations have gone that route.

Romans 10:2-3. Paul prayed for the sincere, religious Jews. There are people in this world who know the Bible, go to church, and give to charity. They are very sincere in what they do, but they are sincerely lost. Having knowledge, zeal, and good works doesn't get me into Heaven (Remember Cornelius in Acts 10?). I must obey according to GOD's way of salvation and not according to MY thoughts of religious behavior. It's either salvation God's way, or salvation no way. There's no room for error here. **I must be saved.**

Romans 10:9-10. The very first step in salvation is confessing with your mouth. I have to acknowledge that God, via Jesus, exists in the first place. Without that basic step, there is no salvation. However, we can't just stop there! The second step is believing. This verse states if I confess and believe, I shall be saved. A lot of people stop right there. The problem is this: Saying that I believe is not the same as actually believing. If I really believe, I will take action. If I really believe my car is going to transport me back and forth to work without mechanical failure, I will get in it and drive. If I really believe the chair is going to support my weight, I will sit down on it. If I really believe my employer is going to pay me on Friday, I will go to work for five full days without getting paid at the end of each day. I don't know why people think they can just say "I believe, I believe" and not do anything about that belief. Keep reading past verse 9. Verse 10 says we believe unto righteousness. That means I take the appropriate, right (correct, lawful) actions. Salvation **begins** with confession. It doesn't end there. Romans 10:13 tells me if I call upon the name of the Lord, I shall be saved. Now, just a few verses prior (vs 9), I was told if I confessed, I would be saved. Which is it? You see, there is a danger in taking out a scripture and using it to suit my purpose. Jesus said there would be those who called His name and He would say He never knew them (Matthew 7:22-23). Is Paul contradicting Jesus? That's not acceptable. Let's look further. Jesus asked why people called him Lord if they wouldn't obey Him (Luke 6:46). I Corinthians 12:3 tells us no one can call Jesus Lord except by the Holy Spirit. I conclude that believing and calling upon Jesus' name is effective only because of my obedience to the word of God. It's not enough just to mouth the words, "I believe Jesus is God". I must obey His word.

Romans 10:17. Faith is developed by my understanding (hearing). How can I understand except by the word of God? Salvation, then, is a progression, begun by a simple confession of Jesus' lordship. That little grain of "mustard seed" faith (Matthew 17:20) then grows as I learn more and more of the Bible. As I understand the Bible, I follow through and progress into salvation.
- I will repent of my sins. I will not only stop sinning, but I will make a U-turn.
- I will be baptized in the name of Jesus in order for my sins to be expunged (taken off my record). I want to ensure my past sins don't follow me up to the judgment throne (I Timothy 5:24).
- I will be filled with the Holy Spirit with the evidence of speaking in other tongues just like they did in the book of Acts (Acts 2:4). The Holy Spirit will give me the power and the victory to overcome the temptations that come my way (Acts 1:8; Romans 8). Why wouldn't I want that?
- Finally, I will continually live a life pleasing unto Jesus (Acts 2:40). I will live a holy life, separated from the world. My salvation is a continual process. I'm really not saved until I have reached Heaven.

Romans 10:18. The people of this world have already had a witness in (1) nature, (2) by Israel (when it was doing well), and (3) by the early church.

Romans 11:4-5. There's always a group of people who will serve God. Sometimes I feel alone and wonder if anyone else is living for God. Oh yes, there are some ... not many .... just a remnant, but all through the ages God has had, and will have, a people. The question is: Am I one of them?

Romans 11:7-8. I must diligently seek God and be willing to obey His word. If I seek for truth, I will find truth (Matthew 7:7). If I don't diligently seek after God, He will blind me to His word. There is no middle ground with God (Revelation 3:16). An encounter with God will forever change me, one way or the other. If I obey God, I am forever changed for the good and my relationship with Him grows. If I spurn God (just a little), I begin a downward progression into sin and deeper sin. I will never just stay the same. Being blinded by God means I can no longer see or understand His word. I will read it with my eyes, but my mind won't grasp what God is saying. I will read the Bible with human understanding and not with spiritual understanding. I will distort the scriptures to say what I want it to say with my human logic. Now, that's a scary place to be!

Romans 11:11. The depth of God's mercy amazes me. Even after the Jews rejected Jesus, God didn't stop trying to woo them. He had tried many tactics through the years. He tried blessings (Canaan land). He tried appealing to their human egos (kings & military victory). In desperation, He tried punishment (captivity). After their rejection of Jesus, He turned to the Gentiles, but He didn't totally reject the Jews. He's still trying to woo them! He's hoping they will be jealous of the relationship the Gentiles are having with Him and they will want Him back! See, all things *do* work together for good (Romans 8:28)! The Jews' rejection of Jesus was a bad thing, but it opened up the door of salvation for the Gentiles, which is a good thing. God turning his back on the Jews is a bad thing, but His turning toward the Gentiles is a good thing because (according to the book of Revelation) it will ultimately cause the Jews to turn back to Him! He will keep His commitment to Abraham at all costs!

Romans 11:18-22. It makes me sad when I see those who have backslidden reaping the consequences of their wrong choice. I have friends who used to live a consecrated life and now, although they profess to believe, don't act that way. It saddens me. Paul felt the same and tells us because of Israel's unbelief, they were broken off. I must take heed I don't follow the same path. God is merciful and good, but there is a severe, judging side of God too!

Romans 11:23. God is merciful. He will restore backsliders if they repent.

Romans 11:25-27. God made a covenant with Israel a very long time ago. God always keeps His end of the bargain. Israel didn't, but ultimately will. Unfortunately, they have to go through a whole lot of tribulations before they will be willing to serve God. Those tribulations will cause them to turn, once again, to God. The fact God is so longsuffering proves His mercy. It is interesting to note when God refers to the sinfulness of His people, he refers to "Jacob". Other times, He calls them Israel! We all, even those living for God, have the potential to be a Jacob. I must be on guard.

Romans 11:29. God never reneges on His promise or a gift. Even if we don't keep up our side of the bargain, God always keeps His word, even if I don't deserve the gift or if I don't use the gift wisely. These gifts are permanent, even if I backslide (Ecclesiastes 2:9). I know drug addicts who can get in the presence of God and operate the spiritual gifts they were given a long time ago. Does this mean God approves of them? No. It means God doesn't take back the gifts He has given. My gifting does not indicate my spirituality. My fruit does.

Romans 11:33-34. It is true God's ways are not our ways (Isaiah 55:8), BUT He does reveal secrets to His friends. If I am close enough to Him, He will let me in on secrets (John 15:12-17).

Romans 12:1-2. Paul begs the believer to:
- Present my outward self as a visible sacrifice to God.
- Not allow my inward self to adopt the mindset of the world.
- Allow my mind to be restored to its original state (as in the Garden of Eden).

To present my body as a living sacrifice to God is an on-going relationship (Ecclesiastes 12:13) and not a one-time commitment. Sacrifice means it is uncomfortable. Sacrifice will cost me. Sacrificing my body means I deny myself of my carnal desires that displease the Lord, whether it is clothing choices or pleasurable choices.

Romans 12:3, 16. *PRIDE* caused Israel to fail. They were **so stinkin' proud** about being God's "chosen", they forgot to maintain the very relationship which caused Abraham's seed to be the chosen nation. I must not let self-righteousness get hold of me or else .... "how art the mighty fallen" (II Samuel 1:19). I've seen churches get puffed up with pride. A 100+ member congregation is capable of being "self-contained". They are capable of having many programs and social activities among themselves. They then run the risk of being prideful of what they have. They begin to lose sight of outreach and worry more about maintaining the status quo. A few years of this kind of attitude results in a church split. I've heard churches brag about being so good, they'll have a special spot in Heaven. Each one of these churches suffered a church split. God doesn't do pride.

Romans 12:3. God gives everyone the opportunity to have faith. It is my choice whether or not to accept that opportunity and act upon it. God doesn't send anyone to hell. People send themselves when they fail to act upon the opportunities God sends their way. The choice on how to exercise that faith is up to me. I can believe in God, I can believe in nature, or I can believe in my own self. People who are atheists really do have faith. Their faith is in and of themselves, which boils down to PRIDE. If someone plops down on a chair, they have faith the chair will hold them up. People have faith. Some people's faith is misguided.

Romans 12:8-15. God has given us (the church) service gifts. There is the five-fold ministry, of course (apostles, prophets, evangelist, teachers, pastors: Ephesians 4:11), but there are also service gifts. These things need to be developed in a local assembly. Everyone can't have a pulpit ministry, but everyone does need to have a service ministry. These ministries are to be done with a cheerful heart full of love and hope. Now, what does my local church need? More acts of mercy? Then, I will

fill that need. It does no good for me to gripe and complain about a deficiency in the church. Whatever hole there is in the church, needs to be filled by someone. Why not me? If I'm not willing to fill that hole, what right do I have to gripe about it?
- Exhort: Encouraging someone. Looking on the bright side of things.
- Giving: Being generous.
- Leading: Taking charge of a project and being faithful to it. This is typical of an administrator.
- Being Merciful. Showing mercy to others with happiness and not grudgingly.
- Love: Love with purity and not pretending.
- Hate evil ~ embrace good.
- Put others first.
- Be astute in business dealings (not a lazy employee or volunteer).
- Have an attitude of thankfulness (rejoice).
- Show patience when in trials.
- Be hospitable to others.
- Be a blessing to others, even if they are being ugly.
- Empathize with others. Everyone needs to feel validated. Their problem is huge to them. Can I show interest and compassion?

Romans 12:13. Reminder. We are to be hospitable. Learn to be a good host(ess) (whether at church or at home). Good leaders make each individual person feel special. We are to be "given to hospitality" (I Timothy 3:2). We are to love being hospitable (Titus 1:8). We are to be hospitable without complaint and without any promise of pay-back (I Peter 4:9)!

Romans 12:19-21. God will avenge me. I simply have to wait upon God. He claimed responsibility for vengeance. I must not take on His responsibility. I am required to maintain my Christianity, to be kind, and to treat the other person with mercy. God will avenge me. For me to take on that responsibility means I would have to be evil back, which means God would have to avenge that person and chastise *me* for the evil I have done to him/her ~~ oh my, what a vicious cycle! I can overcome evil with good! (Hebrews 10:30; I Peter 3:9)

Romans 13:1-8. A Christian is a good citizen. Christians are honest in their taxes. Christians obey the laws of the land (as long as God's laws aren't violated). Christians pay their debts. I'm talking about "real" Christians here, not people who claim to be a Christian. My father started a church in 1987. Services were held in a rented place, but it was very apparent that as the congregation grew, a new facility was needed. A neighboring church folded and there were no members left. My father was asked if he wanted the building and could assume the bank note. If not, the bank would foreclose on the loan. The congregation voted to do just that. As my father learned of the finances of the church, he realized the former pastor had personal debts all over town in the name of the old church. Although it was a completely new church congregation, a different church name, and they were not in any way legally responsible for the debts of the pastor of the church that closed, my father wrote a letter to each creditor. He explained the situation and asked them to give him some time and he would see that all debts were paid. That little congregation made cakes, peanut brittle, and cooked lunches for years. They sent the children's clothing store $5 here and the paint store $10 there. My father was determined those debts would be paid. He didn't want the reproach and stigma that was placed on the building and Christianity to stick. I know there are some rare instances when bankruptcy is completely unavoidable, but for the most part, I don't think that is an option for a Christian. We need to pay our debts. When I was in the legal field, a lady came into the law office wanting to file for bankruptcy over about $2,000 worth of debt. The attorney told her that although she could do that legally, bankruptcy wasn't advisable for such a small amount. About a month later, she came back. She had gone all over town and purchased about $50,000 worth of furniture, etc., and wanted to file for bankruptcy! This is NOT an example of an acceptable bankruptcy. A Christian should be honest in all dealings.

Romans 13:9-10. "For this cause". For what cause? For the cause of love (vs 8). Love causes me not to steal, commit adultery, lie, etc. Love, pure love, will cause me to act right (I Corinthians 13; II John). When I am low on love, I am low on God because God is Love (I John 4:8). This is a mathematical equation. God equals love!

Romans 13:14. My flesh is very selfish. I can't trust myself. I can't give my flesh any chances (Psalm 101:3; I Thessalonians 5:22). I cannot afford to allow myself to get too close to that mailbox! (See essay entitled, "Playing by the Mailbox" in *It's Not Rocket Science, Volume 1*.) This is why the Holy Spirit is so important for me to have. I can't be trusted to live a holy, separated life without the power of the Holy Spirit actively working in me! God hasn't provided the Holy Spirit for me because He can trust me with it. He has provided the infilling of the Holy Spirit because He can't trust me **without** it. On my own, I can't live for God. I try, but I can't. My human nature flares up and I have no choice but to do wrong. I *must have* the Holy Spirit dwelling and active in me in order to consistently live right in God's sight.

Romans 14:1-14. There are going to be disagreements over minor issues. It is not for me to argue with someone over personal convictions. I will be considerate of other's beliefs. Apparently, there was a huge problem in the early church over the eating of food offered first to idols. Although a Christian cannot participate in the offering of food to idols, eating that food is not wrong. However, if a fellow Christian is offended by it, Paul instructs us not to cause contention between fellow Christians. Modern example: If I go to a church where they wish for me to wear a handkerchief on my head, I will do so. I believe the scripture is clear a woman's *long hair* is her covering (I Corinthians 11:15), but if a congregation believes in taking an extra measure to have the head covered by a bit of cloth, I will honor them and do so. As long as I don't sin, I should comply with someone's beliefs when I am with them. I am not to show contempt or superiority (vs 10), nor am I to be a stumbling block to their walk with God (vs 13).

Romans 14:15-21. I need to be considerate of others. What is a temptation to my friend may not be a temptation to me. Susan told me she felt evil every time she crossed over the bridge to New Orleans. I loved New Orleans! In my youth, I insisted that we go down to the Quarter to eat. I shouldn't have done that. I should have respected that for her, it was not good to go. I've repented over my stupidity and have lamented over that for many years. If getting a non-alcoholic drink would give the wrong impression, or would cause someone to stumble, I should not partake. I shouldn't ridicule or show contempt for someone else's weaknesses or temptations. I must be considerate of an individual's personal convictions. Likewise, I must not put MY personal convictions on someone else's shoulders. There are some things that are sin for me but not sin for someone else. (This does not take away from the fact the Bible does spell out some absolute sins and standards of conduct.)

Romans 15:1-3. Sometimes we all just need some "me" time, but overall, it is right to help others and be selfless. Pleasing my neighbor does not mean allowing them to walk all over me and take advantage of me. Pleasing my neighbor does not mean catering to their every whim. What it does mean is I follow Christ's example and help others make it to heaven. It means going to a church function when I don't want to or feel like it just to support the leadership and those who need me. It means lending an ear or stopping to pray for someone in need. The key word in this passage is "to edification". I am to please my neighbor to his/her edification, or spiritual well-being.

Romans 15:4. The Old Testament is a schoolmaster to teach me about God (Galatians 3:24-25). The Old Testament is a shadow of the New (Colossians 2:17; Hebrews 8:5).

Romans 15:6-7. The church body should be unified. Sure, we will have some differences, but we are on the same team. When a church starts bickering among themselves, the ***trajectory*** of the church is not right. When a church starts bickering, they are self-centered and not soul-centered. When a physical body fights its own self, diseases such as cancer spring up. Likewise, nothing good will come out of church members fighting among themselves.

Romans 15:9-12. Thank the Lord there is hope for the Gentiles! Jesus may have come to confirm God's promises for the Jews, but the door was opened up to the rest of the world! YAY!

Romans 15:13-17. Why do I need the Holy Spirit? So I can be the person described in this passage. I cannot be that person without the Holy Spirit. Going back to bickering in the church ~~ When church people get miffed, feel slighted, get offended, gossip, become jealous of each other, and fight among themselves, I know the church (as a whole) is not prayed up. God is not the author of confusion or division. Satan is (I Corinthians 14:33). Focus on God, not on each other!

Romans 15:27. My ministry is not limited to spiritual things. We do, after all, have to live in this life. From time to time, we all fall on hard times. When I am "up", I need to give and help those who are in need. I will reap what I have sowed. If I sow generosity with both my time and money, God will see to it that I reap blessings when it is my turn to go through tough times. When my eldest was a baby, we took the pastorate of a small, struggling church. We personally paid the church bills. I could not afford beautiful dresses for my little girl. God saw my desire and moved upon Estelle to give me her daughter's $100 dresses as she outgrew them. That was back in the 1980s. Those dresses were beautiful! Estelle lived two states away and went to church with a family member. God saw my desire, and without me even verbalizing it, provided.

Romans 15:30-31. Paul was a little nervous about meeting with the saints in Jerusalem! He had insecurities. Perhaps he felt a little bit intimidated by the apostles who had actually been trained by Jesus Himself! He asked the Roman church to pray for him! I think it is healthy for us to have a little insecurity about something. It keeps us from getting too uppity and proud.

Romans 16:17-18. I must avoid those who teach false doctrines or cause division, even if they are "good" people. Their spirit will rub off on me. I must beware lest they influence me into their false doctrines. I must be careful lest they sweep me up in their spirit of strife. I just hid a friend on Facebook. It seemed like every post he writes is to "stir the pot". He makes heaven or hell issues out of his personal convictions and rallies up his friends into a frenzy. I found myself always wanting to comment and try to get him back on track. I decided that it would be better for me to just not see his posts. I'm not going to get him back on track by anything I say on Facebook! Social media is no platform for theological debates. The scripture tells me to avoid those who cause division.

I CORINTHIANS
Written to the church already established in Corinth. Themes: Cleansing of the church ~ Christian practices ~ love ~ Gifts of the Spirit ~ Resurrection.

I Corinthians 1:5-7. My prayer is that all I do be overshadowed by God's presence. I want to be enriched by Him. He wants me to have all gifts. I don't understand why people stop and plateau with a small experience with God. Repentance gives us a clean-feeling heart, but I can't stop there! I've got to keep pressing on until I've received every thing He has for me. It does take some persistence. God doesn't hide from me so I have to chase Him down, but He does withhold understanding from me until I am willing to slow down and search for understanding.

I Corinthians 1:10-11. Whoever thinks that the early church was perfect hasn't read this book! There was disunity in the church in Corinth. Consequently, there were many sinful activities tolerated within the church. We are all on the same team: God's! There is no big I and little you. We are in this together. We all have different roles to play, but we are to be unified in our goal to
- go to Heaven and
- help as many as we can go there too.

When a church begins to bicker, it is time to pray until that spirit leaves. Disunity will destroy.

I Corinthians 1:22. The Gospel of Jesus transcends to all cultures. The prominent cultures during the time of the New Testament were Jewish and Greek. The Jews were more of an emotional culture and the Greeks leaned toward intellect. Regardless of the cultural backgrounds, God will reveal Himself to a hungry heart (vs 24). On the other hand, those who are not hungry will find fault with the Gospel according to their own culture. I need to understand the temperament of the culture I am dealing with and witness accordingly (regardless of geographical location). God's word can't be changed, but my methods may need to be adapted to fit a particular culture or situation.

I Corinthians 1:25. God is made strong in my weakness. This means God can do what I can't! Is my grief too much to bear? God will give me peace (John 14:27). Is my financial despair overwhelming? God will provide my need (Philippians 4:19). Is my hurt too deep? God will heal my broken heart (Luke 4:18). Am I held captive by addictions? God will deliver (Luke 4:18). When I am weak, He is strong!

I Corinthians 1:27-29. The danger is not being educated or smart. The danger is in *thinking* so. I personally know people who lived and taught God's word, but got educated and then ridiculed that which they had previously believed and taught. I am never too smart for God. I am never too smart to know how to handle situations by myself. I am never too educated to not need God. God can use baptized brains, but I must lean upon *His* understanding and not mine. A counseling session should *never* take the place of a good prayer session. Prayer can give more insight into a particular situation than human reasoning. I'm not against counseling, but I wonder if too many people resort to counseling *in lieu of* prayer time with God. It is easier to yack with a fellow human being than to slow down long enough and listen for the voice of God.

I Corinthians 2:1-4. No one likes a know-it-all. Of all of the apostles, Paul appears to be the most learned and had the most clout. He was a Roman citizen (Acts 22:25-26) and he studied under Gamaliel (Acts 22:3). However, he determined he wouldn't be a show-off. He determined the work of Christ would be the center of his ministry. Paul didn't major on intellectualism. He was determined to be "all things to all men" (I Corinthians 9:22). He was determined he would be relatable to people from all walks of life. I must be careful not to look down (my very long nose) at people. I need to validate them at the level they are and bring the Gospel to them in a way they can relate and apply to their lives. Paul's attitude was the same as John the Baptist's: that Jesus would be the focus. Jesus must increase ~ I must decrease (John 3:30). It's not about me. All that I am could be taken away with one quick stroke. It takes us a long time to realize this lesson. Apparently, it took Moses 40 years of the humbling process before God qualified him to be a leader. God needs "baptized brains" in leadership, but I must not allow my "baptized brain" to get puffed up with pride. If God has blessed me with some intellect, it is to use it to help others see Him and come to a relationship with Jesus! On a side note to being "all things to all men" (I Corinthians 9:22), this does NOT give me license to sin. I had a man tell me that he was called to go drink in the bars so he could relate to those there. He related, alright. He died of AIDS. What a sad situation! This scripture means I find a common thread with someone and, building upon that, lead them to Christ. Follow the example of Jesus. He spoke in parables: stories His audience could relate to.

I Corinthians 2:7. Man's wisdom and God's wisdom are two very different things.

I Corinthians 2:10-11. If I spend some time with God, He will direct my thoughts and my prayers (Romans 8:26).

I Corinthians 2:12-14. Why do I need the Holy Spirit? So I can understand God's ways. I don't understand why some ministers downplay the importance of receiving the Holy Spirit. How can I understand and know God's thoughts without it? How can I go to Heaven without it (I John 2:20-27)? The Holy Spirit will filter out error from truth. The Holy Spirit enables us to translate spiritual thoughts into spiritual words.

I Corinthians 2:16. How do we have the mind of Christ? Look to the preceding verses. We have the mind of Christ by the infilling of His spirit. This is why we need to be filled with the Holy Spirit.

I Corinthians 3:3. Isn't it amazing with all of the spiritual gifts within the Corinthian church, they were still very carnal? Remember, the evidence of spiritual gifts is NOT the evidence of the abiding presence or approval of the Holy Spirit. A gift is just that. A gift. If I give someone a gift and they later turn on me and hate me, I can't go and get that gift back. It was a gift and it is theirs to do as they please. They can give it to someone else. They can even throw it away. A spiritual gift is just that: a gift. God doesn't demand His gifts back when I sin. I've seen people who are openly sinning (and freely admit to being sinful) operate with spiritual gifts. The benchmark of a righteous person is not gifts, but the fruit of the spirit (Galatians 5:22-23). Now many people have natural attributes and abilities that mirror the spiritual gifts. Some people are laid back and have patience at birth. That doesn't mean they are born with the spiritual fruit of patience. We all have a measure of each of these fruits because we are made in the image of God (Genesis 1:27). When we bear these fruits *over and beyond our natural inclinations,* we realize we are able to do so only by the power of the abiding spirit of God. Patience is not a natural virtue for me. I'm a redhead with all of the typical stereotypes attached! I can only be patient and long suffering by God's help.

I Corinthians 3:4-9. We all have different ministries not for competition, but for the edification of the whole body. What if my big toe decided it wanted to be on my face so it could see the world from a higher perspective? Not only would I look funny with a toe on my face, but I would lose my balance. The big toe is important for balancing. My body would suffer without my big toe where it belongs. Likewise, the body of Christ suffers when a member tries to engage in a ministry he/she is not a good fit for and is not called to do. I must fulfil the job in the church I am supposed to do. On Judgment Day, I don't want God asking me why I neglected my job and tried to do someone else's. I don't want the church body to suffer because I insisted on having a particular ministry when someone else would have done a better job and had the anointing. We're all on the same team. This is not a competition! The end result is a God-thing (vs 6), not my thing.

I Corinthians 3:10. I must build upon the foundation laid by Jesus. The apostles built the first "floor". I am responsible for my "floor". If I build my floor with fluff, my children and their children will not have shelter from worldly influences and will not be saved. I must keep the truth, not only for myself, but for subsequent generations. I am responsible to do my part in passing the truth from generation to generation.

I Corinthians 3:13. Ultimately, the quality of my work will be manifested for all to see. The ***trajectory of my heart*** will eventually show itself. Whether or not I have built my life upon the truths in God's word, or if I have allowed my heart to stray, will come out in the open sooner or later. There is an old saying that goes, "Give a hang-man enough rope and he will eventually hang himself." If I (or anyone else) does wrong, it will eventually be made manifest.

I Corinthians 3:16-17. If I have the Holy Spirit, my physical body is the dwelling place (temple) of the Spirit. How can I expect God to stay in a dwelling place that I don't keep clean? This passage clearly states if I defile my physical body, God will go ahead and finish the job of destroying it. Is this why there are so many diseases in our bodies? Humanity fulfills the lusts of the flesh by over-eating, drinking, smoking, participating in sexual deviations contrary to the laws of God, etc. How can we think God is okay with that? Just because we get chills when we go to church doesn't mean God is still abiding in us. Feeling God's presence does not mean God approves of my lifestyle. It means that God is trying to woo me back to my original state. God's intended relationship with me is the same as He had with Adam and Eve in the Garden of Eden.

I Corinthians 3:18-21. Vanity is pride. Vanity is foolish. It is good to be educated, but it is not okay to be prideful about it. God's word is absolute truth. For me to reason and philosophize anything contrary to God's word is foolish. How many times has an adult suppressed a smile when a young child insists something he believes is truth? I image God does that when He hears us talk sometimes. Remember when the scientists of the world thought the earth was flat? They insisted it was. Today, we realize how foolish that line of reasoning was. I wonder how many things we think are true today really aren't? Will the scientists of tomorrow debunk our philosophies of today? Probably so.

I Corinthians 4:1-2. There are different ministries in the church. I will be held accountable for the ministry God has given me. I must be a good steward (caregiver) of my ministry. These ministries or talents are not for competition, but for edification of the whole body (I Corinthians 3). We (the church) are all in this together. We are all headed for Heaven. Competition is a very human thing. If used correctly, it can be healthy. If I use competition to sharpen me, to motivate me to better myself, it is a good thing. If I use competition to jockey for a position, it is PRIDE, and is a bad thing. We must have teamwork in the church. A good team player isn't concerned whether or not he/she actually makes a goal (although everyone wants to be the hero). A good team player will throw off the ball to someone else who is in a better position to make that goal. The main thing is God gets the glory (I Corinthians 3:6). It doesn't matter who all played which part. I just need to play MY part ~ the job God has given me to do, whether or not I get the recognition for it. God knows what I've done and He is the one who will ultimately pass out the rewards. At my age, I realize the ministry God has given me has been primarily to lay a foundation for someone else to build upon. When I was younger, it upset me to train people for them to be a blessing to another congregation. Now, I realize I trained them to train others. I can't begin to imagine what all my influence has been, so I don't even think about it! It's all good! It's all for God's kingdom, not mine. One day, God will reveal what sort of work I have done ~ was it quality work, or just a whole lot of nothing (quantity) (I Corinthians 3:13)?

I Corinthians 4:5. Don't worry. Hypocrites are eventually exposed by God. It seems they get away with their hypocrisy, and they might for a little while, but they won't forever. Be patient. God does love them and is trying to woo them to Him. If they won't repent by God dealing with them privately, He will expose them publicly. Their motives and the ***trajectory of heart*** will be revealed.

I Corinthians 4:7. Talents and abilities are from God. Who am I to take pride in my abilities? One well-placed car wreck or one good stroke could take it all away in a moment's time. Some people get a position and think they're all important. I'm not any more important than anyone else. In fact, if I don't do the work/job God has designed for me to do, I'm less important. If I try to do someone else's job and neglect my own, I'm a detriment to the church.

I Corinthians 4:9-13. Paul wrote to the Corinthians how the apostles suffered so many things, and how those who came after the apostles had it relatively easy by comparison. One generation works hard and paves the way for the next generation. This is the way it should be and yet, the generation who has it easier must not take for granted the price that has been paid and the sacrifices made. This is true in the physical world. America's freedom was paid by the blood of its military. It is also very true in the spiritual world. I have not experienced the religious persecution my parents did. My children did not experience the religious persecution I did in school. When we suffer, we tend to rely more on God and tend to pray more. When things are going easy, we tend to relax in our prayer life. This is not as it should be, but this is how it is. I need to recognize this about my human nature and strengthen my grip. I don't want to fumble the ball for my family and my descendants. I don't want to be the generation that loses knowledge of God. I've met people whose grandparents were mighty in the spirit, but they themselves have no knowledge of God. How sad. It just takes one generation to blow it for the upcoming generations.

I Corinthians 4:18. Some in the Corinthian church got offended Paul hadn't come to visit them. You just can't please everyone! The carnal minded will always get offended by something. Don't let it get you down. Love them anyway. Try to help them reach the next level of spiritual maturity, but don't let it get you down. Keep your conscience clean before God and do your best, of course, then let all of the other stuff go.

I Corinthians 5:5-6. It cracks me up when people lament that the church today isn't as spiritual as the "early church". *Really?????* Have they even read the Bible? The church members (notice I didn't say "saints") in Corinth were openly fornicating, a member was in an incestuous relationship, and they were getting drunk during communion! *Every* church has its problems. *Every* church has hypocrites. Where else would you find a hypocrite? Certainly not in the barroom! I just have to make sure I'm not one! I can't run around looking for a perfect church, spiritual in every way. I'll never find that church here on this earth. Sin should be dealt with, of course, as Paul did in I Corinthians. Sin in the camp does affect the whole church.

Remember Achan at Ai (Joshua 7:13)? A church cannot move forward when sin is allowed to fester. Sin permitted sends a message to the others in the congregation that its okay to sin. A pastor must deal with it, but with wisdom. Those who refuse correction ultimately must be asked to take their sin elsewhere (I Corinthians 5:11-12). Paul instructs the church to turn those over to Satan perchance exposure to Satan's world would bring them to their senses (I Timothy 1:20).

I Corinthians 5:10-12 is a call for separation from the world and to be holy. I must stay away from reprobates or they will affect me and cause me to question Biblical teachings. A reprobate is one who has known the truth and who has deliberately rejected it. A backslider is not necessarily a reprobate. Some people backslide and know they are sinning. Others backslide and twist the scriptures to mean what they want it to mean and justify their sin to the point they don't believe it is sin any more. These are reprobates. Paul tells us to stay away from and not to even eat with someone who blatantly defies the Bible (II Thessalonians 3:6, 14-15; also see Hosea 4:17). It appears that God may have a "strike 3 and you're out" policy (Titus 3:10). Perhaps God wants me to try and steer someone back on the right path, but after a few attempts, just lett'em go.

I Corinthians 6:2. This will happen during the millennial reign (Revelation 5:10).

I Corinthians 6:12-20. Just because something is legal doesn't mean I should participate in it. The law of God supersedes the laws of man. When Adam and Eve sinned, they handed over authority to Satan. God had given Adam authority in the Garden of Eden (Genesis 1:26), but we find somehow Satan became the prince and power of the air (Ephesians 2:2). I believe this happened when Adam & Eve sinned. When I sin, I am doing so to my own detriment. Now, God purchased me back with his own blood (Acts 20:28; Hebrews 9:12; 13:12; Revelation 1:5). When I apply that price to my life, I become redeemed. My intended relationship with Him is restored. I belong to Him. I glorify Him, not only by my words, but by my actions. When I do sinful things with my body, I am slapping away His sacrifice. (See essay entitled "Playing by the Mailbox" in *It's Not Rocket Science, Volume 1*.) I glorify God with my body by living a holy life, separated from sin.

I Corinthians 7 deals with marriage. Ideally speaking, celibacy is good (vs 1) so everyone's spare time could be devoted to the work of God (vs 8, 32). Practically speaking, celibacy is impossible for most people (vs 7, 9). Some of Paul's discourse may have had to do with the political conditions at the time. The Christians were being persecuted and having a family complicated things during that time of persecutions. Paul appears to give some personal opinions (as opposed to commandments from God - see vs. 12) in this chapter. Apparently arranged marriages were common in that culture. Paul gives guidelines concerning that too (vs. 36-38). The bottom line is this:
- Marriage partners should have mutual respect towards each other (vs. 3).

- Marriage is until death (vs 39).
- Single life is good if you can contain your passions (vs 9).
- If one spouse doesn't serve God, stay married if they are willing and you may be able to win them and your children (vs 13-15).
- If you're married, don't seek to divorce (vs 10, 27.)
- Life is short. Marriage is for a season. Don't worry about being single: this too shall pass (vs 29-34)!

I Corinthians 7:17-24. Paul tells us to deal with our lot in life and to live for God where we are. He uses slavery as an example. A slave's lot in life is to be subject to his master. However, spiritually speaking, he is equal. If he becomes free, great, but if freedom never happens, he is still equal in Christ. All believers are bound to Christ. This passage isn't condoning slavery. It is acknowledging slavery exists and how to deal with it as a Christian.

I Corinthians 8 discusses knowledge versus love. The message in this chapter is clear: Knowledge brings out pride in us, but love is a healer. I must always remember that as good as I may be, there is always someone who is better than I. I feel a little proud of myself for a beautifully decorated cake until I see the cakes in competitions. Then I realize how pitiful mine really is! Great people play up their strengths and work to hone their weaknesses, but there is always someone who does something better. There is always someone younger, prettier, funnier, more charming, more elegant, smarter, craftier, etc., than I. Likewise, I can be better in any of those areas than someone else. I need to love people and let them be who they are. People are quirky and some people get offended at the oddest things. Some people have convictions over the strangest things. I'm not talking about convictions concerning absolutes the Bible teaches, but personal convictions that aren't really Biblical. I need to love these people. Instead of acting that I am so smart and know better, I need to love them and accept their quirkiness. I don't want to intentionally offend someone so they get discouraged and backslide. If my actions, although not sinful, cause someone to copy my actions, which they THINK are sinful, then they have sinned and I have sinned by leading them astray. The key word here is "intentional". Let's use a more modern example: If I move to an area and begin attending a church where the pastor preaches against Christmas trees, I should obey that teaching, even if I don't personally feel that having a Christmas tree is a sin. If I have one and tempt others in the congregation to get one, I have sinned because (1) I have undermined the authority of the pastor; (2) I have caused them to rebel against the pastor; and (3) I have caused them to go against and do what they have believed is a sin. I must have enough love for that congregation to respect those individual convictions. People aren't going to remember me for how smart or talented I am: They are going to remember me for the love I showed to them.

I Corinthians 9. Apparently, Paul had received quite a bit of criticism for his rebuke of the Corinthian church. He had written a letter prior to the letters recorded in the Bible (I Corinthians 5:9). Paul devoted I Corinthians 9 to defend his actions and defend his authority to rebuke (vs 1-6). He defended the right of ministers to accept wages (vs 12-13). He also set forth the duties of ministers (pastors). They:

- Must preach, if called to do so by God (vs 16).
- Should not become hirelings and abuse the authority God gave them to their own personal gain (vs18).
- Are to serve the people (vs 19).
- Are to relate to the people (vs 21-23).
- Are to show compassion (vs 22).
- Be level headed, disciplined and temperate (vs 25; Proverbs 25:28).
- Are to practice what they preach (vs 27). Preachers are not immune to the same standards they set forth for their congregation. Preacher's kids are not immune to the same standard preachers expected of the congregations.
- Take heed not to backslide while preaching the Gospel (vs 27)!

I Corinthians 10:1-4. Paul explains a little Old Testament typology here. Moses was the redeemer of Israel, by bringing them out of slavery, and thus, is a type of Jesus, who is our (spiritual) redeemer. Apparently, Moses being immersed in the cloud (water) was a type of baptism in Jesus' name. The cloud cover protected them from the sun's harmful rays during the day. The "rock" which Moses struck to give water is a type of Jesus, who gives us living water. Moses was not allowed to go into the promised land because he struck the rock two different times. God specifically told him to the first time (Ex 17:5-6), but God told Moses to speak to the rock the second time (Numbers 20:8). Moses disobeyed. Not only was the disobedience a serious offence, but Moses messed up the perfect typology. Jesus was not going to die twice. (PS: If God was so hard on Moses for his disobedience, what makes me think God is going to turn a blind eye to mine?)

I Corinthians 10:6. The Old Testament records many prime examples of what NOT to do. You would think we would learn from their mistakes, right? Paul tells us to look how God chastised people and not to repeat their mistakes. Must each generation learn the stove is hot for itself? I want to learn from others' mistakes. I don't want to go down the same path. Listen to your elders. They've been down this road called life. Sure, experiences differ, but the ROOT emotions and temptations are all the same. We are all in the same boat, regardless of race, religion, culture, economic status, etc.! All sin falls into one of three categories (1) lust of eye (2) lust of flesh (3) pride of life (I John 2:16). (See essay entitle "Troubles and Trials" in *It's Not Rocket Science Volume 1.)*

I Corinthians 10:9. Tempting God is pushing the envelope. Actually, the word "tempt" in the context of this verse really means to "taunt". Why would I want to do that? Why would I want to push God to His breaking point? Just because He is patient with me doesn't mean He doesn't have a limit. Do I really want Him to reach His limit with me? Nooooooo. When I think I am invincible, I am the most vulnerable and I will most definitely fall (I Corinthians 10:12). The question I should be asking is "what do I need to do to get closer to God" and not "what do I have to do to be saved". It's a matter of the *trajectory of the heart*, and not a matter of keeping a set of rules.

I Corinthians 10:14. There is a lot more to idolatry than bowing to statues. Anything that takes God's place becomes an idol. Exercise, although good for the body, can become an idol when I am consumed with my physique. Food, although necessary for the body, can become an idol when I make it a top focus and priority. What do I spend the most of my free time on? Computer games? Social media? Music? Yard work? None of those in and of themselves are bad, but when it replaces God-time, it becomes an idol. Humans are made to search for spiritual fulfillment. Essential oils are currently the craze. They are good and have medicinal properties. God created plants for our physical well-being. However, I'm noticing how many oil blends are for "meditation", "joy", "calmness", "spiritual health". They cannot take the place of God. (Exercising helps us feel better because oxygen is flowing to the brain, but is no substitute for God.)

I Corinthians 10:20-33. I have a duty or a responsibility to my fellow man. Participation equals endorsement. I could go into a bar and order a soda. I would not be sinning, but the implication is I am endorsing whatever goes on in a bar. (See essay entitled Playing by the Mailbox in *It's Not Rocket Science, Volume 1*.) I must be considerate of others (vs 29). If it appears I am approving of a sinful thing, I must abstain. This passage is a repeat of I Corinthians 8:8-13. We are not under the law, but under grace. We need to ask the question, "What is conducive for Christian living" to guide us in making decisions (vs 31). *Example:* My husband worked a secular job during most of his pastorates. He was teasing his co-worker, a very devout Catholic, about joining him in New Orleans for Mardi Gras. His co-worker was quite alarmed and exclaimed, "NO, Charles! Mardi Gras is no place for a preacher!" Even without committing a sinful act in the eyes of God, my husband's testimony before the whole office would have been destroyed had he gone. We have to be careful to guard and protect our testimonies.

I Corinthians 11. The subject matter of I Corinthians 11 is "Follow Christ". We are to follow our spiritual leadership ONLY as they follow Christ. We are to keep the practical living standards as the apostles handed them down (I Corinthians 11:1-2). To reinforce his statement, Paul uses the examples of (1) hair and (2) communion. What is interesting to me concerning Paul's discourse on hair is long hair on a female is a symbol (King James version uses the word "power") to the angels. I recall another time where a symbol was used. That was in the book of Exodus. Blood smeared on the doorpost was a symbol for the death angel to pass over that house (Exodus 12:13). What is the long hair a symbol of? It is my submission to Biblical authority. (Submission does not mean slavery, by the way!) Of course, my inside must match what my outside is portraying. Things didn't turn out so well for those in Egypt who did not have the correct symbol on their doorposts. What makes me think things will turn out well for me if I don't have my symbol? There was another time in the Old Testament when God marked those who lived right. Those who did not have the mark were condemned (Ezekiel 9:4-6).

I Corinthians 11:5-6. What is the woman's head? The man. When I pray or preach "uncovered", I am dishonoring the man and might as well have a shaved head. Cutting of the hair was used as a symbol of shame to Jerusalem (Jeremiah 7:29). Definition of "covering" is long hair (vs 15). I've heard single women claim they don't have to obey this passage because they are not "under" a man. Not true. This passage has nothing to do with marriage, but with the order of creation (vs 8-10). This passage is not to be misconstrued as a male's right to boss around a female (vs 11-12). The sexes are mutually dependent upon each other. More on that subject at I Peter 3:7.

I Corinthians 11:7. What is the man's head? God. ("Glory" means recognition of authority and leadership.)

I Corinthians 11:10. The woman's long hair is a symbol to the angels because it is evidence of submission. God knows whether or not the *trajectory of my heart* matches my outside appearance. (Deuteronomy 21:12-14 points out the shaving of a woman's head is a sign of being humiliated.) Angels encircle and protect those who are in submission to God (Psalm 34:7; 91:11; 125:2). Why wouldn't I want their protection? Why would I (as a woman) cut my hair and lose my protection?

I Corinthians 11:14-15. God has always demanded a separation of the genders. Long hair on a man is effeminate and brings dishonor to God (I Corinthians 6:9). A woman's long hair is given to her (instead of a cloth veil) for a covering.

I Corinthians 11:16-18. There is God's custom and a world custom. The world is contentious; God is not. When the world custom and the church custom go separate ways, I must follow God's path. God is not the author of confusion (I Corinthians 14:33). Context: The Roman women of Corinth offered hair as a sacrifice to the goddess Diana. This was a pagan custom. Paul says this is not a Christian custom!

I Corinthians 11:28-31. I must judge myself. Participating in communion is a serious matter. It is not party time. If I participate in communion irreverently or irresponsibly, I am condemning myself to sickness. It is much better to judge myself and take corrective actions than for God to judge and have to discipline me. This is not to say that everyone who is sick is receiving the judgment of God. Disease comes from many sources. A flippant attitude toward communion is one of them.

I Corinthians 12:1-11. The gifts of the Spirit (not to be confused with the fruit of the Spirit) are measured out to individuals for the ENTIRE body of Christ to be edified. They are not given to make anyone more important than another. Unfortunately, we tend to put people who operate with the gifts of the Spirit up on a pedestal ~ especially those who operate with the gift of prophecy. People flock to services just hoping that they would get a direct word from God, but are scared God will reveal their innermost thoughts to the messenger! Ha! Ha! Oh, that we would just learn to listen to God for ourselves! (See essay entitled "Me 'N' You Stick Together Like Glue in *It's Not Rocket Science, Volume 1.*) These gifts of the Spirit are not just everyday things, but of the supernatural. I can walk into any congregation and say, "Someone here is in physical pain." That is not a gift in operation. That is my own human knowledge of probabilities. I can also scan the audience and pick out someone with back pain. It's the person who holds onto the pew in front of them when standing up, or that person who is constantly shifting their position on the pew. That is also my own human knowledge and not a spiritual gift of knowledge. There are many charlatans out there who are good at reading an audience. We must be careful not to exploit people. The gifts of the Spirit are a supernatural thing, superseding any natural talent.

I Corinthians 12:8. "Knowledge" is the understanding of secrets. "Wisdom" is the understanding how to apply knowledge. *Example:* God reveals (gift of knowledge) someone is abusing a child. I need to pray for the gift of wisdom to know how to go about confronting the situation so both the child and the abuser have a chance to be rehabilitated.

I Corinthians 12:10. "Interpretation of tongues" is not the same as translating words of a language. "Discerning of spirits". There are 3 types of spirits: (1) God's, (2) Human, (3) devil's. I grew up in a third world country. Mental institutions were not prevalent and those with mental illnesses were kept at home. Many times, while walking home from school, I would encounter someone acting very strangely on the street. Sometimes, I just knew they had a mental illness and were harmless. Other times, I sensed an evil about them and rebuked that spirit as I passed them by.

I Corinthians 12:12-29. There is ONE body of Christ. I am not a medical student. I don't know all the parts of my own body. Dr. Phillip Smith (Gonzales, Louisiana) told us the body communicates via our nerves. A nerve from the brain to the leg tells the leg to move, etc. Sometimes, a nerve gets pinched. Dr. Smith told us only about 10% of our nerves are pain nerves. Therefore, we can have a pinched nerve and not realize it. A pinched nerve is something like a dimmer switch. The body will function, but not at full capacity. Let's say a nerve to the kidney was pinched. I may live for years in that condition and not know it. After a time, I develop kidney failure. This did not happen all of a sudden. My kidney failure is a result of poor communication between the brain and the kidney for *years*. An Alzheimer's patient runs into difficulties because as the brain shrinks, the nerves become detached and communication becomes jumbled ~ like a circuit board shorting out. When the body of Christ has a schism in it, the entire body suffers. I cannot fail to perform my duties in the church. I cannot fail to perform what God has placed me to do on this earth. If I do, the ENTIRE body of Christ will suffer.

I Corinthians 12:13. Spirit baptism is necessary to be a part of the body of Christ. (Water baptism [remission of sins] makes me eligible to become a part of the body of Christ.)

I Corinthians 12:22-23. There are unsung heroes within the body of Christ. They are necessary too! Key words: "*seem* to be feebler" and "*which we think* to be less honorable". The little kindergarten Sunday school child is just as important as the crusade evangelist.

I Corinthians 12:28. Everyone has a gifting. If I don't, I need to get closer to God and get my assignment! What role do I play in the church? I need to find out and fulfil it.

I Corinthians 12:31 really should be part of Chapter 13. Paul tells us to covet all of the gifts. We should diligently ask God for gifts so we can help the body to function as it should. HOWEVER, more than coveting, LOVE is a more excellent way to obtain the gifts. *It's not rocket science!* (See essay entitled, "Did Jesus Get It Wrong?" in *It's Not Rocket Science, Volume 1.*)

I Corinthians 13(a) defines one specific fruit of the Spirit, and yet incorporates *all* fruits of the spirit (Galatians 5:22-23). They are all intertwined with each other. The opposite of love is NOT hate. ***The opposite of love is selfishness.*** Love rules. Good works, without love, is *nothing*. **GOD = LOVE** (I John 4:8). Therefore, if I don't have the following attributes, I do not have God, no matter how long I've warmed a church pew. Period. Love is the underlying theme of ALL of the fruits of the Spirit. A person who loves
- Is patient *(fruit of the spirit is longsuffering)*.
- Is kind *(fruit of the spirit is goodness)*.
- Is not envious *(fruit of the spirit is peace)*.
- Is not prideful & conceited, not haughty and vain, does not draw attention to self, is not self-seeking *(fruit of the spirit is meekness)*.
- Is not rude *(fruit of the spirit is gentleness)*.
- Thinks the best of others (not evil) *(fruit of the spirit is faith)*.
- Doesn't rejoice in unrighteousness, rather rejoices in what is right *(fruit of the spirit is joy)*.
- Takes things in stride and endures gracefully, hoping for the best *(fruit of the*

spirit is temperance).
Now, all of us bear a measure of these attributes because we are made in the image of God. Even a hardened criminal has a soft spot for something ~ be it a child or a pet! A spiritual fruit is something **supernatural.** I will not have this amount of an attribute without the spirit of God dwelling in me. The spirit of God enables me to exhibit these attributes over and beyond my normal human personality and behavior. At some point, the gifts of the Spirit will cease (because there will no longer be a need for the gifts once the church is in Heaven). However, love won't cease because, once again, **GOD = LOVE**. (This is a mathematical equation. What is God? He is love.)

I Corinthians 13(b). If someone declares his/her undying love, measure their love by I Corinthians 13. Is it love or infatuation? Is this suitor in love with me, or is s/he solely looking out for what I can bring to the table (which would be selfish)? What about my love? Can I honestly love this person, even when times are worse than better? Does my love measure up?

I Corinthians 14 primarily refers to the gift of tongues and the gift of tongues & interpretation. This book was written to people who had *already* received the gift of the Holy Spirit (by the evidence of speaking in tongues). There are three types of tongues mentioned in the Bible:
- Praying in tongues (I Corinthians 14:2). This is when the Spirit which is already dwelling within me speaks forth and prays for me. Sometimes I don't know (a) how to pray or (b) what to pray for, so the Spirit takes over. This type of tongues is for the benefit of the individual and not for the corporate church body (I Corinthians 14:6, 9).
- Initial sign of the infilling of the Holy Spirit (Acts 2:4; I Corinthians 14:22).
- Tongues & Interpretation (I Corinthians 14:13). This is when the Spirit speaks forth with authority and then the interpretation goes forth (either by the same person or another person).

I Corinthians 14:5-9. Apparently, some didn't have the gift of tongues. Paul wishes all would have this gift, but states it is more beneficial to the corporate church body for preaching to go forth than for everyone to be praying in tongues all of the time. I cringe when I hear a preacher demand everyone start speaking in tongues. It raises doubt, confusion, and uncertainty in someone's mind if they don't have this gift.

I Corinthians 14:12. More important than receiving the gifts is my ability to give: to edify others.

I Corinthians 14:18-19. Paul admitted he regularly prayed in tongues, *however*, in the presence of others, he would rather teach so others can understand, than to pray in tongues.

I Corinthians 14:26-39 gives instructions for exercising the gifts within a local assembly. Chaos ensues when there is no organization. Uncontrolled and confusing acts are not of God (vs 33, 40).
- When a message in tongues goes forth, the congregation can just feel it and each individual should make a special effort to be in complete unity so the Spirit feels free to speak forth.
- What is said must harmonize with Scripture. God is not going to say anything contradictory to His word. I was in a service once when a person spoke forth boldly. I felt a little funny, but the person in charge of the service didn't say anything. When that same person gave the interpretation, it was way off from the Scripture and we all knew he was a fraud. The interpretation will never contradict Scripture.
- Don't let people prophesy over you in private (vs 29).
- Human vessels choose the verbiage and the personality of the human vessel comes through (vs 32). It really cracks me up when someone gives the interpretation in King James English! God does speak modern English! I currently attend a Hispanic church where everything is spoken in Spanish. Tongues and interpretation went forth recently and the congregation was really blessed. My elderly father leaned over to me and asked why there was no interpretation. I said, "Dad, there was, it was in Spanish!" He replied, "Well, I didn't understand it!" I said, "Dad, this is a Spanish speaking congregation. Apparently, the message wasn't for us!"

I Corinthians 14:34-35. It is easy for some to take I Corinthians 14:34-35 completely out of context and say women can't preach. The subject matter in the surrounding verses concerns the operation of tongues in a congregational setting. If this scripture is to be taken the way these people say, then women can't sing, testify, or make any noise at all. That would be contradictory to all of the other scriptures which indicate there were female prophetesses and deaconesses, singers, etc. (See essay entitled "On Being a Woman" in *It's Not Rocket Science, Volume 1*.) Does the Bible contradict itself? NO! What, then, does this scripture mean? Remember, this whole chapter is devoted to the operation of the gift of tongues and the gift of tongues & interpretation. In the times of this scripture (and even in Mid-East & Asian cultures today), there was the custom where men sat on one side and the women & children sat on the other, with a partition between the two sides. Women could nurse or take care of the children without being seen by the men. Women in those days were largely unschooled and thus, ignorant. There were also no sound systems in that day. If a woman couldn't hear or understand something that was said, she would yell over to her husband for clarification. Paul was telling the women to be silent and ask her husband later at home. God is not the author of confusion. All of the yelling back and forth was creating chaos. In one of the churches we pastored, we had a problem with members of the congregation adding in their two cents when my husband preached, as if we were all just having a discussion in the living room! He had to teach them not to interrupt the sermon.

God likes order. He created the universe to operate under certain laws of physics, mathematics & science. He wants us to do things in an orderly manner (vs 33, 40).

I Corinthians 15:1-2. Speaking of salvation, Paul stated salvation was contingent upon continuing to believe and remembering the plan of salvation. Some people teach that once you are saved, you are always saved. That simply is not true. Salvation is continual. There is no eternal security. I'm not saved until I'm actually in Heaven. Salvation is a daily thing (I Corinthians 15:31). There are numerous scriptures which deal with backsliding, which means someone was once on the path to salvation, but has digressed spiritually to the point they are no longer heaven-bound.

I Corinthians 15:3-4. See. Colossians 2:12. Paul preached the same thing the disciples did. He preached the death of Jesus (repentance - Romans 6:6); the burial of Jesus (baptism - Romans 6:3); and the resurrection of Jesus (receiving the Holy Spirit - Romans 6:4).

I Corinthians 15:14-15. The crux of the matter is not that Jesus was born, and not that He died. Everyone is born and at some point, dies. It's not even that Jesus was martyred. Many people die a cruel death for a cause. It's all about the RESURRECTION! The resurrection completes the story. Without the resurrection, our faith is misplaced. Because He lives, we have the faith, hope and power of the resurrection. Our hope is in eternity. The very reason we deny ourselves the pleasures of sin (albeit there are sorrows associated with those sins), is because of eternity (I Corinthians 15:19). I love Paul's sarcasm! He apparently got exasperated with the Corinthian church. Some were teaching there was no resurrection. Just about the whole 15th chapter of I Corinthians is devoted to this topic. In verse 32, Paul sarcastically says, "If there is no resurrection, why on earth do I engage in spiritual battles? We all might as well sin and die!" (Remember the Sadducees did not believe in the resurrection. That is why they were sad, you see?!) Paul uses several natural examples to prove his point.
- There are different types of seeds.
- The heavenly bodies (stars, etc.) are made up of different materials.
- The earthly bodies (moon, planets) are made up of different materials.

Likewise, mortal flesh and immortal flesh are different. We MUST BE CHANGED (vs. 52-53). This is the hope of the church ~ that we will be changed to immortal and can enter into eternity. This transformation is called the "rapture", although that specific term is not mentioned in the Bible. Death for a believer, is a wonderful thing. Those (believers) who remain will miss loved ones who have died, but are happy the loved one has been changed to immortality (vs 55). This fact is what makes all trials and tribulations worth it. This fact is what makes all sacrifices to win one soul worth the sacrifice!! I am grieved as I type this because an individual I invested an ENORMOUS time with just passed away. Unless she had a deathbed repentance, by all accounts, she died in a backslidden state. My efforts concerning her (although duly noted by God) were in vain. Was it worth it? Well, yes, in the sense that I have to try to help people. I helped her stay on track with God for a long time, but ultimately it was her decision to go back to her life of sin. I'm just sad, because for her, eternity has begun. What a tragedy! I suppose by now she is remembering all of the hours I spent with her trying to help her overcome her trials. Hell is a torturing of both the body and mind. I've got to be an overcomer. I can't let *anything* hinder me from serving God. Just about every person I know who has backslidden (not counting those who have gone into false doctrine) intends to get back on track and live for God "*someday*". Sometimes they get to death before that "someday" arrives. {{sigh}}

I Corinthians 15:24-28. There will come a time when there is no longer a need for a savior, or the office of the "sonship". God manifested Himself in various formats throughout the Bible. The ultimate manifestation was when He took on human form (John 1:14). My late cousin, Michael, liked to say that Jesus was God in work clothes! (See essay entitled "Get Me Out of Here!" in *It's Not Rocket Science, Volume 1.*) God allowed Himself to put on the limitations of humanity so He would identify with us. That takes away all excuses we have that God doesn't understand what we are going through. Oh, yes, He does! A sinless human had to be the atonement for our sins. The blood of animals was not enough (Hebrews 9:12). Any human born naturally has the inherited sin nature from the father (Exodus 34:7). Therefore, a sinless human could not have a sinful father. Hence, Jesus, born of a virgin was conceived by the spirit of God (Isaiah 7:14; Matthew 1:20). Once the redemption of mankind has been completed and time has been declared obsolete, the office (or duties) of the "son-ship" will no longer be necessary. There will no longer be a need for a redeemer or an advocate. Jesus will then deliver up that office to the Spirit. This passage is a little difficult to read because pronouns are used (he & him) instead of proper nouns. Let's look at vs 27 with proper nouns: *"For God hath put all things under Christ's feet. But when the psalmist saith all things are put under Christ, it is manifest that God is excepted (exempt), which did put all things under Christ."* "God" speaks of the Almighty Spirit. "Christ" speaks of the office of the redeemer (the son), which is God robed in flesh. There are not multiple spirits or multiple gods (Deuteronomy 6:4).

I Corinthians 15:31. The old Indian proverb about the evil wolf and the good wolf ends with the little boy asking which wolf wins in the end. The old man replies, "The one you feed the most". Even though I have the spirit of God dwelling within me, I am still a human being. I still have to keep my humanity under subjection. I have to make choices every day that will either feed my spiritual nature or my carnal nature. If I just flow aimlessly, my carnal nature will take over. Look at nature. The weeds won't pull themselves out of the flowerbed! If I don't mow the yard, it returns to its wild state. If I pick out weeds daily, it's not that big of a deal. If I wait until the weeds are taking over, it's a big job that takes days. I usually neglect the yard during the rainy, cold winter season. Spring means a lot of work in the yard which results in days of back pain! Likewise, I must pull the weeds (carnal things) out of my life. If I wait until there is a huge problem, it will be painful and very difficult for me to get myself back on track where God wants me to be. If I "die daily" as Paul said he did, I will maintain a good walk with God. My soul is quite a bit more serious than my flower bed! I MUST keep my carnality in check. I MUST make sure I am ready to meet God whenever my time comes up. The biggest problem I have is my own mind. My mind is my biggest enemy. The *only* stronghold Satan has is on my mind. I must purposefully allow God to have complete and exclusive authority and control over my mind (II Corinthians 11:3). This requires me to die daily to my own desires. This requires me to reign in my imaginations (I Peter 1:13). I may not be able to control what comes across my mind, but I CAN control what I allow my mind to dwell on. There are places I must not allow my mind to go. Period. ***IT'S NOT ROCKET SCIENCE.*** Just do it! No arguing. No rationalizing. No contemplating. No ifs, ands, or buts.

I Corinthians 15:32-34. Human thinking is this: "you're gonna die, so live it up!" A popular song at funerals is "I did it my way". We pat people on the back who dare to break out of the mold and do their own thing. I see bumper stickers stating the owner of the vehicle is going to bust hell wide open. Oh, the fallacy of that train of thought! We do reap what we sow ... both in this life and in the life to come. Paul tells us in verse 33 that evil behavior ("conversation" in the King James language) will ultimately tear down my conscious. Continual sin will result in my conscious no longer being pricked. Back in 1980-81, I taught in a school. I saw a student throw a spit wad at a girl. I went to him and in his ear, whispered he should not throw spit wads. My intent was just a gentle reprimand. He looked up at me and said, "No ma'am. I didn't throw a spit wad." Now, I had seen him with my own eyes. I *knew* he had thrown that spit wad, yet he was so convincing in his denial, I began to second guess myself! The bigger problem was that he had lied so much during his little life that he believed his own lies. I recently checked up on him. He has been in and out of jail. I am not surprised at all. The danger in habitually sinning (the KJV calls it being "froward") is that my conscious is seared (I Timothy 4:2). How can I have a chance to repent, and thus be saved, when I don't even know what I'm doing is wrong?

I Corinthians 15:37-54. All seeds are different and when planted, produce different plants. All flesh is different. The heavenly bodies are different. Likewise, there is a difference between mortal and immortality (vs 42). *We must be changed.* Our mortal flesh cannot live forever because sin has contaminated it (Romans 6:23). My hope lies in my mortal body being changed to immortal. This can only happen if I have lived according to God's word. Death, then, is a joyous event for me because I will have achieved the ultimate prize, reward, and honor.

I Corinthians 15:55-57. Death is final. How I have chosen to live my life determines whether or not death will be a horrid event or a glorious event for me. The "sting" of death - the horribleness of death is sin. Sin will prevent my body from being changed into incorruptible flesh. This will prevent me from joining Jesus in Heaven. I must purge sin from my life constantly. I cannot afford to have my life snuffed out of me in a car wreck, a heart attack, or by some other means while sin is present. I want God to prick my heart when I have done something wrong. I want a guilty conscious. I want to have the opportunity to repent as soon as I have sinned, whether by deed or by thought. When I live for God (100%), I can live a life victorious over sin. I hear people say that it is impossible to not sin. That is only true if I don't stay prayed up and keep up a constant attitude of being God-conscious. Human nature, being what it is, doesn't always want to stay prayed up. I'm so glad God is a forgiving God!

I Corinthians 15:58. Sometimes I feel discouraged and wonder what good I have done ~ if I have impacted anyone's life. *ANYTHING* done for God is not in vain, no matter how small and insignificant it may be. Remember the parable of the workers who came in late but received the same wages as those who had worked all day (Matthew 20)? God knows what I have done for Him, whether I get any recognition or not. I do what I do for God and not for a pat on the back. Pats on the back by my fellow mankind are nice, but that can't be my motivation. I want to hear God say, "Well done, my good and faithful servant" at the end of my day (Matthew 25:21)!

I Corinthians 16:2. The early church was organized. Regularly scheduled meetings were held on the first day of the week. There are groups of people who feel organization is not a good thing. It is true that any man-made thing is flawed. There is no perfect denomination or organization. However, by banding together, we can be more effective in our outreach efforts and in the edification of the church body. The early church had their headquarters in Jerusalem. In Acts 11, Peter was called before the church board to explain his actions concerning Cornelius, a Gentile. Paul was accountable to the church leaders when he completed his missionary trips. In I Corinthians 16:3, we find Paul was collecting an offering to send to Jerusalem. Pooling our resources together is a good thing. Isolation is not. Isolation brings about pride. Preachers who isolate themselves and their congregations more often than not develop a self-righteous spirit about them. Isolation comes from a fear that the congregants would be influenced by another and change church loyalties or doctrines. There are always flaky people who hop from one place to another, usually because they don't want to submit to leadership. Isolating a congregation doesn't stop that. We need to belong to a fellowship which stands for truth and pray against any false doctrines that would try to creep into the group. We need to be more (God's) Kingdom minded and less (my) kingdom minded.

I Corinthians 16:10. Timothy had been vetted by Paul and Paul recommended his ministry to the Corinthians. This is another example of how an organization or denomination can be beneficial. We need to know those who minister to us (I John 4:1). We need to know if they are true spiritual shepherds or are charlatans. Not everyone who calls themselves a preacher is (1) preaching truth or (2) living a moral life. Some are in it for personal gain (Acts 8:8-21).

I Corinthians 16:13-14. In Paul's final exhortation of this letter, he instructs us to act like grownups and stand for truth. A child is easily persuaded, but an adult is able to stand his/her ground. Standing for truth cannot done be in an antagonistic manner, but must be done in LOVE. God is love (I John 4:8). If I stand for truth in a mean and hateful way, I am still wrong. Others will know if I am a true believer by the love I portray, not by how well I articulate truth (John 13:35). If I spout off truth, but not with a loving spirit, God is deficient in my life. My heart has to match my head. It's all about the *trajectory of my heart. It's not Rocket Science!*

II CORINTHIANS
Second letter to the Christians in Corinth containing Paul's exhortations and instructions.

II Corinthians 1:4. God helps me so I can be a help to others. It's all about letting the spirit of God flow through me. If I just receive and never pour out, I will become stagnant. It is a *river of living water* that God gives (John 7:38). If I don't let the river flow through me, mold & bacteria will set in. If I don't let the river flow through me, there will be a mineral build up. Mosquitos and tadpoles will hatch. God gives to me so I will have something to give to others. Trials and sufferings show me how great and powerful God is. These things draw me closer to God; therefore, these things are for my salvation (II Corinthians 1:6). Don't take offense at a trial! God is trying to get me saved! (See also essay entitled, "Troubles and Trials: Escape Route" in *It's Not Rocket Science, Volume 1*.)

II Corinthians 1:10. God is the God of the past, present and the future. He has delivered, is delivering, and will yet deliver. He is the same yesterday, today, and forever (Hebrews 13:8)! YAY!

II Corinthians 1:22. The Holy Spirit we receive is just a taste of what is to come (Heaven). It is similar to a down-payment or earnest money. Banks usually like a 20% down payment on a house. The down payment gives the bank confidence the loan balance will be paid. God gives us His spirit to enable us to overcome sin, but it also serves as God's promise of more to come (Ephesians 1:13-14). I don't think our current physical bodies could stand any more than the portion He gives to us!

II Corinthians 1:24. Pastors are not "lords" over a congregation, but "helpers" to a congregation. Pastors are to help people get to heaven and not to be someone who offends (II Corinthians 6:3). A leadership position in a church is one of servanthood and not lordship. It's easy to let ego get in the way, but the fact of the matter is, none of us are indispensable. If I resign from my position in the church today (or die), someone else will be taking my place tomorrow! The church can do without me. I can't do without the church, the body of Christ. I need to remember this and to keep my attitude in check. What can I do for the Kingdom of God? If I always remember I work for God and not for any person or any church, I can keep my attitude right. If I begin thinking of what all I do for the church, then I start thinking the church owes me back. That is a very dangerous and destructive attitude to have.

II Corinthians 2:4. Just as it grieves a parent to discipline a child, Paul was grieved that he had to, once again, send a letter to fuss at the Corinthian church. He wished his letter could be one of joy, but he had to help to eradicate the serious problems in the church.

II Corinthians 2:6-8. It is hard for a congregation to forgive someone who has hurt it so badly. Unforgiveness is a very human thing. However, we must forgive. There are ways that a person can damage and hurt an entire congregation. We had a situation in one of the churches we pastored. For about three months, we tried to preach, teach, love, and counsel the individual(s) to repentance. The congregation was patient and loving, but the services became heavier and heavier. The open sin was taking its toll on the congregation and affecting the youth group tremendously. My husband had to take action. These people elected to change churches and did their best to get others to change with them. Years later, one of the parties returned to the church and repented. The congregation had to forgive and love. After the punishment, we must confirm our love. This goes for children as well. After they have been punished for wrongdoing, the parent must reiterate love for the child.

II Corinthians 2:11. A good general will study his opponent's strategy and anticipate his opponent's plan of action. A good driver will look down the road and check his mirrors to anticipate possible problems. Only by staying on guard can we take preventative actions. Likewise, we must know Satan's tactics. We must not be ignorant of his strategy. Satan's most powerful strategy is unforgiveness, which comes from an offense. (See essay entitled "Offence/Forgiveness" in *It's Not Rocket Science, Volume 1.*) This scripture comes right on the heels of Paul telling the church at Corinth to forgive the man who had wronged them. I have met countless people who no longer live for God because they were offended by someone.

II Corinthians 2:14-15. God *always* is victorious. My confidence is in God, not in my fellow man, or even in myself. My faith is a light and a sweet savor to both God and mankind.

II Corinthians 2:17. There are many who corrupt the word of God! I want to be careful not to take things out of context and to make a doctrine where there is none. I also want to make sure I don't ignore a doctrine in the Bible! I don't want to handle the word of God deceitfully, but rather, manifest it in my lifestyle (II Corinthians 4:2). I must live the pure word of God.

II Corinthians 3:3. I am a walking, talking billboard for (or against) God. I will either make God attractive to others, or my life will cause others to have negative feelings towards God. When God's word is in my heart, not merely my actions, the *trajectory of my heart* will be on the right course (Ezekiel 11:19; Hebrews 10:15-16).

II Corinthians 3:6-16. God's word must be internalized. An external knowledge of God will not suffice. It amazes me to see how many people can quote the Bible backwards and forwards and how many people have devoted their entire lives to studying the Bible, and still don't live for God as the scriptures direct. It's all about the ***trajectory* of the heart** (II Corinthians 3:3). The word alone brings death because it is a laundry list of rules. Coupled with the Spirit, it becomes a natural way of life for me (verse 7). When God's ways are internalized, it is easy to live for Him. ***It's not rocket science!***

II Corinthians 3:17. God's spirit gives me the freedom or liberty to live righteously. Without God's spirit, I am bound to sin. I can't help myself. Some people have the whole "liberty" thing backwards. They claim their revelation of God's grace gives them freedom to live outside the realm of God's instructions of holy living. On the contrary, when I live opposite to what the word of God instructs, I am bound by sin. My sinful nature means I have a natural inclination to live in unrighteousness. Only when I am full of God's spirit do I have true freedom. Only when I am full of God's spirit am I free to live right.

II Corinthians 3:18. Another reason to being filled with the Holy Spirit is the Holy Spirit will cause my mortal body to be changed so it can break the laws of gravity (II Corinthians 4:14).

II Corinthians 4:4. The Godhead is no mystery. Some people teach we cannot understand the Godhead, but Paul clearly states that if the gospel is hidden, it is hidden only to those who are lost (vs 3). The gospel is that Christ is God incarnate. God does not keep secrets from His friends. (See essay entitled "Me 'N You Stick Together Like Glue" in *It's Not Rocket Science, Volume 1.)* I was talking to a lady about the Godhead. She had been raised in another church and had been taught there were multiple persons of God. I asked her to take some time and to sincerely pray and ask God to show her truth. A few days later, she called me up, so excited she was screaming over the phone, "I SEE IT! I SEE IT!" She then proceeded to tell me all of the scriptures she had found declaring Jesus was God robed in flesh! She said during the course of her searching and praying for truth, God gave her a vision of me baptizing her in Jesus' name! If I'm sincere and really hungry for truth, God will reveal it. If I'm bound and determined to find scriptures to fit my own theology or the doctrines handed down to me by others, God will let the veil stay on my heart (II Corinthians 3:15). I've got to get this for myself. There are a lot of smooth talkers in this world. Just listen to politicians or experts on talk shows! They will contradict each other and convince you they're both right! If someone can convince me of a particular doctrine, someone else can un-convince me. I've got to get this for myself. I need an encounter with God. I need a **personal** experience and conviction. I need to be willing to make the sacrifice to get truth directly from God. There's too much at stake (my soul's salvation for eternity) for me to take someone else's word for truth.

II Corinthians 4:7-14. The knowledge of Jesus being the incarnate expression of God Almighty is truly a treasure to be cherished. Understanding further that this Almighty Spirit will dwell in my heart gives me a bigger picture of my life. Although I may be going through trauma in the natural (health, financial, persecution, etc.), I realize God is with me and will enable me to get to the other side of my trial.

II Corinthians 4:16-18. Everything is either (1) temporal or (2) eternal. The temporal things shall pass. I need to dwell on the eternal. Suicide is such a permanent solution to a temporary problem (although it produces yet another problem in eternity, which is permanent). There is always a solution to every problem. I need to persevere until I find the solution. At any rate, no trial is worth going to hell over. I need to keep my eyes on the eternal! My trial is a refining process. The trial is temporal, but has eternal consequences. I must react to my trial with the right spirit and attitude so as to allow God to work imperfections out of me. This has to do with the ***trajectory of my heart.***

II Corinthians 5:1-4. Most people fear death. However, death for a Christian is a joyous event! We trade a broken old house for a fancy new one! Some things in life do give us pleasure, but for the most part, we all groan over our aches and pains, stress during our financial hardships, worry about our health, retirement, and children, and gripe about our governments. This is universal. All people of all nations and walks of life have these same complaints. Why, then, are we hesitant to trade all of that for Heaven?

II Corinthians 5:5. Imagine the most wonderful experience you have ever had in the presence of God. Remember how euphoric your felt? Remember how clean and pure you felt? That's just the tip of the iceberg. Now, why wouldn't I want that for all of eternity? Why wouldn't I long for that? What small pleasure here on earth is worth giving up Heaven for? I was praying with a lady one time and she suddenly fell back as if in a daze. She said in awe, "This is the best high I've ever had!" She was a drug user and one little experience in the presence of God was the best "high" ever! She didn't even receive the Holy Spirit at that time ~ she just felt a touch God's presence. We tell our children "Pay now, play later" when encouraging them to go for their college degree. The same is true in the spiritual sense. "Pay now" means to deny some things I *think* I want now, but which are not pleasing to God. "Play later" means to enjoy Heaven for eternity. I'm all for that! If the Bible said I had to wear green socks on Thursdays in order to please God, I would do it! (I might not venture out of the house on Thursdays, but I would do it!) Why wouldn't I? I go through surgery for the *possibility* of feeling better. I suffer through school for the *possibility* of obtaining better employment. I work hard in the yard for the *temporary* pleasure of seeing beauty. I struggle managing rental properties on the *supposition* that (1) I will live to enjoy the income in retirement and (2) the properties will not drain my finances. Now, why wouldn't I be willing to sacrifice some for the **GUARANTY** of Heaven and eternal life?

II Corinthians 5:6. If I am comfortable in this world, my *trajectory* is off. This world is not my home. I do not fit in. I am human, so I am "in" the world, but I cannot be "of" the world.

II Corinthians 5:7. It is my faith which sustains me. I may not see things with my natural eyes, but faith sees beyond the natural and trusts upon God's word (Hebrews 11:1).

II Corinthians 5:10. I will be held accountable for the things I have done while here on earth. I will reap what I have sown, whether good or bad. The full reaping of my actions may not happen in this life. It may not happen until the judgment, but it will happen. I can't worry about whether or not someone is punished for doing me wrong. Their punishment may not happen in my lifetime. I *trust* the word of God and *know* God will see to it that I am avenged. I have decided to let God be God and I'm not going to worry about when or how He avenges me. Life is too short for me to stress over whether or not someone is punished for the wrong they have done me. That kind of stress will drag me down. I will be the one who will suffer. Instead, I choose to be happy and live a joyful life. I choose to place all of that stress upon God. He's already offered to take it from me (Matthew 11:28). Why would anyone want to continue to pack it around? It's way too heavy.

II Corinthians 5:11. Judgment is sure. There is a terrible side of God. I don't ever want to get on His wrong side!

II Corinthians 5:12. There is a saying that there are two sure things in life: death and taxes! A third sure thing is hypocrites! Some people are all about the appearance and not the heart. The *trajectory of the heart* must be pointed in the right direction.

My inside must match my outside, and my outside must match my inside. I must be the whole package. God wants *all* of me.

II Corinthians 5:14-15. Jesus died for all of us. My acceptance of Him as my personal savior is not just a verbal declaration. I identify with His death when I am baptized in His name (Romans 6:4). Baptism is a visible action resulting from my verbal declaration. Through baptism, I acknowledge I am no longer bound to and living according to my natural, sinful nature. I am free from all of my sinful self. I am now living for Him!

II Corinthians 5:17-21. I suspect just about everyone, at some point in their life, wishes they could start over. Wouldn't it be nice if we could climb into a time machine and go back and do some things differently? The good news is that we can start over. If we apply the death, burial & resurrection of Jesus to our lives, we become a "new creature". Our desire to sin is replaced by our desire to live righteously before God. When I seek Him, He will give me my desires because they line up with His (Psalm 37:4). I can restore the original relationship Adam severed with God for the entire human race. I can have that same fellowship with God mankind had before the fall. "Impute" means "to charge". God will not charge me with my spiritual crimes, if I have applied the sentence that Jesus has already served to my life.

II Corinthians 6:1. We work WITH God, not FOR God. Without God, we can't do anything and God won't do that which I can do. It's a team effort. In the same verse, Paul pleads with the Corinthians not to receive the grace of God in vain. If I am not to do that, I must first understand what it means to receive the grace of God in vain. It is two-fold: (1) I must not receive and then do nothing about it. Grace is undeserved favor. To act upon God's grace is to (a) live for Him and (b) introduce others to it. (2) Another way to receive the grace of God in vain is to turn away from sound doctrine and tease the mercies of God (see Amplified Bible on this verse). To initially receive the grace of God and then to get involved in false doctrine is to receive God's grace in vain.

II Corinthians 6:2. There is an urgency. I must be saved NOW. I must not wait until tomorrow or some obscure time in the future.

II Corinthians 6:3. I must strive not to be offensive to others. I know, by studying the scripture, that one of Satan's strongest tactics is offense. I don't want anyone to stumble because I offended them. If they take offense, I want it to be because of someone else and not because of me!

II Corinthians 6:12-15. After a laundry list in the preceding verses detailing what all Paul and his crew had gone through to preserve the Gospel, Paul hits them between the eyes with the fact *they* had lost their love and commitment. Life can do that to us. Our fervency can wain and our feelings for God can change when life circumstances are allowed to take dominance. How does that happen? One reason is being unequally partnered with a nonbeliever. This is not only true for a marriage, but for a ministry, a business, or other type of partnership as well. If there is a difference in core beliefs and absolutes, there is going to be a problem in the partnership. My values will be compromised. I won't win them. They will win me. Why? Because I have disobeyed a foremost commandment of God not to be unequally yoked. A friend from my youth decided to take a job in a church that did not teach full truth. Her reasoning was, "you go to work with sinners, why can't I". The danger for her was by worshiping together with them, her doctrine got watered down over time. My job with sinners just required me to sit at a desk, do my work and go home. I did not party or otherwise socialize with my co-workers. She did and lost the majority of her beliefs. We are to show love to unbelievers and to be a light to them. However, we cannot be partners with them.

II Corinthians 6:17. We must live in this world, but we don't have to participate IN the world. We are especially instructed not to be "unequally yoked" (II Corinthians 6:14). Usually, I hear it preached that this scripture applies to marriage, and that certainly is the case. If my spouse and I aren't on the same page doctrinally, there are going to be many fights, especially after the children come along. There is a good chance my children will not live for God if one parent doesn't. However, this scripture also applies to business partnerships. If I go into business with someone and they want to make a business decision that goes against the word of God, what then? If they want to lie on the income tax forms, do I participate in the lie? Of course not, but that would be a huge temptation to overcome. Why would I even want to put myself in that position? This is why I am to be separate.

II Corinthians 7:1. Because of the relationship promises in the preceding verse, I have to purify and cleanse both my flesh (my actions) and my spirit (***trajectory of the heart***). That is real holiness. It is a whole lot easier to clean up my flesh than it is to clean up my spirit. I can dress right and talk right, but if my heart isn't right, I am not holy (II Corinthians 5:12). Others may think I am and I may deceive myself, but God knows I'm not. It's not the persona I portray that counts. God sees who I really am.

II Corinthians 7:2-3; 12. Paul takes great pains to set forth his compassion for the Corinthians, even while chastising them. Whether I am disciplining my children or members of the congregation God has placed me in charge of, I must remember to discipline in love so they understand that I am on their side, trying to get them in the right position to make it to Heaven. The Corinthians apparently received their rebuke well and with the right attitude (II Corinthians 7:15). It is very important when I am rebuked or chastised, that I receive it in the right spirit and don't allow myself to be offended. It is very human to bristle up at correction. We tend to defend ourselves. The Corinthians went through the emotional process (vs

11), but ultimately, accepted instruction and corrected the situation (vs 15). I allow a surgeon to cut bad things out of my body. Why don't I want to allow God to cut out bad things in my spirit? My spirit is eternal. My body is temporal. Which is the most important?

II Corinthians 7:9-10. Being "sorry" and "repenting" are two very different things. Repentance works towards salvation. Repentance is the first step. Tears don't necessarily mean repentance. I was once asked to pray with a Korean lady at a church in the USA. She was sobbing at the altar and those around her were all excited and came and got me to see if she was receiving the Holy Spirit. When I got up to where I could hear her prayer, she was sobbing about how much she missed her mother back in Korea and was asking God to help her get back home! She was sorry she had left home! She had plenty of tears, but was not repenting of sins. There are also people who are just sorry that what they are doing is wrong, but they have no intentions of stopping what they are doing. That's not repentance either. Repentance is when I am sorry I have grieved God by my sin and I am willing to change my ways so I don't commit that sin again. Being a human being, I cannot overcome sin on my own. I need the power of the Holy Spirit to help me overcome! Repentance on its own is not enough because I lack the wherewithal to be victorious on my own. (Acts 1:8; Romans 8)

II Corinthians 8:2-4. Sacrificial giving is a wondrous thing! Sacrificial giving is giving when it hurts to give. Paul prays the Corinthian church would abound in "this grace" (the grace of giving). Sacrificial giving is not a commandment, but rather an act of love (vs 7-8).

II Corinthians 8:12. God's measuring stick is different than mine. Whether talent or money, God measures me according to what He has given me, and not against what He has given another person (II Corinthians 10:12). Am I willing to use what God has equipped me with, or shall I be jealous of what He has given to others and not to me? Will I take action with what I have or will I mope around lamenting what I would do if only I had .... "xyz"? He only requires me to use what I have been given (Luke 12:48; II Corinthians 9:6-7). God sees me as an *individual*. I tend to see myself in a corporate setting, and that's where I get into trouble. I have no basis to compare myself with anyone else, because God has given us each a separate set of circumstances, personality traits, and talents.

II Corinthians 8:13-14. It upsets me when I hear people talk about "their" church or talk about "Bro. XYZ's" church. No! This is all God's church. We are not in competition with each other. Bro. XYZ is the under-shepherd of a congregation, but it is God's flock! There will be times when one church is going through a tough time and a neighboring church is gliding by smoothly. That is the time to rally together and help each other. It is not right to talk badly about another church or to encourage or even accept members from the church going through a corporate trial. Don't we realize people bring problems and spirits with them? We are the body of Christ. We must work together and not against each other. Some pastors forbid their people to participate in section-wide church functions. That's just controlling and very wrong.

II Corinthians 8:16-19, 22-23. Thank God for helpers and for unnamed people! Not only did Titus go to help the Corinthians, he had a helper. This person is unnamed in the Bible, but God knows who he is. This person had a great reputation among the churches in the area. Sometimes God will send a worker to a church for a season. The Synofski family come to our church for 10 years. They were solid Christians and wonderful examples. They helped us in so many ways. They had to travel far for services, but were faithful until their health dictated they go to a closer church. What a blessing they were! Given the choice of this family or an in demand, name brand evangelist, I'd choose this family!

II Corinthians 8:20. Chapter 8 is primarily talking about the love offering being collected. Paul admonishes them not to criticize the administration of the collection. Unfortunately, there are ministers who collect funds and do not administer them correctly. God will judge these people. If I give with love and a willing heart, I am giving unto God and not unto man. If the offering is misused or administered incorrectly, God will judge and deal with that sin.

II Corinthians 9:1-5. Paul had been singing the praises of the generosity of the Corinthian church, but he wrote them to make sure his praise of them wasn't shallow! He knew human nature, didn't he? Sometimes we offer to do something and fail to follow through with our offer. That really amounts to lying. If I make a promise to do something, I must do it unless it is humanly impossible. *Example:* If I put my name down to show up for a church cleaning/maintenance day, I need to be there, even if I later get invited to a birthday party on the same day! Just because something better comes along, or I don't feel like participating that day, doesn't mean I can back out of my commitment. This is a real problem in churches everywhere. Everyone wants church activities, but no one wants to commit to do the work involved in those. Jesus condemned this in Matthew 21:28-32.

II Corinthians 9:6-12. The Law of Harvest is two-fold: (1) I reap what I sow and (2) I reap MORE than what I sow. One apple gives me numerous seeds, which give me numerous trees, which give me numerous apples. Likewise, the good or evil I do is harvested in multiple quantities of whichever I sowed. Verse 7 isn't speaking exclusively about money. Giving of my time and resources is also giving. God loves it when He prompts my heart to give and I respond. My giving makes Him want to give to me. When my children were little and one of them gave all of their birthday money in the offering, it made me, as a parent, buy them what they would have bought with that money. Their generosity made me respond. I wanted to reward them for being generous. That's how God is. When I give mercy, give time, give money, give resources to someone else, He will give unto me. Even though our spiritual lives are eternal, God cares about our physical lives too. He will supply our needs sufficiently, and sometimes even abundantly (Philippians 4:19).

II Corinthians 9:13-15. God has done so much for me and has blessed me so much, I am compelled to be generous to others. I give to others because God has given to me many things, but most importantly, the opportunity for salvation. God keeps giving to me because I give to others. It's a circle of giving. Keeping in mind that the subject matter of this chapter is giving, I think that God's unspeakable gift (vs 15) is the attitude and spirit of giving. God so loved, that He gave (John 3:16).

II Corinthians 10:4-5. The battle we all struggle to fight is not a matter of identifying the enemy and bombing it. It's not all that easy. It is a battle of the mind. The strongholds are thoughts in the mind. Our minds are our greatest enemy. There are two parts to our minds: brain & emotions. Our brains know what is right, but our emotions (heart) wants things that bring pleasure, even if it is temporary pleasure. Case in point: We all KNOW sugar can be poison to our physical bodies. Our bodies are designed to accommodate only about 6 teaspoons (women) to 9 teaspoons (men) PER DAY according to the American Heart Association. I put 3 teaspoons in my coffee! A slice of whole wheat bread has almost 3 teaspoons! Lemon-pepper seasoning has sugar added to it! Our brains technically know not to eat sugar, but our emotions tell us that a little something sweet will make us feel better. Our sugar-free life starts tomorrow! This struggle is true in the spiritual realm too. Our brains know we need to pray (etc.), but our emotions tell us staying in bed a little longer would feel so good. If we can get control of our own emotions, living for God would not be difficult. The struggle is between the brain and the emotions. ***It's not Rocket Science***, but that doesn't mean it is easy. Our imaginations make mountains out of mole hills. To win this war, *EVERY* thought needs to be corralled (I Peter 1:13). We tend to over think things, even theology. We must guard against rationalizing things to make a wrong thing right.

II Corinthians 10:7. Paul established he was (1) not much to look at (vs 10) and (2) timid in person, but bold in his writings (vs 1-2). He is telling them to pay attention to his writings and not his appearance. My father had a way of fussing with a twinkle in his eye. That twinkle didn't mean he was kidding. It meant he was loving. To misconstrue that twinkle for jesting was to invite consequences for disobedience. This scripture is not giving permission to dress any way I want to. Scripture doesn't contradict scripture. I still obey the modesty standards set by scripture. This verse is telling me not to dismiss (judge) someone because they don't look or sound authoritative.

II Corinthians 10:12-13. My source of comparison is God's standard and not the standard of man. When I stand before God on judgment day, He will see how I measure up to the rule which GOD Himself set forth. I will not be able to point my finger at anyone and say, "Well, *they* told me I ......" My actions are weighed by God's standard (I Samuel 2:3; Amos 7:7-8). I must measure up to God's word. There is no excuse. I can't depend on anyone else for my salvation. It's up to me. Just for fun, let's compare churches. If a church with a membership of 30 individuals gains 6 members in a given year, then a church of 3,000 members must gain 600 to be just as "successful" as the smaller church! A church of 1,000 members gives $50,000 to missions and is lauded for giving such a large offering. However, a church of 100 members who gave $6,000 is more successful! All fun aside, there are many other factors involved such as overall spiritual hardness of the city, financial resources of church members, etc. Therefore, there is no way to make an accurate comparison. That's God's job. He knows all things. All He expects of me is to do what I am equipped to do and do it to the best of my abilities.

II Corinthians 11:3-4. The Gospel is simple. It is cut and dry. ***It's not Rocket Science!*** My emotions will try to corrupt the gospel to make it say what I want it to. I must guard against that. This is a reason why there are so many "Christian" doctrines floating around. I must be able to back my theology up with Bible and not by rationalizing. Rationalizing is what got Eve into trouble. Scripture will not contradict scripture, so I must study. Scripture will also interpret scripture, so I must study. When God says "Seek and ye shall find" (Jeremiah 29:13; Matthew 7:7), He's not trying to play hide and go seek with us. He wants us to desire Him enough to spend a little time with Him. How far would any relationship get if all that is said is, "Hi! How are you? Can you give me some money?" None of us wants that kind of relationship! We spend hours on the phone or emailing each other. We go on dates and find ways to spend time with each other. A relationship with God takes a little effort and time on my part. If I seek after the truth in God's word, I will find it.

II Corinthians 11:6-7. Apparently, Paul had a sharp tongue and was abrasive! In his defense, though, he meant well and he sacrificed to preach.

II Corinthians 11:12-13. There are "self" kingdom minded people. That is the spirit of the world (humanism). I must be God's kingdom minded. I need to look out for the bigger picture. Elevating myself to God-status will doom me every time. How do I do that? By judging & condemning people, by pushing my own agenda, and by making sure I get credit for things. There are ideas that I have had for the church body which were implemented on a state-wide level. No one knows those were my ideas. I did the research. I made the proposal, and my ideas were implemented with someone else getting the credit. Initially, I admit getting all huffed up about it at first. Then, I thought that these ideas were good for the church body and did it really matter if I got the credit or not? All that mattered was these ideas got implemented to the edification of the church body. If I am truthful to myself, I realize that those weren't my ideas after all. Those were God's ideas. He allowed me to be the messenger to relay His ideas to others! God gets the credit for those ideas.

II Corinthians 11:13-15. For everything God has, Satan has a counterfeit. The Egyptian magicians were able to duplicate the miracles brought through Moses up to a point (Exodus 7:11, 22). Satan performs "lying wonders" (II Thessalonians 2:9). Remember, Satan has been around a really, really long time. He doesn't know our thoughts nor can he predict the future. However, there is nothing wrong with his hearing! When God speaks, Satan listens. He believes and even trembles (which is more than some humans I know) (James 2:19)! The people passing by on the day of Pentecost accused the 120 of being drunk. Peter didn't deny drunkenness. He just said they were not drunk as everyone *assumed* they were (Acts 2:15). Being drunk on the spirit of God is a whole lot different (and a whole lot better) than being drunk on alcohol. There is a euphoria that can be experienced with drugs, alcohol, and illicit sex. However, those paths lead to destruction. Stick with the real thing. How do I know who is a real messenger from God? Their words and actions must line up with God's word, even when no one is looking!

II Corinthians 11:16-22. I do like Paul's sarcasm! He is quick to point out his boasting is not a word from God, but from his own mouth. He is comparing himself to some of the false teachers the Corinthians were listening to. He is frustrated as to why the Corinthians accepted teachings which went contrary to what he had taught. His credentials were every bit as good as theirs. This situation reminds me that people are fickle. People tend to ride whatever wind comes along. Whatever new doctrine or new idea pops up, people run with it without analyzing it for accuracy or truth. I see that all of the time on the internet! I must not be swayed with human philosophies or rumors and gossip (Colossians 2:8). I must root out the truth.

II Corinthians 11:24-28. Paul was persecuted both by those without the church and those within the church. I shouldn't be surprised when my persecution comes from someone that is supposedly "in church". That happens. I can't allow myself to take offense. It is interesting to note Paul reaped what he had sowed prior to his conversion. He had severely persecuted the church. I don't have automatic immunity from the law of the harvest when I get in church and start serving the Lord.

II Corinthians 12:2. My take on this scripture is Paul wasn't sure if he saw a vision, or if he had heard of this man, but didn't personally know him.

II Corinthians 12:6-10. We like to have heroes and put people on a pedestal. There is an epidemic of celebrities in our culture today, yes, even in the church culture. We all like to receive recognition, validation, and accolades from others. Paul was careful not to allow the hero worship to go to his head and begged the Corinthians not to exalt him and put him on a pedestal. He acknowledged God had allowed a trial to stay in his life to make sure Paul's pride was kept in check. The trial was from Satan, but God allowed it to remain to keep Paul humble. Paul, then, was thankful for the infirmity. Without it, pride, etc., may have prevented him from being saved.

II Corinthians 12:9. I need to be careful and not judge people just because they sin differently than I do! We all have our individual weaknesses. The medical community sometimes calls them "diseases" or identifies a difference in our DNA! We are all born sinners, so I don't doubt there is a difference in our DNA. I need to be careful I don't downplay someone else's temptation just because it is not a temptation to me. What may be a big deal to me may not be problematic to the other person and vice versa. We all have our struggles to overcome. A 2-year old is seriously upset when he doesn't get his meal on time. A teenager understands the meaning of having to wait and is not quite as upset as the 2-year-old. That doesn't mean the 2-year-old isn't really upset! The teenager, on the other hand, gets just as upset over things as the 2-year-old does! The "upsetness" is the same. The reasons may be different, but the emotion is the same. Likewise, the *cause* of a temptation may be different, but the *pull* of the temptation is the same. I need to have compassion. My strength in the weakness of my friend could very well be what will help my friend get through temptation. If we were both tempted alike, we would both fail. Thank God Christ is strong in my weaknesses. He can pull me through the temptation so I do not fall into it because at His very weakest, God is stronger than I (I Corinthians 1:25)! At the same time, I can't allow myself to think no one understands my struggles and temptations. There are others who have been down my road as well.

II Corinthians 12:10. God reminded Paul whatever the trial, God's grace (unmerited favor) was sufficient enough to see Paul through that trial. It is only when I am the weakest can I allow God to shine through. Oh, to get to the place where I just turn to God first and not to my own devices! Wouldn't that make life a whole lot simpler? ***To every problem there is a solution.*** God has a solution for my problem! If I just allow God to work it out, He will and, He will be right there with me every step of the way. I must be patient and allow Him to show me the solution step by step, trusting (even though I can't see the path in front of me) He is leading me down the perfect path.

II Corinthians 12:14-15. I need to always check my motives ~ the ***trajectory of my heart***. Do I truly want what is best for people or do I just want what they can do for me? Sometimes the pastor loves the congregation more than the congregation loves the pastor. I suppose that is because God has given the pastor the burden for that particular group of people.

II Corinthians 12:17-19. A true messenger of God is not in it for the money, but for souls. I've seen pastors hold on to a congregation long after God was finished with them there, because of finances. It is hard to walk away from a "job" that pays well. The problem is if God has lifted a burden, it is time to leave. The minister's finances become God's problem. He will provide. If a pastor stays beyond his usefulness to God in that particular location, the congregation will dwindle down to nothing. I've seen it happen too many times. My husband has resigned as pastor of two churches when God said so, even though it hurt our pocketbook tremendously. Somehow, we survived and didn't miss any meals! God will provide.

II Corinthians 12:21. Does God allow hypocrites in the church to keep a pastor humble??

II Corinthians 13:1. The requirement of two or three witnesses had long been established (Deuteronomy 17:6; 19:15; Matthew 18:16) and was practiced by the early church (I Timothy 5:19; Hebrews 10:28). Some in Corinth wanted forensic proof God was talking to Paul. Paul challenges them to take a deep look at themselves and they would themselves, become the second witness as to their faults.

II Corinthians 13:5. One of my pet peeves is it appears a whole lot of people don't bother to look in the mirror before they leave the house. They grab something, throw it on, and don't bother to see if it looks decent, modest, flattering, etc.! Have you ever been to Wal-Mart? Do these people realize what they look like? Before I go on an all-out rant, perhaps I should examine my own self. Perhaps I should look in the mirror myself. Before I go around pointing a finger at the fault of others in the church, perhaps I should take a deep look inside. If I really did, I would see so many things I needed to improve on, I wouldn't have time to gossip about the faults of others!

II Corinthians 13:8. The truth is unchangeable (Matthew 16:18-19; Deuteronomy 4:2). If I attempt to change the truth to conform to my own philosophy, I am only fooling myself because truth is invincible. God is truth (John 14:6). God doesn't change (Malachi 3:6). If I try to change truth, I am damned by that truth (Galatians 1:9; Revelation 22:18-19).

II Corinthians 13:10. When I read II Corinthians 13:10, I wonder if Paul was afraid he would be too harsh and offensive if he rebuked the Corinthian church in person. He must have spent a lot of time and agony to get the wording just right in his letters. I need to do the same. There is a right way and a wrong way to discipline or chastise others. A child (and a congregation) must be handled like a bar of wet soap in the shower. If held too tightly, it pops out of the hand. If held too loosely, it slithers out of the hand. The soap must be held just right in order to stay where it needs to stay.

GALATIANS

Written to the church established in Galatia. Themes: Justification by faith, Grace, Abolishment of the law.

Galatians deals with the abolishment of the law quite a bit. There were three types of law given to the Israelites.
- Law of Moses. (Exodus 24). This was the ceremonial law.
- Law of God (Exodus 20). This was the Ten Commandments.
- Moral Law (throughout Bible). This is the things that God hates.
- The Ten Commandments were reinstated by Jesus. (See essay entitled "The Old Testament Law" in *It's Not Rocket Science, Volume 1.*) Since God never changes (Malachi 3:6), I believe the Moral Law is still for today (James 2:8-10). What God hated back then, He still hates. I doubt very seriously God would allow something He absolutely abhors and hates to be in Heaven for eternity with Him. What law, then, was fulfilled and thus, abolished by Jesus? It was the Law of Moses, or the ceremonial law. All of the ceremonies and rituals was given to us to point to Calvary (Galatians 3:24-25). Once we live out a life of separation, there is no need for symbolism!

Galatians 1:1. Throughout the epistles, reference is made to Jesus and God (or similar wording). That little word "and" is better translated as "even". The original word is "kia". It is used to contrast natures of God and not to separate deities. In verse 4, the phrase "God and our Father" is used. God and Father are not two separate deities. The word "father" speaks of relationship. God is our father because He created us. There is only one God (Deuteronomy 6:4). When I read "God, even our Father ...", it takes on a personal meaning.

Galatians 1:6-7. It's easy to get off base when I allow myself to listen to reason by my peers. The Bible is the base, not what anyone reasons out through philosophy. There are those who *intentionally* try to change or pervert God's word! When I study God's word, I must couple that with a prayer God would open up my understanding so I would have a revelation of truth. Truths in God's word will jump out at me when I study with a pure heart.

Galatians 1:8-10. The law was given on Mt. Sinai orally by God (Exodus 20:1) and then written by God (Exodus 31:18). Moses broke those tablets when he saw the golden calf. He had to go back up the mountain and rewrite the law (Exodus 34:27). Apparently, the angels stood by as a witness and possibly even explained the law more fully to Moses so he could implement what he had received from God (Psalm 68:17, Acts 7:38, 53; Hebrews 2:2). No one is to add to or take anything away from that law (Deuteronomy 4:2; Revelation 22:19). I am destined to be destroyed if I attempt to change God's word (vs 9)! It is men-pleasers who want to change God's law to fit society's philosophy. God pleasers keep the law (vs 10).

Galatians 1:12. There must be a personal revelation. A cursory glance through the Bible results in many false doctrines. It is only when I diligently seek with a heart searching for truth that I receive the revelation. Without a personal revelation, I perish (Proverbs 29:18). God wants those who will take time to develop a relationship with Him, not a superficial pew-warming relationship. This is why receiving the Holy Spirit is so important. The Holy Spirit will lead and guide me into all truth (John 16:13; Matthew 16:17). Without it, the Bible is confusing. Spending time with Jesus will open up my understanding of His ways and His word (Luke 24:45). When the *trajectory of my heart* is off course, my understanding is darkened (Ephesians 4:18). Without understanding, I automatically live in violation of God's law (Romans 1:31).

Galatians 1:14. God is timeless (Psalm 90:4). How many years went by from the time Paul was in the womb to the point of his conversion? To God, it was no time at all. God had a job for Paul to do from a young age. Paul was very smart and prepared himself for the work God wanted him to do, even if he didn't realize it at the time. God made sure Paul had the educational background in place to later be able to use that education as a tool to witness to educated people. A lot of time and preparation was completed before Paul could fulfil God's plan. Sometimes we worry about spending a lot of time in the preparation stage, but we need that time to be the most effective. Remember, Jesus had thirty years of preparation for only three years of ministry! He spent thirty years gaining the experience necessary to relate to the ordinary human being.

Galatians 1:18; 2:7. I must be a continual student of God's word. After Paul's conversion, he spent three years studying. Then, he presented himself to Peter (who had the keys to the kingdom, remember? Matthew 16:18). Peter "unlocked" Paul's ministry to the Gentiles. It was another 14 years before Paul was sent out on the mission field (Galatians 2:1). There is always preparation work to be done before a ministry is launched. We can't just "wing it". God wants us to study and show that we have "the goods" (II Timothy 2:15). Jesus told the Pharisees to study his words to find their meaning. Matthew 9:13). It's not about *reading* the Bible. It's about *learning* and *applying* the principles to my life. Whenever I see myself in a "holding pattern" and spinning my wheels, I want to remember to seize the opportunity to beef up my spiritual credentials. Who knows but that God is giving me down time to use for future ministry?

Galatians 2. Paul was accountable to church leadership (vs 2). He worked within the confines of church organization (vs 9). The Jewish converts still clung to the ceremonial law of the Old Testament. The Gentile converts realized that Jesus has fulfilled the requirements of the ceremonial law and thus, the ceremonial law was no longer necessary.
- The law demands righteousness (Lev. 19:1-2). Christ provided.
- The law was temporary until Jesus raised up (Deuteronomy 18:15-19).

- The final verdict of law is death. Christ died once and for all (Galatians 3:13).
- Purpose of the law was to point to Christ (Galatians 3:24-25).

Galatians 2:7-10. It was decided Peter would deal with the Jewish Christians and Paul would mentor the Gentile Christians. Paul was given the liberty to not enforce the Jewish ceremonial law upon the Gentiles. He was, however, admonished to remember the poor. This falls in line with God's moral law which says to love others (Matthew 22:39; Mark 12:31; Luke 10:27)!

Galatians 2:11-14. There were racial prejudices even in the early church. I suppose racism is a human condition found everywhere. Paul called Peter out on it and openly rebuked him for the double standard. Even Peter had human shortcomings! We look to Jesus and not to a fellow man/woman for leadership. There will be times when our leader/pastor falls short of perfection! After all, he/she is a human being. I can't let that be a stumbling block for me. I look to Jesus as my premier example, not a fellow human.

Galatians 2:16-20. "Works of the law" refers to the ceremonial law, not the moral law of God. The ceremonial law was insufficient because it could not change the *trajectory of the heart.* It gave the outward appearance of a separated life, but could not change the inside. On the other hand, if the *trajectory of my heart* is right, my outside will reflect it. To live by faith in Jesus, is to obey His words!

Galatians 2:21. I must be careful not to set aside God's grace. Grace is a contrast with the law. No amount of legality will make me worthy of Heaven. God's unmerited favor (grace), however, does make me worthy of Heaven. Grace gives me the opportunity to live right. I must take that opportunity! *Example:* I can go to a buffet hungry. If I don't eat, I will leave hungry. I have to take advantage of the food laid out before me in order to ease my hunger pains! Likewise, God's grace allows me to come in contact with salvation. If I don't take advantage of the opportunity and if I don't participate in the salvational plan, I won't be saved. Some people preach grace is a "get out of hell free card". Some people preach God's grace will allow any and all sins into heaven. That's a nice, warm, cozy thought, but it is not true. Grace allows me to be in the presence of God so that I can live holy before Him. To "frustrate" God's grace is to misuse it. I misuse grace when I redefine it. Grace simply means "unmerited favor". The fact God allows me to speak to Him when I have sin in my life is grace. The fact John 3:16 exists is grace. The fact God speaks to me is grace. The fact I have blessings (food, lodging, etc.) is grace. Thinking God will overlook my habitual sin and disobedience to His word, is frustrating God's grace.

Galatians 3:1. Apparently, the churches in Galatia had the same problem as Corinth. They listened to human reasoning. I must search and live by the scriptures and not allow someone's logic or human reasoning to deceive me and draw me away from the Bible truths.

Galatians 3:2-5. Paul sure goes on a rant here! His lawyer training comes through. He can't believe they have been swayed away from truth by a smooth talker.

Galatians 3:6-9. After Paul's rant, he gently reminds them how, through faith, they are sons of Abraham and thus, entitled to the blessings promised to Abraham.

Galatians 3:10. Jewish Christians were trying to hold Gentile Christians to the Jewish ceremonial law; circumcision in particular. Paul told them they couldn't just pick and choose which part of the ceremonial law to observe. If one part was adopted, it all had to be adopted. There are three sets of laws set forth in the Old Testament:
- Law of Moses consists of Ceremonial Laws (Exodus 24). Jesus fulfilled these (Deuteronomy 18:15-19).
- Law of God consists of The Ten Commandments (Exodus 20), which Jesus reinstated. (See essay entitled, "The Old Testament Law" in *It's Not Rocket Science, Volume 1.*)
- Moral Law consists of Abominations (things that God hates). These are not all collected in one place, but sprinkled throughout the Scripture (I Corinthians 6:9-10; I Peter 4:3; Revelation 21:8).

Galatians 3:11. The age-old question is what came first, the chicken or the egg?! There is no question, however about faith and works. Faith comes first. The "just shall live by faith" concept was not new (Habakkuk 2:4), but over time, the Jewish religious leaders had confused faith and works. Abraham was chosen because of his faith, not because of his works! However, his faith caused him to take action. He left his home and followed the leading of God. Faith comes first. Faith in God is the initial tug on our hearts. Without a measure of faith, even small, I will never take action. God has given us all a measure of faith (Romans 12:3). Works is merely faith-in-action. Faith without works is nothing (James 2:18, 20, 26). (PS: The chicken came first because God created it in Genesis 1!)

Galatians 3:12-14. To merely live by a set of rules is impossible. Jesus gave us the opportunity to be free from the chains of sin when He paid the ultimate price for our sins. I am still bound by the chains of sin and forced to do things which God hates *unless* my sins have been expunged by baptism in Jesus' name and I am filled with the Holy Spirit. The Holy Spirit gives me the freedom NOT to keep on sinning. *(See notes on Romans).*

Galatians 3:15-18. In true lawyer fashion, Paul brings up an example to prove his point. A "Last Will and Testament" is a document written by a human. Yet, when signed properly (sealed), it becomes legal and binding. No one can add to or take away from that document. Likewise, once God gave the promise to Abraham, He was bound to that promise. The promise was Jesus (Abraham's seed) would bring salvation. The law wasn't to take away from the promise.

Galatians 3:19-20. The sole purpose of the law was to reveal how badly mankind needed a savior by identifying sin! Even the most pious of all people found it impossible to obey every single part of the law. They constantly had to go through ceremonies to get their sins rolled ahead. It is similar to rolling in closing costs on a mortgage. You still have to pay the closing costs, but not up front. The price of sin still had to be paid, but since a sinful human could not pay, God allowed an animal without a blemish to be a substitute. These sacrifices were a continual thing until Jesus, the only man without sin, could pay the price. Without a written law, a person could look at another person and figure he/she was a good person by comparison. The law made people realize that they weren't so righteous, after all! When I realize my need for a savior, I look to Jesus!

Galatians 3:28. God is no respecter of persons (Acts 10:34). These things don't matter:
- Race,
- Economic status, or
- Gender.

Galatians 4:1-3. Before Jesus came, the Jews were under the tutelage of the law, such as a child is under the tutelage of the household servants.

Galatians 4:4-7. The "fulness of time" is a phrase only God understands completely. I impatiently wait for God's promises to unfold. They will. I have faith. As I wait, I remember God's timing is not mine. What I think is the right time may or may not be. I have to TRUST God knows what He is doing. When the timing was just right, God bought back humanity from sin through the blood of Jesus. The Jews had been in bondage multiple times, but it was under the Roman bondage that the "fulness of time" actually came. There is another "fulness of time" we are all waiting on and that is the 2nd coming of the Lord. When will it be? The current world climate sure looks like things are wrapping up. I think every generation faces a crisis to jar them. Surely, they preached the coming of the Lord was any minute during their lifetimes. Since then, there have been other "end time" events. I must be ready to meet my maker at any time. He may come today or He may wait another 100 years. I will not attempt to pinpoint a time. I can't even pinpoint when MY time will be up on this earth. I just want to be ready.

Galatians 4:8-11. As a child of God, I am no longer under the bondage of sin (Hebrews 2:14-15). I have the freedom to make the right choices. Paul was aghast to hear the Galatians were returning to their old habits. I've got to keep the Holy Spirit fresh in my heart. I've got to stir it up (II Timothy 1:6). I've got to keep my prayer life going. I can't rely on yesterday's blessings. I can't go backwards. I must move forward!

Galatians 4:12-16. People are fickle. We will believe one thing and when some new idea comes around, we gravitate to that. Case in point: Advertisements. We blindly believe what companies persuade us to believe about a particular product. The whole point of an advertisement campaign is to get us to switch our allegiance. We must stand for truth regardless of what is popular in our culture. We must plant our feet solidly on the Bible and not be shaken by the winds of outside influence. There's no point in shooting the messenger. When my conscious is pricked during the course of a sermon, I must repent and not get mad at the preacher.

Galatians 4:19. The theme of the epistles (letters to Christians) is this: That Christ be formed in us (Colossians 1:27). That is our goal: To Be Like Jesus! Nothing else matters. If I am just like Him, how could I possibly miss heaven? It's not about just barely trying to make it to Heaven. It is a matter of how much like Jesus can I become while here on this earth? ***This isn't rocket science!*** (See also essay entitled, "My Goal is not Heaven" in *It's Not Rocket Science, Volume 1.*)

Galatians 4:23-26. It fascinates me how detailed God is. I get amazed over and over again by His imagination! Not only did He create some really weird looking animals and plants, He pays attention to the smallest of details. He even knows how many hairs I have on my head (Matthew 10:30; Luke 12:7)! Since I brush out a handful daily, He has quite the computer program going on! God even used Abraham's blundering to give us an object lesson. The birth of Ishmael (Genesis 16) was a very carnal, natural birth resulting from a carnal relationship between Abraham and a slave woman. The birth of Isaac (Genesis 21:1-5) was a miraculous birth, resulting from the relationship between Abraham and his (too old to have children) wife. Now, we know the intimacy of marriage between husband and wife is symbolic of the intimate relationship God wants to have with mankind (the church) (Jeremiah 31:32; Ephesians 5:30-31). Isaac was the child of the promise. God was bound by His blanket promise to bless Abraham's seed and therefore did preserve and bless Ishmael, but Ishmael was not THE child promised by God. We can therefore conclude Isaac's birth has a spiritual connotation. We find that there are two covenants given. The (1) law on the tables of stone was given (natural) to Moses in Arabia, and the (2) law written on our hearts (spiritual) was first given in Jerusalem on the Day of Pentecost (Acts 2; II Corinthians 3:3). The carnal will always persecute the spiritual just as Ishmael persecuted Isaac. In fact, Ishmael persecuted Isaac so much, they had to be separated. The carnal persecutes the spiritual so much, they cannot co-exist together. I must separate from carnal things. This is why I need the Holy Spirit. I need the new covenant. I need the law written in my heart so that it becomes a part of me and is internalized.

Galatians 5.
Liberty = freedom to choose to live right
Bondage = bound, enslaved to sin. By my own power, I have no choice but to sin (Galatians 5:1). The Holy Spirit gives me the power to overcome sin

(Hebrews 2:14-15).

I am not to misuse the liberty purchased by Jesus (I Corinthians 7:23). To misuse liberty is to allow myself to think that I have freedom to fulfil the desires of the flesh (Galatians 5:13). Liberty is not the freedom to do what I want! Doing what I want is bondage to the flesh! Liberty is the freedom to make the right choices.

Galatians 5:2-6. The keeping of the ceremonial law doesn't do any spiritual good since the ceremonial law was symbolic of the church's relationship with God. Once the real thing was in place, there is no need for the symbol.

Galatians 5:7-10. A little false doctrine spoils everything. I must guard against any teaching contrary to the word of God. Who introduces me to false doctrine is immaterial. I have to guard against it by examining the scriptures for myself. I can't take anyone's word for what the scripture says. A lady told me one time if her pastor began teaching false doctrine, she would probably follow because she trusted him. NO! My standard of measure must be the word of God and not what a smooth talking "salesman" preaches!

Galatians 5:11. The cross is offensive. Not too many songs are sung and not too many sermons are preached about the cross, because it exposes my sin. My sinful nature doesn't want to stop sinning. Sinning is pleasurable (for a season - Hebrews 11:25). An encounter with the cross demands I recognize myself as a sinner. People get offended by that.

Galatians 5:13. To misuse liberty is to allow myself to think that I have "freedom" to fulfil the desires of the flesh.

Galatians 5:14. Everything about the law points to one thing: LOVE. Why? Because God is love (I John 4:8). The absence of love means the absence of God. When I have hatred in my heart for someone, I don't have God. When I do things which displease God, I don't have love. The Ten Commandments are divided into two sections:
- relationship with God and
- relationship with my fellow man.

If I have God, I have love and I don't have a problem with relationships. When I have a relationship problem in my life, I need to examine my relationship with God! Sometimes I need a little more love than other times!!

Galatians 5:16. My inner motivation must be to walk in the Spirit ~ which comprises both truth and attitude. If my attitude *(trajectory of the heart)* is to walk after the Spirit and please God, I will not succumb to the natural instincts of the flesh.

Galatians 5:19-23. There is fruit of the flesh (vs 19-21) and fruit of the spirit (vs 22-23). What fruit am I producing? It's pretty simple. I need to analyze my life and see which category my actions fall under. The actions of my life will fall under one category or the other. ***This isn't rocket science!***

Galatians 5:22. Every one of the fruits of the spirit comes under the umbrella of love. God is love (I John 4:8). Every one of the fruits is mentioned in the "love chapter". *(See notes at I Corinthians 13.)*

Galatians 5:26. It is interesting to note immediately after the listing of the fruit of the spirit Paul admonishes them not to allow pride to rise up! Pride is the first step in backsliding. It is tough to keep at bay. Perhaps that is why God allows so many trials. Perhaps He is trying to knock the pride out of me! It would behoove me to remember I am dispensable and my talents could be taken away in one swift second. Without God, I am nothing.

Galatians 6. When things are tough,
- Don't faint (vs 9).
- Do good (vs 10).
- Don't get offended (vs 17).
- Let God be with my spirit (vs 18).

Galatians 6:1. When I help to restore someone to God, I must do so in a humble manner. If my pride rises up, I will fall as well.

Galatians 6:2. What is the practical application of loving my neighbor? To love my neighbor means to help them bear their burdens. The Greek word for burden in Galatians 6:2 means excessive load. The Greek word for burden in Galatians 6:5 means burdensome routine. If I read these two verses in English, it sounds contradictory. The Bible NEVER contradicts itself. (When it appears the Bible does contradict itself, I need to dig a little deeper and find out the true meaning.) When I see someone with an excessive load, I need to help shoulder that load and get them through to victory. I pray with them. I visit with them. I let them cry or vent to me. I help them financially. I give of my time to run errands for them. I do whatever I am capable of doing to help them carry that load.

Galatians 6:9. The law of the harvest is I reap what I sow ***and*** I reap more than what I sow.

Galatians 6:14. The summary of Paul's message to the Galatians is this: (1) I will not allow pride to enter into my heart; and (2) It's all about the cross and the price Jesus paid for me.

EPHESIANS

Written to the church already established. Themes: Grace; Unity of believers & Christians living.

Ephesians. Some early manuscripts say "Laodicea". Maybe this was a form letter of sorts? Paul was in Rome and in prison (3:1; 6:20).

Ephesians 1:3. Blessings aren't always physical! The ultimate blessing is life in Heaven, free from the tugs of sin!

Ephesians 1:4. "Chosen us in him". It is not a rejection of others, per se, but favor. God loves ALL human beings, even the worst ones! However, He responds favorably to those who seek Him out.

Ephesians 1:6-7. "Accepted". The blood of Jesus makes us "worthy to be adopted." The ransom (redemption) was paid by Jesus.

Ephesians 1:4-10. Let's talk again about "predestination" or "foreordained". There are a few things that are foreordained by God. At the beginning of time, God knew mankind would sin, so He provided for the "Lamb" to be slain. God also foreordained there would be a body of believers. Whether or not any particular individual will be in that body of believers is up to the person. God didn't go down the human line and say, "You're in; you're out", etc. Some religions teach you have no control over whether you go to heaven or hell. You can only do good and hope that if you're in the slot to go to hell, your good behavior will get you a lesser punishment. That's not true. It is the church body which is predestined, not the individual.

Ephesians 1:11. Have you ever talked to yourself? Have you ever uttered, "Let's see ..."? I have! Apparently, God does too! There are not multiple gods counseling with each other.

Ephesians 1:13. We (1) hear, (2) trust, (3) believe, and are (4) sealed by the word of God (Romans 10:17). Studying scripture is important.

Ephesians 1:14. What spiritual things we experience here on earth is only the tip of the iceberg. The Holy Spirit is a (a) foretaste of glory; (b) sample of reality; (c) preview of eternity; (d) partial payment! Things will be different when I experience the Holy Spirit (Romans 8:19-23; Philippians 3:21).

Ephesians 1:15-18. Paul prayed for fellow believers. I need to pray for my fellow church members. I need to:
- give thanks that they are serving God.

- pray they grow in wisdom and spiritual knowledge.
- pray they understand the scripture.
- pray they realize the awesome riches in serving God!

We need to pray for each other ~ not only for the temporal requests that we all have, but for eternal issues.

Ephesians 1:19-23. There are no words to adequately express how great, wonderful and powerful God is. I don't even know if the human mind can fully comprehend His greatness.

Ephesians 2:1-5. Satan, for the time being, is the prince and power of the air. God intended for mankind to have dominion (Genesis 1:26), but Adam turned that authority over to Satan back in the Garden. God has been trying to get us back on track ever since (vs. 5)! God is "rich in mercy" (vs. 4). Mercy is compassion so strong it restrains judgment. He has made the Holy Spirit available, which gives me the power to override the pull of sin! We are "quickened", or made alive by the Holy Spirit.

Ephesians 2:6. Even though we have a sinful nature and even though we have sin in our lives, God allows us to have a glimpse and a taste of heavenly places. I have experienced an overpowering presence of God in my life from time to time. I have felt God so strongly that I couldn't stand up and I felt like I would burst open! I can't even imagine what it would be like to have that 24/7. It's a good thing our bodies will be changed (I Corinthians 15:51-52)! I don't think our physical bodies can handle pure, 100% God's presence!

Ephesians 2:9-10. When I act upon the faith imbedded in me by God, God's favor is extended to me, even though it is unmerited. I can't do enough good works to earn my salvation. There are a lot of good people doing good things in this world. However, their good deeds don't reserve their spot in Heaven. I am God's "good deed" (vs 10), therefore, any good deed I do is from Him. The closer I get to God, the more good deeds I will do. My relationship with God will produce good deeds, but my good deeds don't produce a relationship with God. Some people get the cart before the horse and put people in Heaven because they were "good". Not so. Our goodness is like a filthy rag compared to God (Isaiah 64:6). I can't get good to get God. I get God to get good!

Ephesians 2:11-19. God made mankind. He did not make Jews or Gentiles. He made mankind. However, through the course of time, God chose to specifically communicate with a particular person, Abraham, because of Abraham's extraordinary faith. God made certain promises to Abraham concerning Abraham's descendants. How God loves us to respond to Him! How many billions of people have been blessed because of Abraham's faith? His descendants don't all live for God and yet, they are blessed because God does not go back on His promises. Abraham's descendants are the Jews. God's plan was for the Jews to be so blessed other nations would want to live for God (Malachi 3:12). For a period of time, from Moses to Jesus, there was a very strict set of ceremonial laws in place which separated the Jewish people from other religions. Outsiders had to convert to Judaism in order to be saved. When Jesus came, He fulfilled the law. The ceremonial laws of Moses were abolished and God's moral law was written on our hearts by the infilling of the Holy Spirit (vs 18). (See discussion in Galatians.) Jews and Gentiles alike can experience salvation through the same Spirit!

Ephesians 2:20-22. My foundation must be upon Jesus and the teachings of the apostles. Matthew, Mark, Luke and John are biographies of the life of Jesus, written by His disciples, and mostly recorded what Jesus DID. I note Jesus had a lot of teaching time with the disciples. The content of all his teaching isn't recorded (John 21:25). I'm sure their time together wasn't spent playing Monopoly! Through the letters of the apostles to the body of believers (Romans-Revelation), we can learn what all Jesus instructed them to teach. Jesus only had three years to get people to "buy in" to the idea of a spiritual redeemer. This was very radical! The Jews at that time were looking for a physical redeemer, not a spiritual one. They thought they were (spiritually) just fine! Jesus was only able to get them to first base (belief)! Peter got them to second base (plan of salvation). The teachings of the apostles got them to third base (holy living). The still-abiding Holy Spirit dwelling inside gets us home (to Heaven). I cannot discount the teachings of the Apostles. Jesus is the corner stone, sure, but the teachings of the Apostles are also part of the whole foundation.

Ephesians 3:7. Is the power of God within me working effectively? Am I allowing for that, or do I quench the Spirit (I Thessalonians 5:19)? God is only able to do what I allow Him to do (Ephesians 3:20). He is able, but only according to the amount of His power I allow to work in my life. Do I quench the flow, or is my faucet wide open, allowing Him to do a great work in me?

Ephesians 3:8. God's riches cannot be exhausted! It is mind blowing to think about that. God has *everything* at His disposal. Well, He is everything!! There is no limit to His love. There is no limit to His ability to provide. There is no limit to His healing powers. There is no limit to His strength. There is no limit with God!! If I will partner with God, nothing is impossible (Philippians 4:13).

Ephesians 3:11-14. The eternal purpose of God is for everything to come under His lordship. Mankind put itself under the lordship of Satan, so God had to buy us back. Whatever trials and troubles I go through for the kingdom of God is nothing.

Ephesians 3:17-19. "Christianity" means to be full of Christ's character. Since God is love (I John 4:8), to be a Christian, I must be full of love. I must pray for an understanding of true, pure love. I must unlearn man's definition of love (conditional), and learn God's definition of love (unconditional). Love (like grace) is not to be misconstrued to mean that God loves us so much He will allow our sinful selves to be in Heaven with Him. Love means He loves us so much, He gives us the opportunity to be saved (John 3:16).

Ephesians 3:20. This scripture is often misused! God is able to do anything, yes. However, He won't do what I can do. God is not a magic wand I can waive around and things happen. I must do what I can do. *Example:* God can cause someone to give me an awesome job. However, unless I am qualified and actually apply for that job, I will never get that call! The same goes for spiritual things. God can reveal things to me, however, unless I spend some time learning to hear His voice, He won't speak to me. I qualify myself by:
- praying, talking to God.
- studying His word.
- thinking (meditating) upon spiritual things.

The question this verse poses is this: Is the power of God at work in MY life?

Ephesians 4:3-6. I don't have a kingdom. I am a part of God's kingdom. I have a role to play. It doesn't matter how small or large my role is. Too many Christians are out to build their own kingdoms. Who has the largest church? Whose choir is the best? What churches have the best dramas? NO, NO, NO! It is not about what position I hold. It is about whether or not I perform my duties well, as unto the Lord. Sometimes we get so cocky God has to knock us down a notch or two so we can be saved! I've seen whole churches become full of pride, God had to allow them to split. That's painful. Wouldn't it be better if I humbled myself?

Ephesians 4:11-13. The five-fold ministry was a gift to the church, given *after* Jesus ascended.

The *purpose* of this ministry is to:
- perfect the church body in order that the body will minister to others.
- uplift and edify the church body.

The *goal* is to:
- Be unified in the doctrine, and
- have an intimate relationship with Jesus so we can be mature.

The goal for each believer is set in verse 13. The believer's goal is not to make it to heaven. The believer's goal is to BE LIKE JESUS!

Ephesians 4:14; 5:6. We have to be careful not to be swayed by the great oratory skills of another. The Scripture has been given. Who am I to argue with it? There are so many doctrines floating around, how can I know which is right? I must be a student of the Scripture and not another's interpretation of it. Satan's greatest tactic is to deceive. That's the trick he pulled in the Garden with Eve, remember? My spiritual house must be built upon the rock and not sand (Matthew 7:24-27). Sand is ground up particles of rock. Spiritual sand is bits and pieces of truth, but not solid truth.

There are enough impurities in sand to render it soft and movable. I cannot afford to have a little bit of truth mixed with false doctrine. I must be on solid rock. Jesus plainly declared "the rock" was the revelation of who He is (Matthew 16:18).

Ephesians 4:15-16. There's a right way and a wrong way to expound on truth. The cut and dry harsh statement of facts leads to pharisee-ism. The right way to present truth is in LOVE (John 15:12-17). I must be mature and explain things in love to a hungry heart, not beat them up over the head! My teaching must edify.

Ephesians 4:17-19. The mindset of the sinner is:
- Pride.
- Ignorant of God's ways.
- *Trajectory of heart* pointed in the wrong direction.
- Sexual perversions.
- Greedy.

Ephesians 4:22-25. To be like Jesus! This requires a mind transplant! My mind must be renewed. This means to begin anew - to get back to its original state! God wants me to get back to the original state He intended for man to be in the Garden! The *trajectory of my heart* dictates the thoughts of my mind, which in turn, dictates my actions.

Ephesians 4:27. I really like this verse. It is pretty cut and dry ~ simple ~ *IT'S NOT ROCKET SCIENCE*!! Don't give the devil an inch; he'll take a mile. Sin will take you/me further than we ever intended to go (II Timothy 2:16). (See essay entitled, "Playing by the Mailbox" in *It's Not Rocket Science, Volume 1.*)

Ephesians 4:29-32. Sandwiched between verses which talk about sins of the mouth, is a sentence that says "grieve not the holy Spirit of God". This leads me to believe the vile things that come out of my mouth are grievous to God. The *trajectory of my heart* is (eventually) exposed by my mouth (Matthew 12:34; Luke 6:45). I can't control my tongue ~ whatever is inside just blurts out (James 3:8). I need to surrender to the Holy Spirit so good things will burst forth from me! The mindset of a believer is to:
- Be honest;
- Not to allow anger to give way to sin;
- Not to steal;
- Be a hard worker;
- Only speak of good and edifying things;
- Not to grieve the Holy Spirit *(See notes at Galatians 2:21; 5:31; and Philippians 4:5.)*
- Not to be bitter;
- Not to always be angry and wrathful;

- Not to constantly complain or join others in an uproar (clamor);
- Not to want to "get back" at someone (malice);
- Not to speak evil of others;
- Be kind;
- Be compassionate (tenderhearted); and
- Be forgiving.

Ephesians 5:3-5. People who joke about holy things make me uncomfortable. In the list of ungodly things, "foolish talking" and "jesting" are mentioned. I don't think this means we can never tell a joke. I believe this has to do with spiritual matters. I shouldn't make fun of the way someone worships, etc. ~ or make fun of the way someone sins. I've known of people who jested about certain sins in their youth, only to succumb to the same sin later in life.

Ephesians 5:6-7, 11-12. We've talked before about not allowing people to deceive us into believing something contrary to the word of God. The best way to prevent that is to not associate with them! I must be friendly and loving to all, but I can't be buddy-buddy with an apostate. My focus and *trajectory* are in an opposite direction than theirs and they will get me off track, if I am not careful. Apostates are those who have once believed the truth and departed from it. Apostates or reprobates are on a mission to convince me to go down their path. That's how they justify themselves. The more they can get to walk with them, the more their conscience is soothed. The disobedient will experience the wrath of God. Why would I want to be anywhere close to them when that happens? I am to separate myself and have no fellowship with them. It's even a shame to talk about their activities! Oops! Sandwiched between these two passages (vs 9-10) is an admonition that my actions (my behavior) proves my heart. Ultimately, the *trajectory of the heart* plays out in my actions. I may be able to cover up my trajectory for a little while and fake out others, but ultimately, it comes out through my behavior.

Ephesians 5:16-21. How do I stay full of the Spirit? How can I be wise? How can I make the most of my time here on earth? How do I understand what is God's will for me? I do that by:
- Not getting drunk with wine (Satan's counterfeit for the Spirit), but with the Spirit (vs 18),
- Speaking of spiritual things (vs 19),
- Singing of spiritual things (vs 19),
- Having an attitude of thanksgiving (vs 20), and
- Submitting to each other (vs 21).

Ephesians 5:22-25. What does it mean to submit? What does it mean to love? The famous scripture that has been lorded over females for years is found in Ephesians 5:22-25. Wives are to submit. Some people overlook the fact that husbands are to love! First of all, wives are to submit to their own husbands, not everyone else's (Titus 2:5)! This is not a statement that all women must kowtow to all men. Now, having gotten that out of the way, let's talk about the difference between submitting and loving. Whenever I see the blue lights in my rear-view mirror, I submit and pull over. I have no particular love for the police officer, but I submit. It is quite possible to submit without love. On the other hand, it is impossible to love without submitting! Christ loved the church so much that He submitted His life to the cross (Philippians 2:8; 3:10; Hebrews 5:8). When you love someone, you put their desires before your own. How many times has a mother given her piece of cake (or her last dollar) to her child? Loving someone is a whole lot harder than submitting. Love requires more. This scripture comes on the heels of (1) being filled with the Spirit, (2) singing spiritual songs, and (3) giving thanks always (vs. 18-20). It also comes right after the admonition for us all to submit to each other (vs 21). This submission to each other is actually the subject matter. The marital submission is an example used to enforce the concept of submission. When my vertical relationship with God is correct, my horizontal relationship with others, including my spouse, will be correct. The *reason* for the submit/love relationship is found in verse 26-27: That the church would be the spotless bride of Christ. This is why men should love their wives as much as they love themselves (vs 28-29, 33). Love is a more excellent way than submitting (I Corinthians 13). My father is the epitome of loving so much he submits. When it became apparent that Mother (with Alzheimer's) had to go into a nursing home to receive proper care, Dad wrestled with whether or not he had to go as well. He really wanted to stay in the assisted living facility. We all knew without Mother's help, he could not stay by himself in an assisted living facility but, I dreaded having to tell him he had to go to a nursing home too. I also didn't want the facility to kick him out. He ultimately made the decision for himself. He called me after a few days and stated that he felt he was not keeping his marital vows if he was in a different place than Mother! He goes to her unit and visits her multiple times a day. It is so difficult for him since she rambles, gets confused, and stresses over everything, real or imagined. However, he faithfully subjects himself to all of that because of love! He epitomizes the love Christ has for the church. It amazes me.

Ephesians 5:29-33. Marriage is a God-made institution and not a man-made one. For mankind to try to redefine marriage is to highjack God's creation. Marriage is a symbol of and is to reflect the relationship between Christ & the church. This is why sexual sins are so grievous to God. Sexual activity outside of a marital relationship between a husband and wife is symbolic of a spiritual condition with something other than God (Jeremiah 3). God hates that and punishes that! This is why Satan tempts mankind so strongly with any type of sexual sin. It blows my mind at the number of tenants I have who are not married, and yet are faithful and active members of a church. Somebody is not reading or preaching the Bible! I don't know why God chose the marital relationship to represent His relationship with us ~ neither did Paul (vs 32)!

Ephesians 6:1-3. Once the marital relationship is correct, the relationship between parents and children will fall into place. Honoring parents contains a promise of longevity (Exodus 20:12). Parents are to nurture (care for) the spiritual life of the child (vs 4). There is a difference between making a child angry and provoking a child to wrath. Anytime a parent disagrees with a child, the child will get angry. Damaging their spirits provokes a child to wrath. A child may, from time to time, not like a parent, but honoring is a commandment.

Ephesians 6:5-9. The Bible does not promote slavery. The Bible recognizes that slavery exists and gives guidelines on how slaves should be treated and how slaves should act. *[Slavery is actually condemned in I Timothy 1:10.]* In cultures where slavery, per se, does not exist, this scripture would apply to the employee/employer relationship. Employees are to give the employer an honest day and the employer should treat the employee well. We all reap what we sow (vs 8) and there is no respecter of persons with God (vs 9).

Ephesians 6:11-17. God has given us a suit of armor. It is up to ME to put it on. It won't do me any good stuffed in the pages of the Bible! I've got to put it on and be ready for battle. Ready or not, Satan is coming at me from all sides! He will even attack me through the wickedness of my leaders (vs 12)! I know this. I have been duly warned. Therefore, I must put on and WEAR the WHOLE armor of God. I must also keep an attitude of God consciousness at all times (vs 18). The only part of me that the armor of God does not cover is my back. I have no protection if I turn around. I can't go back to my sin. The glory of the Lord is my rear guard (Isaiah 58:8). His glory pushes me from behind. I must guard His glory. Ezekiel 28 talks about a war being waged in Heaven. Besides being a chief musician, Lucifer's primary ministry was to cover or protect. God gave him this job (Ezekiel 28:14). Lucifer was honored above all of the other angels, but his vanity caused him to rebel. Vanity marred Lucifer's ability to reason (Ezekiel 28:17). He was so proud of his beauty, he forgot about his relationship with God, his maker. When Lucifer was cast out of Heaven, he lost his job of being the guard of God's glory. God subsequently delegated that job to mankind. In the Old Testament, the guarding of the glory was symbolized by the cherubim who covered the mercy seat in the tabernacle (Exodus 25:20-22). God promised to meet and talk with man at that place. The guarding of the glory is now symbolized by hair (I Corinthians 11:7, 10, 15). As all jilted or jealous people, Lucifer tempts men and women to meddle with the covering because it symbolizes to Lucifer everything he lost. Hair signals to the spirit world whether we are in rebellion or in submission. The angels can tell by looking (I Corinthians 11:10). The armor of God protects my front. The glory of God pushes and sustains me from behind. I MUST protect the glory.

PHILIPPIANS

Written to the church already established. Themes: Triumph in suffering. Joy, Christian living.

Philippians 1:6. It is a comfort to know the Holy Spirit CONTINUES to work in me! God is not finished molding and making me. It is a process. He is timeless, so He sees me as the finished product. I'm not there yet, but He keeps working on me! On the flip side, God is not finished with everyone else, either. Therefore, I must be patient with others. As long as I continue to ALLOW God to move, He will keep moving and working! We are continually to strive for perfection in Christ (Philippians 3:14).

Philippians 1:9-11. Love is the ever-recurring theme of the Bible. Love must be front and center of all of my judgments, perceptions, and sensibilities. The REASON love must rule is so I don't offend others. Since God is Love (I John 4:8), it stands to reason I must have the Holy Spirit of God dwelling in me to the fullest (vs 11). When I am disgusted with someone, I must check my "love-o-meter" and pray for love and compassion for them. Without love, my judgment, sense, and perception will be off kilter.

Philippians 1:12-14. Bad things happen to good people. God can use those bad things to advance the gospel. I must look at the big picture. Am I willing to go through bad times in order for someone to be saved? Is the ***trajectory of my heart*** in the right place? Am I willing to go through cancer treatment in order to witness to a doctor, nurse or technician? People can intentionally do me wrong, but God can use that for good (Genesis 50:20; Romans 8:28). Royalty would have never had a witness if Paul had not been bound and brought before them. Fellow Christians received strength and boldness from Paul's attitude in his situation. My father is steadily witnessing in the nursing home and has submitted some names to a local pastor to follow up. These are people he would have never come in contact with if he was not living there. What if he was their only witness? Surely eternity is worth a few years of temporary suffering. I don't have a wish to suffer, of course, but if I am faced with that in my life, will I have the right attitude? Can I be content in my horrible situation (Philippians 4:11), trusting God has a master plan and I am playing a role in it?

Philippians 1:15-18. Regardless of the motive, if the gospel is being preached, then souls are being saved. Some preachers do have the wrong motives. Some are just trying to make some money. Love is the *correct* motive. However, if the true gospel is being preached (even with the wrong motive) and the listener receives it and is saved, it is a good thing. God will anoint His word. This does NOT mean God approves of the messenger. It simply means the message (gospel) is approved.

I can't get my eyes on people. There are hypocrites even within ministerial ranks. I can't discount the gospel just because the messenger is not living right. I must not confuse God's anointing with God's approval. God will continue to "woo" and "court" people. God will allow people to feel His presence even if they are not living right. God will respond to praise and worship by people who aren't living right. God will respond to faith by people who aren't living right. They will feel His presence and will be touched. Their prayer of faith will even get answered. This doesn't mean He approves or condones that life. It just means He is honoring His word. My mother related an incident to me. She was 17 when she first began living for God. There was a musician in the church who she KNEW (for a fact) was living in sin. Marvin would be greatly moved on by God and would shout and talk in tongues when the spirit of God moved. Mother was very confused by this and went to God for an answer. God told her He wasn't condoning Marvin's life, but He (God) was trying to show Marvin that living for Him would be a more rewarding life. God was trying to "woo" Marvin into fully surrendering to Him. Marvin didn't, and eventually quit going to church. An encounter with God will change me. I cannot leave the same. God will deal with me for a long time, but I can't straddle the fence indefinitely. I will either surrender to God, or fall off into deeper sin.

Philippians 1:21-26. I live to die! That sounds strange, doesn't it? My death is inevitable. Therefore, I must die right. I have absolutely no control over what happens to me AFTER I die. I have control of my destiny BEFORE I die. Therefore, I live with death in mind. I have made up my mind that Heaven is my destination. Therefore, death is a welcome thing. Death is free from pain and worries and life with Jesus! What joy! In the meantime, I do have some joy here on earth. The advantage of staying here on earth is to help someone else on their journey to Heaven. The people I want to help the most are my family and loved ones. Hopefully, my writings will help someone.

Philippians 1:27. Does my behavior, my lifestyle, reflect Christ? Do I fight for the faith? Can I live Christ-like even if no one around me does? Can I stand with God? Will I fight for the faith (Jude 1:3)?

Philippians 1:28. My Christian life is a beacon to sinners and a reminder they are not living right. I will not be intimidated by sneers or persecution from them. This world is not my home! I am only passing through it on my way to Heaven!

Philippians 1:29. Living for God is not always fun. Even a bed of roses, as beautiful and fragrant as it is, has thorns! There is some suffering in living for God; either by specific persecution from others, or by denying myself of carnal pleasures. My Christian lifestyle is a sacrifice unto God. I am willing to live a life pleasing to God because He has made a way for me to enter into Heaven.

Philippians 2:1-11. Here we go with love again! Love is putting others above myself. Love is NOT being selfish or conceited. If I have the mind of Christ (who is God, and God is love – I John 4:8), I will love. To emphasize the importance of love, Paul spells out exactly how Jesus put His love in action. Because of that love, God exalted the flesh of Jesus. Mankind will ultimately bow and acknowledge His lordship (vs. 5-11).

QUESTIONS (vs 1):
- Does your life in Christ give you strength?
- Does his love comfort you?
- Do we share together in the Spirit?
- Do you have mercy and kindness?

THEN make me (Paul) happy by (vs 2-4):
- Sharing my thought.
- Sharing the same love.
- Having one mind [heart; soul].
- Having the same purpose.
- Being ruled by humility.
- Having the mind of Christ..

Philippians 2:5-8. What does it mean to have the mind of Christ? Verse 5 plainly states I am to have the same mental state as Christ. What does that entail? Jesus knew exactly who He was. He was God Almighty. However, He took on the attitude of a servant and lived as a human man. He took the humble route and even submitted Himself to the cross. He could have zapped His opponents into oblivion, but He yielded His almighty power to their puny power and submitted to the cross. This goes against all of the "name it and claim it" preaching, doesn't it? I hear preachers tout that a child of God doesn't have to put up with ... xyz. Jesus sure did!

Philippians 2:12. I must be serious about working out my own personal convictions. There are some absolutes I adhere to from Biblical principles. However, there are some things that are sin for me and not for someone else. These things have to do with my personal temptations and my personality. I must judge myself and analyze myself in order to see what areas I am weak in (I Corinthians 11:28-31). My weaknesses may not be the same as someone else's. I must take a harsh, critical look at my tendencies. We all have sin in our lives and we all have a predominate sin particularly difficult to overcome (Psalm 51:5). The obvious ones are addictions or immorality. The less obvious ones are a tendency to not be truthful, a tendency to be judgmental of others, etc. The scientific community tells us some of these things are "diseases" (such as addiction to alcohol). The scientific/medical communities tell us a gene is different in people with addictions and they just can't help it. Yep! I agree. That "gene" is called "sin". When I honestly examine my own self and identify MY sinful tendencies, I can work on overcoming them through the power of the Holy Spirit. *THE* Judgment Day is later, but we have to make choices daily. When I have an encounter with God, I have to judge myself. When I have an encounter with God, I realize my sin and have the opportunity to repent and get it eradicated from my life. That point is the beginning of the daily judging of myself. Judgment begins with the household of God (I Peter 4:17). When I am a member of the household of God, I realize the need for self-judgment. When I hear a convicting sermon preached, I realize my need for repentance. When I have an intimate relationship with God, I realize my need for *trajectory* correction. God established that precedent in the Old Testament (Amos 5:15; Ezekiel 9:4-6). In other words, a Christian must judge him/herself first before judging others. This is consistent with Jesus' teachings (John 8:7-9).

Philippians 2:14-15. Did you know an attitude can be a sin? Griping, complaining, and arguing are not holy attributes. Those are the attributes of a worldly system. Look through a newspaper! There's a lot of strife in this world and very few peacemakers. I am supposed to be the light in darkness. I am supposed to be a peacemaker (Matthew 5:9). My parents taught us to look for the other side of every argument. They taught us to look for a reason why a person acts the way they do, so we would have a greater understanding and compassion for them. My husband and I own a shipping business. One of our drivers always comes in grumbling about how many packages we have to ship out. She mutters under her breath the entire time she is in the store. We dread her coming in every day. A Christian should not be like that! The joy of the Lord should be bubbling up in us (John 7:38; Nehemiah 8:10).

Philippians 2:15. I am a light to the world (Matthew 5:14). If I don't shine brightly, how will others see the pathway to Christ? My countenance, my actions and my appearance reflect my inward attitude, which reveals the *trajectory of my heart*. It serves no purpose to appear holy and have a sour look on my face! Jesus said He was the light of the world (John 8:12). On the surface, it appears that the Bible is contradicting itself, however that is never the correct train of thought. I must dig deeper. Jesus is the light. When I have His spirit dwelling inside of me, I reflect His light. The moon does not have light in itself. It merely reflects the light of the sun. When nothing is obstructing the rays from the sun, the moon reflects the light bright enough to illuminate the path. Likewise, I must not allow anything to obstruct my reflection of Jesus. What is an obstruction? Sin. *It's not rocket science!*

Philippians 2:21; 1:15; 3:2. I get tired of people lamenting and longing for the church of today to be just like the early church. They had the same problems! They had plenty of minsters who had the wrong motives. In fact, to hear Paul tell it, it sounds like ALL of them except for Timothy were corrupt (vs 19-20)! People are people. There is nothing new under the sun (Ecclesiastes 1:9). There is no point in longing for the past. The grass wasn't any greener than it is right now. I just need to make sure I'm not the corrupt one and make sure that the ***trajectory of my heart*** is right.

Philippians 2:27. We all go through sorrow. Life beats us up some times. In the midst of our sorrow, however, God is there with mercy!

Philippians 2:25-30. Apparently Epaphroditus ministered to Paul without regard of his own health. Others should have stepped up to the plate (vs 30), but didn't, so Epaphroditus trudged on. He shares Paul's reward (Matthew 25:40-45). It doesn't matter which role I play in the kingdom of God. What matters is I play my role well and faithfully.

Philippians 3:2. FYI: Body mutilation (concision in the KJV) is wrong (Leviticus 19:28; 21:5). We are to stay away from that. Those things are associated with spiritual (evil) practices.

Philippians 3:4-7. Spiritual pedigree does not bring salvation. I must have my own experience with God! God has children, but no grand-children. At some point, if a child raised by devout Christian parents does not develop his/her own relationship, s/he will not live for God as an adult. This is personal.

Philippians 3:10. Suffering can bring me closer to Jesus, if I will let it. Suffering will either make me bitter or better. It's my choice. Suffering can help me relate to Christ more and I develop a deeper understanding and appreciation for what He did for me. Shared experiences bring two people closer. They can relate to what each other has gone through. There is fellowship with Christ in my suffering.

Philippians 3:12-14. My battle with sin isn't over. I won't be saved until my life is over. However, I pursue salvation so I can ultimately lay hold of it. How? By
- Discarding my previous shortcomings,
- Looking to future victories, and
- Pressing forward and pursuing the goal of Christ being duplicated in me!

This is God's goal for me (Colossians 1:27).

Philippians 3:15-17. I can't take a frivolous attitude about my salvation. I can't blindly follow someone's lead just because they have great personality. I must carefully mark those who believe and preach the truth. I must ask God to reveal to me those who do not practice pure Christianity. We all have people we look up to. I must be careful who I look up to and who I allow to lead me in life.

Philippians 3:18-19. Those who stray from the truth are enemies of Christ. Wow! That's not politically correct, but that's the truth. Hanging around them will do me no good, because they are headed in the wrong direction. I don't want to get tangled up in their trajectory. I often tell people who don't believe a portion of the Bible to just take a pair of scissors and cut it out. They are appalled and say they could never do that, but by their disobedience, they are doing exactly that! When I was a teenager, there was a girl in the seminary who got mad at someone and slashed her Bible with a knife. An evil spirit entered her. Her family refused to let her live with them, so she had no place to go but to stay at the church. She required constant watching so she wouldn't destroy herself. I took a turn babysitting her. She would eat the linoleum and lunge at me, snarling and clawing. When I spoke the name of Jesus, she would cower in the corner like a wounded animal. During times of sanity, I would talk to her about Jesus and try to get her to repent. I wasn't with her the day she finally repented. When she did, the evil spirit was cast out and she came back to her right mind. This is a very drastic example of what happens when I cut out the Bible, whether literally or by my disobedience. I may not become demon possessed and lose my sanity as this girl did, but it is still sin and puts me on the wrong side of God!

Philippians 3:20-21. Guess what!!! My future looks bright! There is a great reward ahead if I hold fast to the faith. It will be worth it all when I see Jesus.

Philippians 4:3. *News flash*! There were women on Paul's ministerial team!

Philippians 4:5. More and more I'm seeing articles in magazines touting the reasons when a little lie would be okay. They are teaching the public that the ends justify the means. It really makes me angry when I see these articles. This rationale also goes with other little sins. When the apostle said "let your moderation be known", he wasn't giving us license to sin moderately. I wonder what your friend would say if you told her/him you had spent a little time with her/his spouse: Not a full-blown affair, but just "a little"; a moderate affair. Crazy, right? But that's what people do with God. People diligently go to church and go through the motions of religion, but they turn around and "sin a little", assuming God will overlook their sin because of their church attendance. That is a misuse of God's grace and mercy! I can't sin moderately and go to Heaven. The Bible defines sin; not humans. *Example:* A white lie is still a lie and will cost me my soul's salvation (Revelation 21:8). I had a boss who always told me to tell callers that he was in court if he was concentrating on something and couldn't talk to them. I told him I couldn't lie. He agreed to let me say, "Mr. XYZ is unable to take your call right now." [PS: "Moderation" in Philippians 4:5 is also translated as: gentleness; kindness; consideration; patience; modesty; graciousness... puts a different spin on it, eh?]

Philippians 4:5-9. We are to think on good things. What is in my heart will come out (Luke 6:45; Matthew 12:34). It will come out in my speech and what I post on social media. It will show on my face. I need to control my mind so it dwells on pure things. I need to feed my mind so it dwells on pure things. I will be careful what I watch, read, and see (Psalm 101:3). What is the correct attitude (<u>*trajectory of my heart*</u>) I should have?
- Be moderate (not excessive, but gentle; kind; considerate; patient; modest;

gracious).
- Not worry.
- Pray.
- Be filled with peace.

Philippians 4:12-13. When I have the correct attitude, I can get through the tough times because Christ strengthens me. I receive strength by waiting on God's timing (Isaiah 40:31).

Philippians 4:19. This scripture has a two-fold meaning. (1) God will take care of our basic needs (Matthew 6:28; Luke 12:27). (2) All that I really need is God because HE is the source of all blessings (Matthew 6:33). If my daughter goes to the mall with $25.00 in her pocket and sees a shirt she wants for $24.95, she is out of luck because she won't have enough to pay for the shirt with tax. However, if she goes to the mall *with me* and $25.00 in her pocket, she can get that shirt because I am her source. I will happily give her the extra few dollars to add to her $25.00. If I get the source (God), blessings will flow (Proverbs 22:4). God knows exactly what I need (Matthew 6:32). He also knows what I want, but sometimes what I want and what I need are in conflict with each other. Sometimes what I want may end up being a detriment to my spiritual life. I trust Him to give me what I need.

COLOSSIANS
Written to the church already established. Themes: Duties & life of the Christian; Refuting a particular heresy (Chapter 2).

The **deity of Christ** is outlined in Colossians. Jesus is ...
- Image of invisible God (1:15).
- First born (preeminent) of creation (1:15).
- Creator of all (1:16).
- Goal of creation (1:16).
- Omnipresent (1:17).
- Eternal (1:17).
- Head of the church (1:18; 2:19).
- Beginning (1:18).
- Victorious over death (1:18).
- Fulness of Godhead (1:19; 2:9).
- Reconciler (1:20).
- Spirit dwelling in man (1:27).
- Omniscient (2:3).

- Object of my faith (2:5).
- Realm of spiritual life (2:6).
- Source of spiritual nourishment (2:7) and life (3:4).
- Foundation (2:7).
- Omnipotent (2:10).
- Completeness (2:10).
- Coming in glory (3:4).

Social Climate. By the time the book of Colossians was written, heresy had crept into the church. It doesn't take long for the secular to influence the church, does it? We must be careful not to allow worldly influences affect the church. It has been an ongoing problem. Gnosticism was the prevailing philosophy at the time. Gnosticism was a mixture of Greek, Oriental and mystical ideas with Jewish and Christian thoughts adopted in ... a layer cake religion! The basic theology of Gnosticism is:
- ALL matter is evil, and
- ALL spirit is good.

Therefore, the Gnostics believed:
- Since the human body is made of matter, it could never do good. Therefore, the body can do anything it wants. As long as the spirit was in tune with God, what the body did was okay. This makes for very loose morals!
- Since flesh and spirit could not intermingle, Jesus could not have been both God and human.
- The Gnostics based salvation on a mystical experience and knowledge (gnosis). Scriptures were not to be interpreted literally.

This theology sounds a lot like today's theology. I live in an area that embraces Mardi Gras. The idea is that you can live the way you wish and just confess to a "man of God", who will forgive you. It's all the same spirit as in Paul's day. There's nothing new under the sun (Ecclesiastes 1:9). It may be a different verse, but it is all part of the same song.

Pros of "being in Christ". A huge theme of Colossians is being one with Christ. Truly, if we would all be like Jesus, there wouldn't be any church problems!!! Being like Him is a goal. Heaven is my destination, but being like Him is my goal.
- It is Heaven's dream (1:27).
- I will be complete (perfect) (2:10).
- I will have wisdom & knowledge (2:2-3).
- I will be dead to sin (2:12, 20).
- I will be raised with Him (2:12).
- I will appear with Him in glory (3:4).
- I will have peace (3:15).
- I will receive the reward of inheritance (3:24).

How to become *in* Christ. A goal is nice to have, but without a plan to achieve that goal, it will fizzle into just a dream. Fortunately, Paul teaches us the steps to becoming one with Christ.
- Continue in the original doctrine that was taught (1:23).
- Guard against false doctrine (2:4, 8, 18).
- Be thankful (2:7; 3:15, 17; 4:2).
- Get *trajectory* pointed to Heaven (3:2).
- Take precautions and strengthen myself against sin (3:5).
- Put off ungodly emotions & sin (3:8).
- Forgive others (3:13).
- Be gentle and gracious with others (3:12).
- Love others (3:14).
- Treat others right (4:1)
- Be prayerful (4:2).
- Speak wisely (4:6) - that means think before speaking!

Colossians 1:3-9. Intercessory prayer is always accompanied by love and thanksgiving. Intercessory prayer is really just praying for others. I am interceding on behalf of someone else. Many times, it does go in to travail (deep, fervent prayers), but all praying on behalf of others is interceding.

Colossians 1:4. "In" Christ. The word "in" comes from the Greek preposition "en", which denotes a fixed position. This is consistent with other scriptures which tell us to be rooted, grounded, and unshakeable (Psalm 1:3; Ephesians 3:17). Regardless of the way the winds of society and culture blow, I must be fixed with Jesus. He is my anchor and the anchor holds well in all storms! When I am fixed with Christ, I will be a conduit for His love of others. Love is the supreme evidence of ongoing salvation (John 13:34-35). Love for God will cause me to live a life pleasing to Him. Love for others will cause me to treat my neighbor right. *ALL* sin is a result of a lack of love in one of those two areas. This is consistent with Jesus' teaching in Luke 10:27-28.

Colossians 1:9-14. Full knowledge of God, both intellectual and via experience, enables me to be transformed and to live right. It is not enough to have a head knowledge of God. The Israelites had a head knowledge of God (Psalm 103:7). I must know Him by experience. Moses had the experience (Psalm 103:7). When I internalize Him, I become one with Him and He puts HIS desires into my heart (Psalm 37:4). I must be "in Christ" (Colossians 1:14), which means to be surrounded by Christ ~ a continual relationship! When I am surrounded by Him, I will have:
- Wisdom.
- Spiritual understanding.
- A worthy walk.

- Increasing in knowledge.
- Fruitfulness (re: fruit of the Spirit ~ Galatians 5:22-24, which is love, joy, peace, longsuffering, gentleness, goodness, faith, meekness, temperance).
- Strength (according to His power).
- Patience.
- Longsuffering accompanied by joyfulness.
- Thankfulness.
- Qualification to inherit eternal life.
- Deliverance from power of darkness.
- Translated into the kingdom.
- Redemption & forgiveness.

Now, why wouldn't I want to develop all of these characteristics? We've got to change our outlook on things. Instead of focusing on the negative (can't do this and can't do that or I'll go to hell), let's focus on the BENEFITS of living for God while here on this earth! Why wouldn't I want those attributes in my life?

Colossians 1:13-19. Jesus is the visible image of an invisible Spirit. It's that simple. *It's not rocket science!*

Colossians 1:20. Sin separates us from God (Psalm 5:4). The blood of Jesus reconciles us to God. Since we are all sinners (Romans 3:23; 5:12), how could God even tolerate us? There had to be a mediator. Who is qualified to bridge the gap between sinful man and a holy God? A bull or goat? No! Only a sinless man could bridge the gap. Who could that possibly be since all men are sinners? God had to come Himself in flesh. Jesus is the visible expression of God (John 1:1-14). Therefore, although Jesus had a fleshly body and was tempted (Hebrews 4:15), He was not under the BONDAGE of sin, which was passed on from the human father's blood (Exodus 34:7). He was tempted, yes, but not forced (bondage) to sin, because His father was the spirit of God (Matthew 1:18). When Jesus died, He was sinless. He had overcome all of his temptations. The role or office of the son is one of redemption. This "sonship" is what mediates between God and man (I Timothy 2:5; Hebrews 8:6; 9:15; 12:24). The flesh of Jesus is the common denominator between God and man (Colossians 1:22). Jesus is the head of the church and thus, holds it all together (Colossians 1:17).

Colossians 1:23. I can be reconciled to God ONLY if I am rooted and grounded in the faith *and* I don't depart from it.

Colossians 1:27. The absolute theme of all of the Epistles (letters to the church: Romans - Jude) is summed up in Colossians 1:27 (Also Galatians 4:19): Christ in Me! That is the hope of Heaven. Up until the infilling of the Spirit in Acts, the hope of Heaven wasn't clear. The Old Testament was merely a glimpse of hope. The only way I can live a life that overcomes sin is to be filled with, and surrender to, His spirit. The first recording of this happening was in Acts 2:4. God longs for me to be so full of Him that I am an extension of Him (Luke 6:40). I am only complete when I am IN Him. I am "in Him" when His precepts are in my heart. Circumcision of the heart is when my sinful nature is cut off and He is grafted in my heart. How does this happen? When I am baptized and receive the Holy Spirit (Colossians 2:11-12).

Colossians 2:4. Do I want to be smart & wise? I need to get to know Jesus. God "hid all the treasures of wisdom and knowledge" in Jesus. Again, my goal is to be like Jesus! Wisdom and knowledge will come when I develop my relationship with Him!

Colossians 2:4-8. It is possible for me to get off course through human reasoning and logic. I am to BEWARE of:
- Man-made traditions and
- Rationalization.

So many times, we talk to each other instead of taking things to God. Sometimes that is okay, but other times, we can get off track doctrinally. I must remember to compare everything to God's WORD and not to a person's philosophy. Even if I don't understand the "why" of something in the scripture, I must obey. The understanding will come later. Either God will reveal it to me, or I will understand once I get to Heaven (I Corinthians 13:12). Scripture interprets scripture. When I don't understand a certain scripture, I can find its meaning within the Bible itself. I need to dig a little and pray that God will open up my understanding. This is what is meant by "seek and ye shall find" (Matthew 7:7; Luke 11:9). God is not playing hide and go seek with us, but He wants us to search out the scriptures and hew out a relationship with Him. It takes some effort on my part. Some passages are difficult to understand and require research. I must *want* this enough to work on it. I can't take the lazy way out and just expect to learn everything I need to know from another person. What if they're wrong? I must know for myself what the word of God says!

Colossians 2:9-15. Paul fully declares the deity of Jesus (vs. 9) and that I can only be made perfect if I am full of His spirit (vs. 10). How? By allowing the ***trajectory of my heart*** to be completely changed. In the Old Testament, the symbol of the covenant God made with Abraham was circumcision (Genesis 17:10). The New Testament explains that the physical circumcision of the Old Testament was symbolic of a circumcision of the heart (vs 11). The sinfulness of my heart must be cut away. I must cut away pride and other attitudes. The initial circumcision of my heart is when I am baptized and filled with His Spirit (vs 12). A Jewish male child was not given a name until he was circumcised. I take on the name of Jesus at baptism!

Colossians 2:16-17; 20-22. The ceremonial law (ordinances) of the Old Testament were a tangible (physical) evidence of a spiritual thing. It is fine to commemorate and remember events, but remembering those things without living out those things is hypocrisy. *Example:* There's nothing sinful about keeping the Sabbath. However, the book of Hebrews clearly identifies the physical rest day (Sabbath) as a symbol of the spiritual resting (ceasing) from sin (Hebrews 4:8-10). I live out the Sabbath by not sinning. Thus, I (spiritually) keep the Sabbath on a daily basis. Demanding obedience to a symbolic ordinance without obedience to its spiritual application is non-Biblical. God instituted the ceremony of the Sabbath as a sign of Israel's separation unto God (Ezekiel 20:12). I must separate myself unto God on a daily basis by not sinning!

Colossians 2:18-19. I've seen so many different movements sweep through the Church in my lifetime. These are fads which are not Biblical. A few years ago, it was popular to dispatch angels here and there. That is not my job. That is God's job. Angels are not errand boys to tend to my every whim. It is pure vanity and PRIDE to think that I can order angels around and totally by-pass Jesus. I need to make sure my theology is Bible-based and not just adopt a theology because it sounds good.

Colossians 3:1-2. I do like pretty, elegant and unusual things. My home is decorated with such things from all over the world. I must keep in mind that these things which are precious to me and make me feel all warm and fuzzy with happy memories, are temporal. This was especially brought home to me when my parents had to move into an assisted living facility. Deciding what few things they could take with them was very difficult. After 10 months, we had to move them into a nursing home and all they could bring were a few clothes and pictures. I had to downsize them again! It reminded me of what Job said, "Naked came I ... and naked shall I return" (Job 1:21). Mother kept lamenting that you accumulate things all your life for what? Just to give it to your heirs. What would I grab if my house caught on fire? I think it would be my laptop and my Bible. My laptop because it has most of our pictures digitalized on it and my Bible because it contains a lot of my research and studying. I can't get too bent out of shape with the stuff I've accumulated over the years. This world is not my home! (UPDATE: In 2016, we realized our house would flood overnight. I grabbed my Bible, my laptop, and five days of clothing.)

Colossians 3 is pretty much a repeat of Ephesians chapters 5 & 6 and Philippians chapter 4. The message must be important if it is repeated multiple times.

- Get rid of sins of the mind.
- Be renewed with the mind of Christ (back to the original state of mind God intended mankind to have in the Garden of Eden).
- Love others.
- Be thankful.

- Sing.
- Have correct relationships (both family and employment).
- In all I do, do it with (a) heart and energy, (b) in the name of Jesus, and (c) do it as if I was doing it for God Himself.

Colossians 3:5-6. God's wrath falls on those practicing idolatry. What is idolatry?
- Sexual immorality.
- Impurity (deals with *trajectory of the heart*).
- Lust (Lust is when a desire for "xyz" overwhelms the desire to please God. This can be success, money, fame, sexual pleasure, addictions, etc.).
- Evil desires.
- Greed.

Colossians 3:7. *News Flash!* We have *all* been guilty of sin!

Colossians 3:8-9. There are other weights we need to rid ourselves. They serve only to derail us from the correct *trajectory* (Hebrews 12:1). Isn't it interesting that anger, rage, malice, slander, filthy language, and lying all go hand in hand?

Colossians 3:10-15. Instead of having the attitudes and sins outlined in the above verses, God desires we return to the original state of mind He intended for us to have when we were first created. We were created in HIS image (Genesis 1:27). What characteristics does God have?
- Not a respecter of persons.
- Merciful.
- Kind.
- Humble.
- Gentle.
- Patient.
- Holds back judgment (forbearance).
- Forgiveness.
- Love.

Colossians 4:1. The Scripture isn't so much condoning slavery here as it is telling people how to treat slaves. A Christian is to treat others, including those in a lower social standing, with respect.

Colossians 4:3-5. My prayer is for God to give me wisdom in my speech so I can recognize and seize an opportunity to witness to someone. I don't want to squander away my time here on earth. I want to make it count for something in the kingdom of God.

Colossians 4:6. I must be careful how I talk to people. I must be careful of my tone of voice. Sometimes I can be a little sharp, especially when I am stressed or harried. Sometimes it is not what is said, but HOW it is said that is offensive. If I need to chastise someone, I must do so in the right spirit and the right way (I Thessalonians 2:7; 10-11).

Colossians 4:17. This is a really neat story (in a way). I had a cousin who was an evangelist. He evangelized a lot in Alabama and wherever he went, he worked to spruce up the church. He planted flowers and did cosmetic repairs. He even went to small churches other evangelists didn't want to go to. He was in his 20s and was accidently shot and killed by a good friend in a hunting accident. I was in college at the time. There were some other students there who were from Alabama and who knew Tommy's ministry. They were very distraught and gathered together to pray. I couldn't join them because I had a huge paper due. I was cramming to get it done so I could go to the funeral. During the prayer meeting (as it was told to me later), there were tongues and interpretation that went forth. The message was this: "Why are you crying? He finished the work I put him on this earth to do. When you are finished with the job I have for you, I will come and get you too!" WOW! God has a job for me. I must fulfil it.

I THESSALONIANS

Themes: The 2nd coming and the believer. Continue in holiness and truth until the Lord's return.

I Thessalonians 1:3-9. I am a spiritual billboard. I hope I'm a good one! What am I known for? The Thessalonians had a good record and their influence stretched far and wide (vs 8). They were known for their:
- Work of faith.
- Labor of love.
- Patience.
- Gospel in (a) word (b) power (c) conviction.
- Imitators of Paul and of God .
- Missionaries.
- Turned from idolatry to serve God.

Whether I am a good billboard or a bad one, I will still influence people!

I Thessalonians 2:4. God will judge me by my motives and not by my results. Humans judge each other by results. The human philosophy is the ends justify the means. Not so in God's book! The means (the path to the end result) is just as important. The strength of my ministry is only as good as the strength of my character.

I Thessalonians 2:6. All humans have a need to feel important and crave validation. However, God gets all of the glory. I have to realize any good thing I have done is because God has allowed me to do so. One quick car wreck or a stroke can put an end to my works. I can only do as much as God allows and enables me to do. Therefore, any credit belongs to God. I can't go around like a prima Dona expecting special treatment because of who/what I am. Without God, I am nothing.

I Thessalonians 2:7-9. The attitude of a minister or leader of a group of people is to be one of humble servanthood and not lordship. A true minister will give of him/herself and not demand of others. Humility is not thinking less of oneself, but thinking of oneself less.

I Thessalonians 2:10-12. When my attitude is right, I will influence others to walk righteously before God.

I Thessalonians 2:18. Sometimes Satan does hinder me. Other times, the Holy Spirit constrains me (Acts 16:6-7). Do I know the difference?

I Thessalonians 2:19. God is the only sovereign being. What then, is meant by a "crown of rejoicing"? The word "crown" comes from the Greek word, "stephanos", which most often refers to a Roman crown of victory, not a sovereign crown. We will be victorious through Jesus! We will rejoice in our victory!

I Thessalonians 3:3. Why are we so surprised when we go through trials and afflictions? We know trials are a part of life (Colossians 1:24). Brace yourself. A trial is on its way. The question is: Am I ready for it? I need to buckle up and store up resources when things are going well. I can't stop training for battle when it is not a time of war! No, every army practices war games. An army cannot afford to be lax in its training during times of peace. Likewise, when things are well with me, I need to study and pray just as hard as when I am in the middle of a trial. Actually, when I am in the middle of a trial, it's a little hard to pray. My battle must be won BEFORE I ever face the trial. My actions during a trial must be second nature. If not, I will fail.

I Thessalonians 3:8. My salvation is contingent upon my faithfulness. When I am faithful to pray and study while things are going well, I will have those resources to fall back on. When the storm of a trial blows me over, my anchor will hold and I will be safe. When I am faithful to live according to God's word, heaven awaits me!

I Thessalonians 3:13. I can live a holy life without blame before God. It is possible. It is possible to live without habitually sinning. Good to know I'm not trying to do the impossible!

I Thessalonians 4:1. I must walk the walk and not just talk the talk. My *actions* prove the *trajectory of my heart* - not what comes out of my mouth. Does my walk please God? I can fool people with my talk. I can make people think I am the utmost Christian. However, God knows what I do in secret. God knows whether or not my walk pleases Him.

I Thessalonians 4:2. Some Christians balk at rules and regulations. They only focus on the message of loving others. Paul gave commandments. The church at Thessalonica received those commandments. That sounds like rules and regulations to me! God's rules and regulations are not grievous if the *trajectory of my heart* is right (I John 5:3).

I Thessalonians 4:3-6. To "sanctify" means to set apart for a specific purpose. One of the ways I set myself aside for God's purpose, is to abstain from sexual sins. This is God's will, plain and simple. *It's not rocket science!* I don't understand how people who claim to be Christians live in sexual sin and think it is okay. Over the years, I've had tenants in all leadership positions at their respective churches, who think nothing of participating in all sorts of sexual sins. If I participate in sexual sins, I am not only disobeying and offending God, but I am defrauding my own self and I am defrauding the other person.

I Thessalonians 4:7. God has called me to holiness! I can do this. Since I still have human frailties, there is the probability I will mess up from time to time. Thank God for the privilege of repentance! He is faithful to forgive (I John 1:9) when I repent. Repentance gives me a clean slate again. Remember, though, repentance is not saying "sorry"; it is making a U-turn. There is an old saying, "Sometimes it is easier to beg forgiveness than to get permission." That doesn't work with God. Saying, "sorry" after a premeditated sin is not repentance. True repentance is a change of character. True repentance is both saying "sorry" *and* changing my ways.

I Thessalonians 4:11-12. Mind your own business! Study to be quiet! I don't need to broadcast my business all over social media or at the work place (Proverbs 21:23).

I Thessalonians 4:13-18. We take comfort in knowing there is a future beyond this life. Life is a culling ground. It is a space of time which separates those whose *trajectory of the heart* is pointed heavenward. No one will be forced into Heaven. It is for those who actually want to go and prove it by their actions. It will be so wonderful to be in a place where everyone wants to be in God's presence! It will be wonderful to not have sin tainting our lives!

I Thessalonians 5:1-4. This is a continuation of the discussion concerning the coming of the Lord. When the Lord comes, it will be quick and for those who are ready. There won't be time for repentance then! Now is the time to get right with God (II

Corinthians 6:2)!

I Thessalonians 5:6. A sobering thought is that there is a judgment day. I must be careful who I allow to speak into my life or mentor me (vs 12). Jesus is coming and I intend to meet Him (I Thessalonians 4:14 - I Thessalonians 5:2). I don't know when, but I know He is. I won't allow talks of peace lull me into thinking that all is well (vs 3). Just because peace treaties have been signed doesn't mean there is peace. Worldly contracts are broken on a daily basis. The only contract I can rely upon is my contract with God. If I keep up my end of the bargain, He will keep His.

I Thessalonians 5:8. The hope of our salvation is the 2nd coming of Christ! This is what must be in the forefront of our minds! Faith in God's word and a love for Him protects our hearts.

I Thessalonians 5:9. The Cajuns are fond of saying "It's all good!" People will say it even after a terrible thing has happened. It is a state of mind acknowledging that (1) things don't stay bad and (2) ultimately things work out. There is no point in getting all angry and worked up over temporal things. We look to Jesus, who makes things all good!

I Thessalonians 5:12. It is so important to vet those who have leadership or mentoring positions in my life. They *must* line up with the scripture, or I cannot allow them to influence me, no matter who they are. I should pray over a job before I accept it. I should pray before I turn an acquaintance into a friend. This is serious.

I Thessalonians 5:16-22. The basic attitude and spirit of being a Christian is summed up here. This speaks of the inner attitudes. My inner spirit will eventually show up on the outside, but my outside appearance can be initially deceptive. My inner self will:
- Rejoice.
- Pray.
- Thankful heart.
- Let the Spirit of God flow.
- Love preaching (prophesying).
- Prove and challenge everything to see if it is the truth.
- Stay away from even an appearance of evil (also Romans 13:14).
- Control the tongue (also James 1:26).

I Thessalonians 5:18. Have you ever wondered about the will of God for your life? Wonder no more. It is God's will for me to maintain a thankful heart.

I Thessalonians 5:24. God is faithful to do what He promised. Just wait.

II THESSALONIANS
Themes: 2nd coming of Christ. The Antichrist. Discipline. Admonitions.

II Thessalonians 1:3-4. In the midst of persecutions and trials, the Thessalonians stood firm on the faith and showed love to all. Troubles separate the real from the fake. Hard times will either make or break someone. Hard times force us to either lean on God more *or* push God away. Trials reveal the ***trajectory of my heart.*** Will I become bitter? Or better?

II Thessalonians 1:6-9. Persecutors reap what they sow. God sees to that. It may come later than sooner, but God will punish. I don't have to fret.

II Thessalonians 1:12. This is an indication of God's investment in the church. God wants me to be on the same page as He. God wants me to have the mind of Christ (Philippians 2:5). God wants me to be full of His spirit (Colossians 1:27).

II Thessalonians 2:2. Satan tries to wear us out (Daniel 7:25). He gnaws at our minds and tries to shake us off our *trajectory*. Can I be shaken? Will I remain steadfast on God's word (Hebrews 12:27)? I will take control of my mind and my imagination and not allow Satan to have any time (I Peter 1:13). I will not allow anything to deter me: Not even by human personality (spirit), nor human philosophy (word), nor even by my spiritual mentor! I will stand on the word of God!

II Thessalonians 2:3. It is deceptive to think all who profess Christianity will be saved! There will be a separation of the wheat and the chaff. There will be a separation according to the ***trajectory of the heart,*** and obedience to the word.

II Thessalonians 2:4. The spirit of the antichrist has always been around ever since Satan pulled his stunt in heaven. He wanted to be God. He wanted to usurp God. There are plenty of glory-seeking, self-promoting people in the world. The "celebrity spirit" creeps into the church. I can't get caught up in such a mentality.

II Thessalonians 2:6-7. The lawlessness sin brings is restrained by the people of God. Once the church is removed from this world, chaos will ensue and the world will embark on a quicker descent into a very dark place. The church is the salt and the light of the world (Matthew 5:13-14). The church is what is preserving God's presence on this planet. Once God's presence is removed, only evil will prevail. We think this world is evil now, but the church prevents evil from completely taking over.

II Thessalonians 2:9. I've been to magic shows before where the magician acknowledged all magic is just an illusion and a sleight of hand; that he is not *really* performing miracles. So it is with Satan. He is not powerful, but he is smart. He knows how to trick people into believing something false. He did that with Moses & Pharaoh. He was able to imitate the true miracles God performed through Moses up to a point (Exodus 9:11). Satan will deceive as many as possible through presumed miracles. His most successful stunt is to get me to condemn myself. If Satan can get me to do something God hates, I will have condemned myself.

II Thessalonians 2:10-12. Loving the TRUTH as it has been taught by the Bible is paramount. If I don't LOVE it, God will send the delusion (Isaiah 66:4; Romans 1:28). Delusion won't come from Satan. It will come from God. If I don't love the truth, I will take pleasure in sin (Romans 1:24-28; II Timothy 4:4; Psalm 81:11-12). I have to constantly be on guard against anything that will cause my love for truth to get cold.

II Thessalonians 2:13-15.
- God has chosen salvation for me (vs 13; Ephesians 1:4).
- God has a process of salvation (vs 13; I Peter 1:18-20).
- God's call is available to me (vs 14; Romans 8:28).
- I must believe, stand upon, and protect the truth (vs 15).

II Thessalonians 3:1. Pray for leadership.

II Thessalonians 3:2. Everyone has been given a measure of faith (Romans 12:3), but all men don't have faith. Are these scriptures contradictory? It is impossible for the scripture to contradict itself. These are people who were given faith but at some point, lost it.

II Thessalonians 3:3-5. My daily prayer is God will protect the *trajectory of my heart* from evil.

II Thessalonians 3:6-15. The rest of II Thessalonians chapter 3 warns me to stay away from those who have walked away from the truth. Taking the context of this chapter into account, I believe if I walk away from truth, I gradually and eventually lose the faith. I am to love those who walk away from the truth (vs. 15), but I am to separate myself from those who do not obey the word of God (vs. 6, 14; I Corinthians 5:11; I Thessalonians 5:22; Hosea 4:17). I can't socialize with them. They will bring me down. Their attitude and spirit will rub off on me.

II Thessalonians 3:10. God is not going to take care of my needs if I don't help myself. I have to work for my income. Money just isn't going to rain down from the sky! Idleness breeds sin, which is what happened to Sodom (Ezekiel 16:49). This scripture is two-fold. (1) I must work for my financial blessings and (2) I must work for my spiritual blessings.

II Thessalonians 3:13. We do get tired of working! I was the chair of a committee within the Louisiana Alliance for Education Reform. I worked hard to improve the public educational system. A parent asked me one time, "Karen, why are you trying so hard?" I have asked myself that question over and over since then! In that particular instance, I was trying so hard because my children were in school and I wanted them to have the best education possible. I try hard in many areas. Sometimes, I just want to quit and give up. However, there is a reward both in the natural and spiritual (Galatians 6:9). I need to keep on keeping on!

I TIMOTHY
Themes: Advice to ministers. Christian living. Qualifications of ministers.

I Timothy 1:3-4. I cannot teach any other doctrine than what is in the Bible. The *trajectory of my heart* must be pure. I must have pure doctrine, not deluded with other trains of thought. We are all somewhat influenced by the mindset of the society we live in. I cannot allow myself to be swayed by the current social climate if it clashes with God's word.

I Timothy 1:5-8. The showing of love must be genuine and not fake. Remember the definition of love? (See notes at I Corinthians 13.) Love reveals the true *trajectory of my heart*. My life will reveal if my conscience is pure and my faith is sound. Too many people have been sidetracked by useless arguments and empty discussions. Just as a good attorney can argue both sides of a case, each one of us is capable of twisting scripture to say what we want it to say to justify our sins. I've got to stay founded on the scripture. I must adjust MYself to match God's word and not the other way around.

I Timothy 1:9. If God knew mankind wouldn't be able to keep the law, why did He institute it? The reason for the law was to identify sin and thus, point to Christ (Galatians 3:24-25). The law is like a fence to separate property. It is difficult to know exactly where one property begins and another ends without a fence. The fence defines the space. God allowed mankind to live according to his conscience for a long time. Man's conscience became so diluted and deteriorated (because of sin) to the point man did not know right from wrong. Thus, God had to spell out the law. The law helps us to realize our goodness is really not good at all (Isaiah 64:6). The best of men are still just men at their best. I can't get good to get God. I get God in order to get good! I need the Holy Spirit!

I Timothy 1:10. Even though the Bible teaches how a slave is to be treated, it also lists slavery as evil. The Bible doesn't condone slavery, but acknowledges it exists, and spells out how to treat a slave properly.

I Timothy 1:13. Paul is quick to add his name to the list of sinners! I can never feel self-righteous. God has shown me mercy by allowing me to experience salvation. I cannot take that privilege lightly. There is a huge difference between someone who sins but does so out of ignorance and someone who knowingly sins. I think God will judge those who know the truth a little bit harsher than those who don't (Luke 12:47-48).

I Timothy 1:16. Paul firmly believed if God could save him, God could save anybody!

I Timothy 1:19-20. When someone walks away from God, things spiral downward. Sometimes, a person will stop living for God, but the *trajectory of their heart* is still God-ward and they still believe the truth. These people are more likely to live for God again, unless they procrastinate too long and life devours them (II Samuel 18:8). Then, there are other people who stop living for God because they don't love the truth. These people are on very dangerous ground (Romans 1:28) and ultimately become apostates or reprobates.

I Timothy 2:1-3. God wants us to pray for our secular & political leadership so we can have a good and quiet life. The political climate of a country dictates its economic climate and its social climate. "God, speak to our leaders and help them to have godly thoughts. Put them in contact with people who can guide them in the right direction. Better yet, bring them to salvation!"

I Timothy 2:4. What is God's will? That *everyone* be saved. Unfortunately, God won't get His way because some people just don't want to be saved. I need to remember that the next time I don't get what I want. God doesn't get want He wants either!

I Timothy 2:5. What does God, being the Supreme Being, and I have in common? Absolutely nothing without Jesus! There is such a vast disparity between God and I. There is nothing I could do to get even close to God's level. Therefore, God robed Himself in flesh (John 1:14; I Timothy 3:16) and called that manifestation Jesus (Matthew 1:21). This incarnation enabled God to get down to my level. He forced Himself to the limitations of the human body so He could know and experience what I do (Hebrews 4:15). While here on earth, Jesus could have played the "God-card" and gotten himself out of trouble! Jesus performed miracles for other people and not for Himself. Now that the flesh of Jesus has ascended and is no longer on this earth, when the Spirit of God gets frustrated with me, the flesh nature (Jesus) acts as my lawyer and mediates on my behalf. Now, God and I have something in common! When I am weary, He knows. When I am frustrated, He knows. When I am hungry, He knows. When I'm in a financial bind, He knows. When I am discouraged, He knows. When I am in pain, He knows. When I am grieving, He knows! When I have been betrayed, He knows! HE KNOWS!

I Timothy 2:8-9. There is a difference between male and female. God created us to complement each other (Genesis 2:18). Men and women have different traits and thus, different temptations.
- Male temptation: Men are prone to anger, arguing, and aggression.
- Female temptation: Women are tempted to worry about appearance.

Both men and women must overcome their natural inclinations. Paul tells the men to lift up holy hands without anger and disputing and for women to be modest (without extreme hair, jewelry & expensive clothing). This scripture recognizes the temptation of the sexes and teaches us to overcome those so we can be holy before God.

I Timothy 2:11-12. Here we go with women being silent again. Does this mean women are not allowed to sing, praise or speak? Such interpretation would contradict other scriptures, so we know it is not correct. Women are to be subject to her authority. I recently heard of a couple who are in charge of a camp. The husband made a ruling and the wife disagreed. On the surface, the wife repeated the rule her husband set forth, but in private, she undermined his authority and pushed her own agenda. This story is not going to end well. She is usurping her husband's authority. She may get her way for the time being, but if she stays on this path, she will be out of the will of God. The NIV Bible interprets "woman" and "man" as "wife" and "husband", which is in agreement with Ephesians 5:22-25.

I Timothy 2:13-14. Paul brought forth the example of Adam and Eve to further illustrate his point. He reminded Timothy that Adam could have and should have stopped Eve. Adam was the one who had originally received the commandment directly from God. He had a responsibility to not let Eve go that far.

I Timothy 3. It's too bad Paul felt the need to put the qualifications for church leadership in writing. Really, every Christian, not just leadership, should exhibit these qualifications!

I Timothy 3:2-7. Remember that scripture which said to know those in authority over you (I Thessalonians 5:12)? How do I do that? The qualifications of a minister are:
- Above reproach (no grounds for accusations).
- Husband of one wife.
- Self-controlled.
- Disciplined life.
- Loving.
- A capable teacher.

- A non-alcoholic.
- Not out for dishonest gain.
- Not antagonistic, but peaceful.
- Earning the respect (therefore control) of family at home.
- Experienced.
- Have a good reputation within the community.

I Timothy 3:8-13. The qualifications for lay leadership positions are:
- Worthy of respect
- Honest (no half-truths)
- Not an alcoholic
- Honest in business dealings
- Uphold the doctrine and faith taught by the Bible
- Must stand the test of time
- Be blameless and without reproach
- Wives must also exhibit the same qualities and not be a gossip
- Husband of one wife
- Earn the respect (therefore control) of family at home

I Timothy 3:16. The great "mystery of godliness" is simple. God put on flesh and came to the earth! *It's not rocket science!* Mysteries refer to divine truths previously unknown to man but revealed by God's servants via the Holy Spirit (Mark 4:11; Romans 11:25; Romans 16:25; I Corinthians 4:1; Ephesians 3:7-9).

I Timothy 4:1-3. Plenty of false doctrines pop up. I just wish people who don't want to obey the Bible would go start a totally different religion and not claim to be Christian (which means Christ-like). Unfortunately, Satan likes to build upon truth and distort truth, so he will twist scriptures up in people's minds and people will believe what they want a scripture to say and not do what the scripture actually says to do. When I hear of a church group forbidding things (such as eating of meat and forbidding to marry - vs 3) that aren't in the Bible, I know it's a man-made church (Matthew 23:4). When I hear people prayer by rote (Matthew 6:7), I know it is man-made and there is no real relationship with God. I like the wording of the King James Version of I Timothy 1:6. Paul calls it "vain jangling"!!

I Timothy 4:6-7. The duty of a minister is not only to preach the truth to unbelievers, but re-teach believers the truth. We always have to go back to the root of our beliefs. We must always be reminded of what the BIBLE says and not what someone has philosophized as truth. Most professions require continuing education. A Christian does too!

I Timothy 4:12-16. I must be true to:
- Myself and

- The doctrine

For me to neglect what I have been called to do is not being true to myself. I will never be happy if I don't exercise the gift and calling God has on my life. My calling is a gift and needs to be "stirred" (II Timothy 1:6). In deputational travels, we met three families who had felt a call to the mission field of South Korea long before my parents ever did. Had they gone when they were called, property could have been purchased very cheaply and the church would have been much further along. Unfortunately, these three families elected not to follow the calling of God. Things did not go well for them. Their marriages had or were falling apart, their children had backslid, and/or sickness had overtaken their bodies. For me to be true to myself means I must be true to God. I must praise & worship God. I must fast & pray. I must read His word. I must be stirred.

I Timothy 5:1-3. I must always be respectful of others with a pure heart. The church is to help the (real) widows.

I Timothy 5:4. My responsibility is to my family first and then to the church. God instituted the family unit (Adam & Eve) long before He instituted a church (tabernacle worship in the wilderness). God intends for the father to be the priest of his own home and lead the family into a relationship with God, which is God's Plan "A". God's Plan "B" is to have corporate worship (church) and a leader of the corporate body (pastor). A pastor can only do so much, though. If the parent(s) undermine(s) the authority of the pastor at home, the children will not survive. Even the fatherless needs to learn respect for authority at home.

I Timothy 5:8. If I don't provide for my family, I am a sinner! In fact, many sinners do provide for their families. If I don't, I am worse than a sinner! Wow! There are circumstances, of course, that warrant government assistance, however, an able-bodied Christian should strive to provide for his/her own family.

I Timothy 5:9-10. Families are supposed to help each other. However, in the absence of family help, the church should help the elders, widows, who are TRUE widows, provided they are living for God 100%. The church should provide a venue in which older widows can minister. Qualifications for assistance are:
- Reputation for good works.
- Raised children.
- Been hospitable to strangers.
- Ministered to the saints.
- Assisted those in distress.
- Devoted to doing good.

I Timothy 5:11-14. Young widows should devote themselves to God's work, but are more likely to get into trouble by gossiping and being a busy body if left idle. Younger widows should remarry.

I Timothy 5:18. This scripture repeats the admonition given in verse 8. Provide for your own household!

I Timothy 5:18-21. I must respect those who labor for God. I must respect God's will too! I don't begrudge the salary a minister makes. He and his family have to live and deserve to live at least as decently as I do! I must be careful not to talk about or listen to talk about a minister (vs 19), unless those accusations are made by multiple witnesses. A leader must not promote anyone (think: nepotism) (vs 21). I must allow God to raise up my children if He so chooses. Unfortunately, there's always a minister who will take advantage of his position and perhaps take a larger-than-necessary salary and/or promote family members. God will deal with him, not I. That's not my job.

I Timothy 5:22. There is a danger in ordaining someone too hastily. A person must be proven before given a leadership position.

I Timothy 5:23. Water is not potable in many countries, even to this day. The drinking of contaminated water causes many illnesses. There are properties in wine which can help with those illnesses. However, this is not license to drink alcohol all of the time. Other scriptures warn against being drunk. This scripture gives license to use substances for MEDICAL purposes and not for pleasure. I believe this can also carry over to modern medicines. Morphine and other drugs are used in hospital settings. In a pleasurable setting, these drugs are highly addictive and highly destructive to the human body, however, under medically controlled situations, are beneficial. Nothing is to "own" me except for the Holy Spirit (Romans 6:16; I Corinthians 6:12). Therefore, anything potentially addictive is for medicinal purposes only. I cannot allow anything to become an addiction and thus, gain control over me.

I Timothy 5:24. I want my sins cleansed BEFORE I meet God. My sins are expunged at baptism (Acts 2:38). If I take care of that, I will be clean before God. If I neglect to do that, my sins follow me. I'm doomed if I go to trial with the evidence stacked against me! I need my record cleared beforehand! On judgment day, I don't want a record to be found by my name.

I Timothy 6:1-3. This scripture isn't condoning slavery. It is simply teaching how the employee/employer relationship should be. An employee should be respectful to his/her employer, even if that employer is not a believer. If the employer is a believer, the employee should not begrudge the status of the employer. In God's eyes, all souls are equal, but in the workforce, the employer does have authority over the employee. When the employer and employee both go to the same church, the relationship is different at work and at church. The early church leaders were reprimanded for treating the big givers better. God looks at the percentage of giving, not the amount (Mark 12:41-43). If I give $50 and my income was $500 for the week, I have given 10%. However, if my income was $5,000 for the week, I have only given 1%, which is considerably less.

I Timothy 6:4-5. What is the characteristic of a false teacher?
- Proud.
- Throws out questions which cause contentions.
- Encourages friction.
- Encourages twisting of words.
- Misuses godliness for financial gain.

Stay away from those people as much as possible. We can't avoid those people totally. They are in all aspects of life and are especially concentrated in academia. Understand, however, some professors enjoy challenging everything and their mission is to dislodge students from the rock of truth. I need to use that as an opportunity to dig into the scriptures and become even more grounded. I may have to go to class to get a grade, but I don't have to hang out with them afterwards and philosophize with them. I taught my children to give the teacher the answer s/he wanted on a test, but to write a protest in the margin that they believed otherwise. The teachers all respected their stand.

I Timothy 6:6-8. There will always be someone who is more privileged than I. There will always be someone who has less than I. I will be content with what God has allowed me to have (Philippians 4:11). It is all temporary anyway (Job 1:21)!

I Timothy 6:9-19. Money is okay. Being rich is okay. After all, some of the most spiritual people in the Bible were rich (Abraham, Job). It is the LOVE of money which is the basis of evil. Trusting in riches instead of trusting in God will get me in trouble. I need money in this life. I believe God blesses us because He enjoys seeing us have pleasure in His creation. However, He also expects me to be a good steward (Luke 16; Titus 1:7). Just because I can afford something doesn't mean I should buy it. God blesses me so I can be a blessing to others. Am I not blessed as much because I am stingy with what I already have? Did God just give me a raise on the job so I can buy a larger house or did He give me a raise so I can give more to missions (vs.18)? Where is the **_trajectory of my heart_** aimed? Isn't it interesting that this discourse on money comes on the heels of identifying false teachers? Sandwiched between the verses about money is an admonishment to keep the eternal things in the forefront of my mind, not the temporal (vs. 12). Money can affect my soul's salvation if it is not kept in perspective. It is not a sin to be rich - just don't trust in riches and don't lord it over others (vs. 17). God can take away my riches quicker than He gave them to me. Remember Job? Remember the stock market crash? God is no respecter of persons (Acts 10:34; Romans 2:11). God knows how to humble me if I get too proud. (God knows how to humble a church body if it gets too proud, too!) Money spent on myself is temporal. Money invested in spiritual matters is eternal (vs 19).

II TIMOTHY
Themes: Apostates. Advice to ministers. Experiences of Paul.

II Timothy 1:1-5. This is a beautiful example of mentorship. Each generation should take care to pass the baton to the next. It only takes one generation to lose the truth. Everyone should have three people in their lives (1) a mentor, (2) a peer, and (3) someone they are mentoring. Mentoring takes time, and perhaps more importantly, a willingness to let go. I am happy when my protégé does better than I! I want my protégé to stand on my shoulders and be taller than I! I want to give the next generation a rich heritage. A good leader knows when it is time to step down and let someone s/he has trained take over. An insecure leader will hang on and take back the responsibility given to another. The next person isn't going to do things exactly the way I would have done them, but that's ok!

II Timothy 1:6. I have to keep the gift God has given me stirred up. A body of water must be continually stirred and moving or it will become stagnant and a breeding ground for illnesses. The manna sent in the wilderness had to be gathered fresh each day. Day-old manna was full of worms (Exodus 16). I can't allow myself to receive the beautiful gift of God's holy spirit and then just sit on it. A person who does that becomes highly critical of everything and everyone in the church. How, then, do I keep this precious gift stirred up within me?
- Pray
- Fast
- Read and meditate upon the Word
- Pour out myself to others

II Timothy 1:7. If fear is not from God, then who is it from? It's from the other guy. Satan likes to keep me in a state of turmoil. This is why so many people are addicted. They are fearful and are trying to find some measure of peace. Many turn to narcotics or some other addictive behavior. Satan is a liar and the source of all lies (John 8:44). God will keep me safe in all situations (II Timothy 1:12). I have no need to fear. God is with me (Psalm 23:4; Psalm 34:7).

II Timothy 1:8. Persecution over my faith may come. If it does, I can be confident God will supply the courage I need at the time (Philippians 4:19) and what He gives me will be sufficient to carry me through (II Corinthians 12:9). How do persecuted Christians manage to stay strong in the face of such horrible atrocities? God carries them through by His power. He will carry me through as well, *IF* I hold to His hand.

II Timothy 1:9-10. God:
- Has saved us.
- Has called us.
- Gave us these things in Jesus.
- Was made manifest .
- Abolished death.
- Brought life.
- Brought immortality.

II Timothy 2:2. I've seen many a great man/woman pass on into eternity during my life time and these individuals are sorely missed. As one generation moves on, the cry is "Oh no! Who is going to take their place?" I trust God. I trust God's timing. I trust God knows what He is doing. God has always had a spokesman. God has always raised up leaders. So, the answer to the question is this: My generation will take their place and when the time comes for me to move on, I trust that my children's generation will carry on. God's got this thing. He is in control. Don't worry. (Be sad for the loss, but don't worry.) I must pass the torch to the next generation (and be wise enough to know when to officially hand it over).

II Timothy 2:12. God is able to keep me through *any* storm, PROVIDED I have surrendered into His care. He can only keep safe the areas of my life I have given unto Him. He will not rip anything out of my control. God doesn't just take over my life. He is a gentleman. He will safely keep that which I have given unto Him. Doesn't it make sense to surrender myself 100% to Him?

II Timothy 2:13-14. There are so many various doctrines within Christianity. How do I know which one is right? I will cling to the doctrine God delivered through His apostles. Biblical principles and concepts have been established and apply to every age, every culture and every social climate. *Example:* When we first went to Korea as missionaries, the people balked at demonstrative worship, claiming that it was an American custom and Koreans weren't emotional. My parents showed them where it was not an American custom, but a Biblical custom. Once that understanding was illuminated, they danced under the power of God as much as anyone! Biblical principles of a life of holiness apply and stand through the ages and changes in technology. Technology in and of itself is not sinful. Its application can be sinful if it violates Biblical principles.

II Timothy 2:15-16. It is good to study and be educated, *however,* my education must be God-approved! There is a right way and a wrong way to learn truth. The right way is through scripture. The wrong way is through philosophy, which leads away from truth. Human philosophy and sin will take me further than I ever intended to go. I know ministers whom I greatly admired at one time, who began philosophizing the Bible. They began veering away from the truths of the Bible.

Then, small sins appeared in their lives. Now, they are not recognizable as Christians. How sad!

II Timothy 2:17-18. Even the early church had to deal with false doctrine! I suppose Satan realized he couldn't stop the church, so he decided to do the next best thing ~ delude it. It takes some seeking out truth to really find it. There are so many untruths floating around. I have to take the time to dig out the truth from underneath all of the falsehoods.

II Timothy 2:19. God knows who is His! He sees me. He knows the *trajectory of my heart*. He takes note when I make a stand for truth, even if it is just in my daily life and not always verbal.

II Timothy 2:20-22. There are always hypocrites in the church. I don't want to be a vessel of dishonor. I want to be someone God can use. I have to separate myself from the hypocrites. Just because someone comes to church and participates in worship doesn't mean they are honorable vessels of God. If they don't live for God outside of a 1½ hour church service, they are a hypocrite. I have to align myself and partner with people who have the right *trajectory.*

II Timothy 2:24. It serves no useful purpose to be contentious. There is no point in arguing scripture. I am to patiently teach. Some people are argumentative and are just not teachable.

II Timothy 2:26. Those who are teachable have a chance of being saved. If someone's *trajectory* is on the right course, God will give them a chance to repent of their actions and be saved.

II Timothy 3:1-4 outlines characteristics of humanity prevalent in the last days. These characteristics have always been around, but are increased in the last days. There have always been wars and natural disasters. There has always been sin. It's just that as less and less people practice true Christianity, the "salt" and "light" of the world are less and less, and darkness increases. However, I MUST continue in the faith, even if NO ONE ELSE does (vs. 14). I must stick with the scripture, for it (and it alone) is of God. I must allow the scripture to convict me (vs. 16; Hebrews 4:12), or God will allow me to become a reprobate (II Timothy 4:3-4; Romans 1:24, 26, 28; II Thessalonians 2:11). How can the scripture convict me if I never read it?

II Timothy 3:5-7. The wickedness listed in the preceding verses are even in the church! These people are religious, but don't allow the power of God to rule their lives. They live the way they want to live and not the way God wants them to live. This is not a new thing, either. Cain was religious. Cain offered sacrifices to God. Cain's problem was he wanted to define his own religion and didn't want to serve God according to God's commandments. These people are not content to keep their self-made religion to themselves, but prey on gullible people. These gullible ("silly" in the KJV) people like the new doctrine being taught because it coincides with their own fleshly desires. It is amusing to me in a sad sort of way that these people appear to be more spiritual than they ever were when living in the truth! They are always going to conferences, getting together for Bible studies, etc., but get further and further away from the truth.

II Timothy 3:8-9. Here's an interesting tidbit. Jewish custom says Janes and Jambres were Pharaoh's magicians. They could replicate some of the miracles God performed through Moses because of their sleight of hand. The difference between these men and Moses was the power source. Janes and Jambres depended upon their own power. Moses was merely the vessel of God's power. A savvy individual can scan a congregation and know by his/her own powers of deduction, which individuals are in pain or emotional distress. This minister will call the person out for special prayer, and viola, the minister is perceived as a man of God. Don't be derailed by these people. If a self-proclaimed minister does not live according to the word of God, run! His/Her power will only go so far.

II Timothy 3:11. Paul sure did reap what he had sowed prior to his conversion, didn't he?

II Timothy 3:13-14. False doctrine will prevail more and more. It is like a cancer. It grows and spreads. I must keep going back to the root. I must measure all doctrines by studying them out in the Bible. It is very easy to take a phrase out of the Bible and make a doctrine of it. It takes some in-depth studying to discover the truths in the Bible. My ***heart's true trajectory*** is made manifest. Do I want to know for myself or am I willing to gamble on someone else's doctrine? There is a televangelist who is known and admired worldwide. My husband was listening to his program on the radio while driving one day. He emotionally declared how he had a vision and saw two thrones in Heaven. My, my~ he saw more than John saw! There is only one throne in Heaven and only one upon the throne (Revelation 4:2)! The popularity of this televangelist doesn't impress God. This man is working for his own kingdom and not for God's kingdom. This is a false prophet. It is very sad so many people don't bother to check out his doctrine. They are blindly following him.

II Timothy 4:3-4. People want to hear what pleases them. No one is happy when sin is pointed out. The scripture illuminates my sin (II Timothy 3:16). It is good when I am convicted. I have a chance to correct my course when my sins and/or omissions are brought to light. I can't get mad at the preacher when he steps on my toes! Unfortunately, people want to hear sermons that give them a warm and fuzzy feeling. My father pastored a congregation consisting of a powerful family. He preached on something that displeased them and one day during testimony service, the old matriarch of that family stood up and stated, "We Kremcofts donated the land for this church and we want a preacher who will preach what we want to hear!" (My father promptly resigned! He knew as long as that family fought to control the church, there was no way he could pastor them and bring the church to revival.) God will eventually quit dealing with that attitude. God will turn us over to a reprobate mind if we resist truth and refuse to repent (Romans 1:24, 26, 28; II Thessalonians 2:11).

II Timothy 4:6. Am I like Paul? Am I willing to be poured out? Am I willing to be a vessel of honor (II Timothy 2:20)?

II Timothy 4:7-8. I, like Paul, intend to finish my life's journey in good standing with God. It is a spiritual fight (Ephesians 6:12). Satan is a parasite (I Peter 5:8). I must be vigilant; on guard. I know his tactics, so I must stay prepared.

II Timothy 4:16-17. It is very hurtful when your friends don't stand by you. I suppose that experience is common among mankind. God doesn't forsake us, though.

TITUS

Themes: Christian doctrine. Advice to ministers; Qualifications & characteristics of leaders and Christians in general.

Titus 1:2. Guess what? God can't lie! Remember all of those promises from God? They will come to pass because God can't lie! Remember all of the prophecies? They will come to pass because God can't lie!

Titus 1:3. I should never discount preaching. God reveals His word through preaching *and* has chosen preaching as a mechanism whereby we can hear of salvation and thereby be saved (I Corinthians 1:21). Don't mock preaching. Don't scorn preaching. (I do admit that some of the antics of preachers are amusing!)

Titus 1:5-6. Qualifications of elders:
- Husband of one wife.
- Faithful children (blameless).

Titus 1:7-9. Qualifications of bishops:
- Blameless.
- Submitted, not over bearing.
- Level headed.
- Not an alcoholic.

- Not prone to fight.
- Not pursuing dishonest gain.
- Hospitable.
- Loves the sensible.
- Fair.
- Devoted (to God).
- Self-disciplined.
- Sticks to original teaching of God's word.
- Capable teacher, mentor.

Titus 1:10-15. Paul is not very pleased with the apparent discord which had been sown in the church! There are always people who gossip, run their mouths, and spout off every new doctrine that comes along without thought of whether or not it lines up with the word of God. In my lifetime, I've seen various little ideas spring forth and spread like wildfire within the church. We must stop that sort of thing. Whether it is gossip about another person, twisting scriptures around, or taking scriptures out of context to try and prove a doctrine, we must stop that. Paul is not talking about unchurched people! He is talking about those who profess to serve God!

Titus 1:16. Beware. Not everyone who claims to be Christian is actually serving God or is saved (Matthew 7:21). I can sit in McDonald's all day long. At the end of the day, I might smell like a hamburger, but sitting there doesn't make me one. Actions prove the *trajectory of one's heart*, not words.

Titus 2:1-10. What is sound doctrine? It is the practical application of Biblical teachings. Why? So that the reputation of Christianity is upheld (vs 8).
Old men:
- Temperate.
- Dignified.
- Sensible.
- Solid in faith.
- Solid in love.
- Christlike character.

Old women:
- Similar to their male counterparts.
- Not malicious gossipers.
- Not alcoholics.
- Teach younger women.

Younger women:
- Love family.
- Sensible.
- Pure.
- Maintain a godly atmosphere in the home.

- Good natured.
- Submitted to own husband (Ephesians 5:22).

Younger men:
- Ditto the above.
- Sensible & serious about life.
- Self-controlled.
- Integrity in doctrine & honesty.
- Do good deeds.
- Dignified.

Servants (employees):
- Obedient to employers.
- No back-talk.
- No stealing from employers.
- Trustworthy.
- Adorned with the doctrine of God.

Titus 2:11-12. There are people who preach grace releases me from the ordinances of God. However, this scripture defines grace and it is very different from what is being touted. Grace TEACHES me to live holy.
- When I live unholy, I live under the knowledge of guilt. Holiness gives me the freedom to worship.
- Holiness does not bring me under bondage.
- Grace demands holiness (not the law).
- He who despises holiness has never learned to despise worldliness.
- Under grace, holiness is the discipline of love.

Titus 2:14. The sole purpose of mankind was so God could have a relationship based upon love. God already had creation which was programmed (or forced) to praise Him (Luke 19:40). He wanted a relationship of choice. When man fell in the garden, sin severed that relationship (Exodus 33:3; Revelation 21:27). The sole purpose of Jesus coming to earth and paying the penalty of sin was to give me the opportunity to restore my relationship with God (II Corinthians 5:19). It is my choice. The more intimate my relationship with God is, the more I act like Him and thus, become a little peculiar to the world. (I Peter 2:9; Deuteronomy 14:2). God has always demanded a separation between His people and the world. I should be easily identifiable by an initial glance, my attitudes and thus, my conduct.

Titus 2:15. I can't allow myself to be intimidated when I am teaching the word of God. This is God's word. I'm merely the messenger. I am not allowed to change it, only present it. It doesn't matter if the hearer doesn't like it.

Titus 3:1-2. General characteristics of a Christian:
- Law-abiding citizen (albeit God's law comes first).

- Not to slander.
- Gentle.
- Courteous to all.

Titus 3:3. General characteristics of a non-Christian:
- Foolish.
- Disobedient.
- Deceived.
- Slave to sinful pleasures/desires.
- Hateful.
- Going through life with malice & envy.

Titus 3:5-8. Good works don't save us, but they are profitable to us and God will remember them (Hebrews 6:10). We are saved by water baptism and receiving the Holy Spirit.

Titus 3:9. Some things are just not worth wasting time on. There is no real conclusion to these things and serve no useful purpose. Avoid them.
- Ill-informed controversies
- Genealogies (ancestor worship)
- Legal quarrels

Titus 3:10. Does God have a "strike three and you're out" policy? It sure seems so! To quote a deceased elder minister, "Don't waste your time with stupid people!" There is a time for teaching and mercy, but someone who habitually sins ("froward" in the KJV) is not going to change. The word "froward" is used 24 times, and it is not nice. Move on to someone who will accept teaching.

Titus 3:11. Christians are sometimes accused of being judgmental. Sometimes they are, but a Christian cannot condemn anyone. God doesn't even condemn anyone. People condemn themselves. In the USA, there are certain laws. Generally speaking, there is a penalty for murder. If I commit murder, I can expect to be punished. This is common knowledge. No one can claim the "I didn't know" defense. The prosecution would retort, "You should have known". Likewise, God has set forth His laws. If I don't know them, I should (Romans 1:20)! If I disobey, I am condemning myself. When I disobey, I am, in effect, telling God that I WANT to be punished. It's that simple. ***It isn't Rocket Science.***

PHILEMON
Theme: The good character of Philemon; Appeal to forgive Onesimus.

Philemon was man who was:
- Loved by Paul (vs 1).
- Worked for God (vs 1).
- Had a church in his home (vs 2).
- Had a love for the truth and was devoted (vs 5).
- His actions bore fruit of the *trajectory of his heart* (vs 6).
- Was compassionate of the needs of others (vs 7).
- Elderly (vs 9).
- Submitted to Paul (vs 21).
- Hospitable (vs 22).

Because of his character, Paul was confident Philemon would do what was right concerning Oneimus (vs 8)

Oneimus was:
- Convert of Paul while Paul was in prison (vs 10). Whether he was a prisoner also or a guard, we don't know.
- Wasn't much use to Philemon in the past, but now is (vs 11). Had he been a trouble-maker before his conversion? We don't know.

Paul's appeal:
- Paul would have preferred Oneimus stayed with him, but was sending him to Philemon because he was Philemon's slave. (vs 12-16).
- Paul makes an appeal that Philemon accept Oneimus back, not as a slave, but as a brother in Christ and forgive him (vs 17-18).
- Paul was willing to pay whatever debt Oneimus owed Philemon (vs 19).
- Paul reminded Philemon that he (Philemon) was indebted to Paul (vs 19).

HEBREWS

Theme: "Better": better high priest, better sacrifice, better tabernacle, better covenant.
Doctrinal theme: The just live by faith (Hebrews 2:4).
Companion book is Leviticus.

The book of Hebrews is devoted to explaining why the New Covenant is better than the old. There was no literal son of God until Bethlehem, but the idea was born before creation (Psalm 2:7; John 17:24; I Peter 1:20). Jesus is a little lower than the angels (Hebrews 2:9) because He took on flesh (Hebrews 2:16-18). This is why He came - it was a choice He made.

Hebrews 1:1-3. God, by His son, who was the express (visible) image of God, purged our sins.

Hebrews 1:4-8; 14. Here the scripture states Jesus was better than the angels, but in Hebrews 2:9, it states that He was made lower than the angels. Which is it? Is the Bible contradicting itself? That is impossible, so we must delve deeper. Jesus was made lower than the angels in the sense that He confined Himself to a human form. However, since He was the express image of God, He is better than the angels. It's all about perspective. The angels are ministering spirits and not heirs of salvation.

Hebrews 1:9. Have I mentioned before that God hates sin? He couldn't stand it in the Old Testament (Psalm 5:4; Isaiah 59:2) and He still can't stand it. He doesn't change (Malachi 3:9). Don't sin. It's that simple! ***It's not rocket science!***

Hebrews 2:1, 3. I bear a responsibility for my own salvation. The sacrifice of Jesus isn't enough. That's sounds like heresy, but it is true. The sacrifice of Jesus IS enough to pay the penalty for my sins, but if I neglect to utilize His sacrifice, I cannot be saved. I can't neglect or procrastinate. This is serious. Eternity is at stake. As time goes on, I need to actually dig in *deeper* lest I slip and fail.

Hebrews 2:8. If Jesus and God (Father) are two separate entities, then this scripture demotes God. If God put *all* things under Jesus, then God Himself would be subject to Jesus! That would be in violation of every scripture which talks about there being no god but God. Scripture does not contradict scripture. When it seems confusing, it is time to study and seek out the truth. Jesus is merely God wearing flesh so He could be visible in the natural world.

Hebrews 2:9. Jesus was made lower than the angels simply because of His human nature. God confined Himself to a human body. This does not mean that angels are spiritually superior to Jesus. Human nature is lower than angelic nature. Jesus took *every* man's place in death. In His humanity, Jesus is lower than the angels. (In His deity, Jesus is far superior to the angels.)

Hebrews 2:14-15. In my unregenerated state, I am in bondage to sin. I have no choice but to do wrong. Through His sacrifice, Jesus freed me from sin. Now, I have the freedom to do the right thing: to live righteously before God.

Hebrews 2:16-18. The very reason Jesus came to this earth was to give me the freedom to reconcile my relationship with God which had been severed because of sin. This was *His* choice. He made the choice to suffer for me so I could make the choice to live for Him.

Hebrews 3:2-6. Proof that Jesus is better than Moses, whom the Jews revered greatly.

Hebrews 3:10-11. I don't want to be guilty of not knowing God's ways. It is not enough to merely know His works. I must know HIM! Many people know, and believe in, God's works. They pray for and even receive miracles. That sort of superficial relationship is not enough. God wants an intimate relationship with me. We all have people and family members in our lives with whom we eat, laugh, etc., but with whom we don't share our innermost thoughts. These are not intimate friendships or relationship. God doesn't want a superficial relationship with me. God wants intimacy. He wants to be more than an object of worship. Although God enjoys blessing us, He doesn't want to be "used". He wants in my heart. When I develop that close relationship with Him, I will know *His* heart. When I am that close to Him, I know what He likes and dislikes without even asking. A lack of this type of relationship will result in my not being allowed into Heaven. Relationships are two-way streets. What am I giving God in return?

Hebrews 3:12-14. I don't want my heart hardened. Sin is deceitful. Not too many people wake up in the morning intending to sin. Most of us justify our sins. No sin is justifiable, but we tend to make excuses for ourselves and rationalize our actions to the point we no longer view them as sin. There is a big "IF" in verse 14. Yes, I will partake with Christ, but **only IF** I stay on the right course.

Hebrews 3:15-16. Has anyone ever provoked you to do something you didn't really want to do? How many of us have given in to our children at the check-out line in the grocery store because they provoked us? How many of us have lashed out at someone because they nagged us to death? The children of Israel were guilty of provoking God in the wilderness. How? By their lack of faith and their constant complaining. Am I guilty of doing the same?

Hebrews 3:18. An entire generation of Israelites was not allowed in the promised land because of their unbelief. What about me? Do I have unbelief too? What is unbelief? Whatever it is, it is very serious! Do I really trust God with all things? Do I pray about something and then take it into my own hands and try to answer my own prayer? Sarah did that and Ishmael was born. That didn't turn out so well, did it? Neither will my flimsy attempts to fix my situations. It is easy to verbally say, "I believe", but living in belief is not so easy. I get impatient when God doesn't rush to my rescue the minute I pray. Trusting God means I not only take my hands off a situation, but I *keep* my hands off that situation. I have to learn to pray, but then sit back and allow God to have complete control. I need to rest on His word (II Chronicles 32:8). My soul's salvation depends upon my patience with God (Luke 21:19).

Hebrews 4:5, 9-10; 8:8-10. What is God's rest? The Sabbath is an Old Testament symbol of the Holy Spirit. The keeping of the Sabbath is the only one of the Ten Commandments that is not specifically reinstated as a literal event in the New

Testament. Without going into a deep discussion here, we find there were many Sabbaths in the Old Testament. Not only was there a weekly "day of rest", but every cycle of 7 weeks (49 days), there was a feast, or a 2-day Sabbath. Then, the 7-day cycle began again. Example: Let's say the Sabbath was on a Saturday. There were 7 weeks of the Sabbath falling on a Saturday. Then, there was a 2-day Sabbath (Saturday and Sunday), followed by the 7-day cycle again. Thus, the Sabbath would fall on Sunday for 7 weeks until the next 2-day Sabbath. We realize that eventually, the Sabbath fell on every single day of the week. (See Leviticus 23.) In Hebrews, we are told the Holy Spirit is our rest. We rest (cease) from the works of our flesh (sin). The rest of the Old Testament was a physical rest. It is true that our bodies need rest, but the New Testament rest is more than a physical rest. It is:

- Physical.
- Spiritual (ceasing from sin).
- Eternal (Heaven awaits).
- Emotional (because I have ceased from sin).
- Mental (because my trust is in God, not myself).

Hebrews 4:12. This is one of the first scriptures I memorized! The word of God reveals the *trajectory of the heart.*

Hebrews 4:14. Since Jesus is my high priest, I will hold fast to the doctrine and not faint.

Hebrews 4:15-16; 5:2. Jesus knows what I'm going through. I can barge in and talk to Him and He will have compassion on me. He is my mediator (Lamentations 3:58; I Timothy 2:5). What a relief!

Hebrews 5:2. One of the key doctrines of the New Testament is having love and compassion upon others, especially those who are less fortunate. Jesus was afflicted. He knows.

Hebrews 5:3-8. There are so many charlatans in Christianity. A God-called minister (as opposed to a self-appointed one) will intercede with "strong crying and tears (vs 7) and obeys (vs 8) the voice of God.

Hebrews 5:12-14. News Flash! Church is not about me. Church is about bringing OTHERS to Christ! Church is about HIM! It's not what can the church provide for me and my family. I am not to sit back and just enjoy church. The Anderson family came to our church for a while. He was a backslider from another city and she had never been in church before. They were a great family. After a while, she began comparing our little church to the large church her husband had grown up in. That pastor had a ranch and took groups of church members there to camp and hunt. They had all kinds of social events at their church. This couple left our church because there weren't enough social activities for them. Eventually, they left that big church, went to another, and then ultimately quit going to church altogether. Apparently, our lack of social activities wasn't the problem. I must grow up and understand that the church isn't about me and the pastor isn't responsible for my entertainment! The pastor is responsible for my soul! I must become a teacher of others. I must get off the baby bottle and be a mature Christian (I Corinthians 3:2-3). I must be ever growing (II Peter 1:5-8). If I am growing (in the spirit), I cannot fall.

Hebrews 6:1-2. I must not ever forget about my foundation. I must build upon it and go on to completeness. What are the most basic doctrinal foundations?
- Repentance (initially preached by John the Baptist).
- Baptisms (water & spirit) (introduced by Jesus in John 3).
- Laying on of hands (miracles - introduced by Jesus).
- Resurrection (introduced in the Old Testament).
- Judgment (introduced in the Old Testament).
- Life of separation (introduced in the Old Testament).

Hebrews 6:4-8. The perils of apostasy are real. There is a doctrine in "Christian" circles teaching once you're saved, you're always saved. That doctrine is in direct conflict with this scripture. Someone can get to the point they can't get back to good standing with God. I don't ever want to get to that place. I don't ever want my conscience to be seared so I don't know right from wrong (I Timothy 4:2). I don't ever want to believe in some twisted doctrine contrary to the word of God.

Hebrews 6:10. God keeps track of my work for His kingdom. I may never be appreciated by my peers, but God takes note.

Hebrews 6:11-15. God has an ideal in mind. He hopes I will consistently, until death do me part:
- Not be spiritually apathetic.
- Imitate heroes of faith.
- Patiently endure.
- Be faithful (because He is faithful).

Hebrews 6:18-19. There are two unchangeable basics in life:
- God can't lie.
- There is hope.

Since God can't lie, why don't I take Him at His word?

Hebrews 7:4-5. Abraham paid his tithes. Tithing is simple and easy, really, when you realize 100% of everything belongs to God. He lets me keep 90%! The attitude of "I have to pay my tithes" is burdensome. My attitude shall be, "Great! I get to keep 90%!" It's all a matter of the ***trajectory of the heart!***

Hebrews 7:8-22. The book of Hebrews is generally attributed to Paul. This passage is very "lawyer-y". The writer is logically walking us through the idea tithing was instituted in the Old Testament and it could be argued that Levi (future generation of Abraham), both received tithes and paid tithes! The bottom line is this: There is a better priesthood than Levi, and that is Jesus!

Hebrews 7:24-28. The reason Jesus is a better priest than anyone else is. He:
- is eternal.
- is unchangeable.
- is able to save others.
- is holy.
- does not need to offer sacrifices for himself.

Hebrews 8:5. The tabernacle Moses built was a replica, inasmuch as is possible here on earth, of the tabernacle in heaven. Every minute detail in the tabernacle is a representative of something in heaven. God instructed Moses not to leave out *any* detail. If God cared enough about a *shadow of the real thing* to insist it be executed in a precise manner, how much more does He care about how I live? It does matter that I live a holy, separated live unto Him.

Hebrews 8:7-8. Under the law, the priests had no power to overcome sin. If they had had the power, there would have been no need for a second covenant! The new covenant gives the believer the power to overcome sin on a daily basis.

Hebrews 8:10. The new birth experience (repentance, baptism by water & by spirit) wipes my sin slate clean and enables me to live a holy life. My whole mind set is changed. My inclination is no longer to sin, but to live my life pleasing to God.

Hebrews 8:13. The new covenant makes the old one obsolete. That is not to say God has changed. God cannot change (Malachi 3:6). His laws do not change, but the method or execution of those laws has. In the Old Testament, God's people exhibited their holiness by the ceremonial laws. The ceremonial laws were made obsolete by Jesus (Matthew 5:17). Today, we still must exhibit our holiness ~ holiness meaning a separation unto God. God has always required a visual separation of His people. I don't understand why people today think a visual separation is no longer necessary. When I walk into a room, before I even utter a word, people should be able to tell there is something "holy" about me. They may not be able to pinpoint what it is that is different about me, but they should be able to sense and see I have the aura of God's holy presence in my life. Over the years, we have had guests in our home. Some of them have been churched people and others have zero knowledge of God. The comment we hear from them all is, "Your home is so peaceful. There is a good atmosphere in your home." What a great opportunity to introduce them to Jesus!

Hebrews 9:1, 8-9. The tabernacle of the Old Testament had certain rules pertaining to how worship was to be conducted. These rituals have given way to worship from the heart. The rituals of the tabernacle were symbolic. This is another reason I need the Holy Spirit. I need to understand the rituals of old and apply their concepts to my heart and life. In keeping with the theme of Hebrews, the tabernacle of the New Testament is better than the tabernacle of the Old.

Hebrews 9:11-14. Jesus is a better sacrifice than the sacrifices of the Old Testament. The blood of animals gave temporary respite from the consequences of sin, but the blood of Jesus gives permanent relief. How can a spirit (God) shed blood? By coming in flesh, human form, of course! God robed in flesh is Jesus! God provided the perfect sacrifice required by the law, just like He provided the sacrifice for Abraham (Genesis 22:14). Jesus is *JHVH-Jireh*.

Hebrews 9:15. The sacrifice of Jesus qualifies Him to be the mediator between us (mankind) and God (the spirit) (Hebrews 8:6, 12:24; I Timothy 2:5).

Hebrews 9:16-22. If there is a testament, there must be a testator. A testament cannot be executed until the testator has died. The inheritance is not passed down until the testator has died. The blood of animals pacified the sentence of sin temporarily. God, in spirit form, cannot shed blood. Therefore, He put on flesh. That flesh, which we call Jesus, was the ultimate, and final sacrifice necessary to remit sin. The blood of Jesus is applied to my life at baptism (Acts 2:38). The Hebrew children had to apply the blood to their own doorposts in order for the death angel to pass over their house. It wasn't enough for the animal to be sacrificed. The animal's blood had to be applied. Likewise, I must apply the sacrifice of Jesus to *my personal* life. Without the application, Jesus' sacrifice is of no avail to me.

Hebrews 9:24-28. It is not necessary for Jesus to be a sacrificed over and over again such as animals were in the Old Testament. Jesus only had to shed His blood once and when He did, it was enough to cover the sins of all mankind! Jesus is the better sacrifice!

Hebrews 10:1. So many people discount the law and refuse to study the Old Testament. That shouldn't be. The Old Testament gives insight into our daily walk with God today. It was a *shadow* and an *example* (Galatians 3:24) to teach mankind how to get back to a relationship with God that mankind had in the Garden of Eden. Sin left unattended for so many years had taken mankind farther and farther away from that relationship point. The relationship of the Garden was "heaven" for God. That's what He intended when He made mankind. That's what He wants. We have our individual ideas of what heaven will be. Heaven for God is the relationship He intended when He first created me.

Hebrews 10:1-3. The purpose of the sacrifices of the Old Testament was merely to remind mankind of his sin. It was a continual reminder that no one ~ no human being ~ could by his/her own power and resolve, live a life free from sin.

Hebrews 10:4-5. The blood of animals could not atone for sin. Only the blood of a sinless human could. What human is sinless? God had to prepare a body for Himself (vs 20) to get the job done.

Hebrews 10:6-8. God did not enjoy seeing the animals (His creation) slaughtered. Millions of innocent creatures were slaughtered over the years because of the sin of mankind. My sin has far reaching consequences. Adam and Eve had no idea how many people would be affected by their moment of sin. How could I possibly know the long-term effects of my sin? I simply need to allow the Holy Spirit to operate in my life and live for God. *It's not rocket science!*

Hebrews 10:9-10. The blood of the body of Jesus sanctifies me. It sets me apart, so I have the opportunity to be saved. When I receive a jury summons, I am being set apart to serve on a jury. Whether or not I actually serve on the jury is contingent upon some variables, however, that summons "sanctifies" me (sets me apart) from the rest of the population. I can't just show up for jury duty without a summons! Likewise, the blood of Jesus sets me apart. Whether or not I am ultimately saved depends on some variables (my actions), but the opportunity for salvation has been made possible. Jesus is *JHVH-M'kadedesh*, the Lord who Sanctifies (Leviticus 20:7-8).

Hebrews 10:12. The "right hand of God" denotes the position of power. This is not a literal place. This scripture says that Jesus "sat down"; others stay He is standing. Is the Bible contradictory? That is impossible, so the figurative interpretation is correct. (See notes at Exodus 15:6, Psalm 110, and Isaiah 62:8 in *It's Not Rocket Science, Volume 3.*)

Hebrews 10:13. Jesus is waiting until His work is completely finished. His work (the work of His flesh in redemption) is not finished until Satan is completely put in his place. At that time, there will be no more need for the office of the sonship (redeemer) and this office will cease (I Corinthians 15:28).

Hebrews 10:14. Jesus' sole sacrifice was enough to complete salvation of all those who had obeyed the plan of salvation for both the Old and New Testament eras. The plan of salvation sets apart (sanctifies) those who obey it. Full and complete salvation does not occur until after the price for sin has been paid (Jesus' death) and the physical death of the individual.

Hebrews 10:15-16. The Holy Spirit confirmed what Jesus had taught while on earth: that is, the laws of God are written in our hearts. It is a matter of the *trajectory of* *the heart.* Is my heart on the right path? Has my mind been changed to the mind of Christ, or do I live by a set of rules and regulations set forth by a priest or leader? Is my heart in a place where I intuitively *know* what pleases God? When I read concepts in the scripture, can I apply them to my life? *Example*: The scripture teaches modesty and even defines it somewhat. When I study the Old Testament, I find that exposing the thigh was equated with prostitution. If I have the mind of God, I will not wear anything that is immodest. No preacher has to preach against various clothing. I will know what not to wear, if my heart is right with God. Immodest apparel will make me uncomfortable.

Hebrews 10:17-21. The shedding of Jesus' blood remits sins. Once I apply Jesus' blood to my life, my sins are expunged from my record and God can't remember them! God can't remember sins that have been repented of, remitted by baptism, and not committed again by the power of the Holy Spirit!!! It takes all three components to live a sin-less life. There is no need for additional blood sacrifices (as in the Old Testament) because Jesus paid the price once and for all. The blood of animals was a temporary fix until Jesus came. The expungement of my sins gives me the power to go directly to God with my petitions. *Jesus is the better high priest!*

Hebrews 10:24-25. We must motivate each other in our walk with God. When a brother/sister in Christ is discouraged, I encourage them. When they are hurting, I help them. I attend church to:
- Get fed. Although personal devotions are good and necessary, it is through preaching that my mind is engaged (Romans 10:14).
- Encourage others
- Corporate worship

Hebrews 10:26-29. Intentional sinning is a dangerous thing to do. Some people think they can just repent really quickly so it is okay to sin. I heard the women's director at a nearby church, tell a lie and immediately, under her breath, mutter, "Forgive me, Father." Uhm. It doesn't work that way. God is quick to forgive when we genuinely repent, but intentionally sinning and then asking for forgiveness is not repentance. Just as there was no mercy for those who knew, but transgressed, the law of the Old Testament, there will be no excuse and no mercy for those who intentionally sin. In modern courtrooms, there is a concept of "mitigating circumstances". If there is sufficient evidence someone has committed a crime, he/she is deemed guilty. Before a sentence is handed down the judge or jury will consider mitigating circumstances. A lighter punishment will be considered if someone snapped because of years of abuse, or has a history of mental illness, etc. This scripture states for those who know better, there is no mitigating circumstance which will reduce their punishment. I fear for those who use the grace of God as an excuse to sin.

Hebrews 10:30-31. I am so thankful no human (including me) has the responsibility to judge or to repay sins. That's God's job (Romans 12:19)! If it was up to me, I would have flicked this planet off its axis years ago! God will, in His own timing, judge. God's judgment will be pretty rough if the *trajectory of my heart* isn't right.

Hebrews 10:32-38. I will stand fast through the good times and the bad. I will be confident in God through the good times and the bad. I will have faith God will bring me through all types of circumstances which will pop up in my life. I will live a life that gives God pleasure! My end result is redemption and eternity in Heaven!

Hebrews 11 is the big Faith Chapter.

Hebrews 11:1. Faith is the realization of my prayers.

Hebrews 11:3. The word of God is powerful. God created all things by His word. Why do I think I can do better with human philosophy and reasoning? I must be true to His word!

Hebrews 11:6. It is also impossible to please God by walking after the flesh. Real faith means walking after the Spirit (Romans 8:8). If I have faith, I will seek after God. Faith demands action (works).

Hebrews 11:7. Healthy faith is a positive respect ("fear") for God's word. The ark was not for God's benefit. It was for Noah's benefit. Noah believed God's word, and therefore took action. My faith requires my action of obedience and not just lip service.

Hebrews 11:11. Even though Sarah originally laughed at the prospect of being a first-time mother in her 90s, she somehow came around to the idea and believed. That faith gave her strength to go through pregnancy and childbirth!

Hebrews 11:13. These Old Testament saints not only obeyed, but *embraced* the promises of God. I've got to jump in and give God 100%. Reading through the Bible is not enough. I must embrace it and internalize it. I must make it my own story.

Hebrews 11:15. There will always be an opportunity to look around and be sidetracked away from His word. There is always the opportunity to go back to the old paths. Lot's wife looked back at the last minute (Genesis 19:26). More than curiosity, I believe the *trajectory of her heart* caused her to look back.

Hebrews 11:17-19. The story of Abraham and Isaac is an intriguing one. We assume God told Abraham to sacrifice his son and he readily agreed. I'm not so sure it was like that. Abraham was just as human as I am. I think he really struggled to obey, but his final conclusion was God would raise Isaac from the dead. Isn't it interesting how we think things through and come up with the wrong conclusion sometimes? God didn't raise Isaac from the dead! He did over and beyond what Abraham could have hoped (Ephesians 3:20). He provided an alternate sacrifice so Abraham didn't have to actually sacrifice Isaac. All Abraham had to do was to offer up Isaac.

Hebrews 11:25. There is some pleasure in the world. Sin is fun for a season (Job 20:5). Unfortunately, once that season has had its run, the "wages of sin is death" (Romans 6:23). When I sin, I must bear the consequences. There is a small measure of peace in the world, but Jesus gives ultimate peace when I trust in Him (John 14:27). People come to my house and exclaim how peaceful it is. I don't really recognize it because I'm used to having the peace of God in my life. I guess I could compare it to someone who is extremely overweight. After they lose 100 pounds, they exclaim, "Wow! I feel great!" They didn't realize those extra pounds put a hardship on their bodies. I need to understand others don't have the peace that I do. I must be compassionate with them. I can't judge something based upon my feelings. I hear people say, "I just feel good about this." There is no place in scripture which holds my feelings as the plumb line. The Bible is the measuring stick (Psalm 138:2; Amos 7:8; Deuteronomy 6:18).

Hebrews 11:35-40. Unlike the previous verses in this great chapter of faith, these people did not receive deliverance or victory. This is a deep faith. This is a faith that looks beyond suffering and to the resurrection. The previous verses talk about people who fought battles by faith and won. These scriptures talk about people who kept the faith in the midst of their suffering. These people chose to suffer and obtain eternal life than to accept temporary relief and lose their soul. They had faith God had something better for them than this world.

Hebrews 11:40-12:1. I have a responsibility to the Old Testament saints to discharge the sins that drag and entangle me (Colossians 3:8-15). Some of these heroes are not named in the scripture, but God knows their names! How did they manage to stay strong and endure these horrific hardships? Could I hold up to that persecution? I think not, but then I am reminded of the scripture that says God's grace is sufficient (II Corinthians 12:9). In my flesh, I could not, but I trust God will give me what I need at the moment I need it!

Hebrews 12:2-3. If I compare myself to my fellow mankind, all types of negative feelings pop up (II Corinthians 10:12). I feel jealousy that my trials are harder than theirs. I feel lonely. I feel discouraged. All of these feelings are incorrect, of course, because they have trials that I don't have. We all have different triggers, but *everyone* has hard times. My struggles may be financial. Yours may be over health. Someone else's may be relationship issues. When I compare my trials to those of Jesus', however, my trials pale! My trials are small compared to His! When I look to Jesus, my trials no longer overwhelm me. I can make it through with His help! He overcame and so can I. I can do this!! The glories of Heaven await me! Heven will be worth whatever hardships I have to go through (Romans 8:18)!

Hebrews 12:5-11. No one likes to be disciplined! No one. No one thinks they are wrong. How does God chastise? How can God get my attention?
- The first thing He does is talk my heart. My own conscience and the prompting of the Holy Spirit should alert me that I am wrong (John 8:9). I must make a choice whether or not to listen to my conscience. If I decide not to correct myself, then
- God will talk to me through someone else. God sent the prophet, Nathan, to talk to King David (II Samuel 12).
- God may deal with me several times through various trials. (See essay entitled, "Troubles and Trials: Escape Route", in *It's Not Rocket Science, Volume 1.*)
- God then allows public exposure (Matthew 23:28-33, 26:24-25).
- Finally, God just turns me over to a reprobate mind (Romans 1:28).

I should never bristle with God's chastisement. He corrects me because He cares about me. He wants me to make it to heaven (II Peter 3:9). Just as I have a right to correct my own children and not someone else's, so God has a right to correct me, if I am His child (Deuteronomy 8:5). It's my choice whether or not I want to be His child. Will I accept correction from him? When I go through trials, it is a good time to examine the ***trajectory of my heart*** to see if my trial is God trying to get me back on course, or if the trial is a temptation from the enemy.

Hebrews 12:12-13. The attitude to have during a disciplinary trial is to be grateful I have the opportunity to make the necessary corrections to get myself back on track! God cares about me enough to take the time to discipline me.

Hebrews 12:14. I must be holy or I can't see God. That is rather difficult to do since I am a sinful human. It is only by the power of the Holy Spirit that I can live a holy life. I can't do it on my own. The Old Testament proved that point.

Hebrews 12:15-17. It is very, very easy to become bitter. Once bitterness has taken root, however, it is extremely difficult to dig it out. It is difficult to recognize bitterness in one's own life. It is good to have an accountability friend or mentor to help me identify problem areas in my spirit. I cannot avoid the tinge of bitterness that comes from betrayal, or other issues. I CAN, however, determine I will not allow bitterness to take root. Bitterness is like a cancer. It will ultimately destroy every relationship I have. It first kills the relationship I had with the person who did me wrong. It then kills my relationship with God. It ultimately drives away my family and friends. I might allow myself to wallow for a day or two, but I have to quickly get up, brush off, FORGIVE that person, and let God worry about avenging me. (PS: The best way to begin forgiving the person is to pray *for* them (Job 42:10; Matthew 5:44; Luke 6:28). I cannot allow someone to steal my relationship with God, family, and friends. We see in this passage Esau finally got around to repenting, but it was too late. He had allowed his bitterness to go unchecked so long he missed his opportunity to repent.

Hebrews 12:19-20. There are two types of backsliders:
- one who sins and knows he is sinning and
- one who turns away from truth and has become a reprobate.

Rejecting the word of God turns me into a reprobate. It is impossible for a reprobate or an apostate to be renewed (Hebrews 6:4-6). There comes a point of no return because they will not obey.

Hebrews 12:24-27. The blood of Abel cried out unto God from the ground (Genesis 4:10). The blood of Jesus speaks for me. *The shed blood of Jesus is better than the shed blood of Abel.* I must see to it I don't refuse the sacrifice of Jesus. How do I do that? By refusing to obey His words. I shall not be moved and shaken by every wind of doctrine that comes along, whether it be by public opinion or by a fellow "Christian". I will stand firm and not let the blood of Jesus be shed for me in vain.

Hebrews 12:29. There is another side of God besides the loving God. He is also a God of judgment. God has given me instructions on how to live a holy life, separated unto Him. He has also spelled out the consequences of NOT obeying His word. When I elect to sin, I am actually asking God to give me the punishment to fit my crime. God doesn't condemn anyone (John 8:11). We condemn ourselves. When we ask God to punish us, he obliges.

Hebrews 13. The concluding remarks of this book on faith are:
- Love each other.
- Remember those who are persecuted.
- Love your marriage.
- Behave.
- Be content. God is with me, what else do I need?
- Honor my spiritual leadership.
- *Reminder* God doesn't change!
- Stick to the original doctrine of the church.
- This world is not our home.
- Give verbal thanks (Psalm 116:17; Leviticus 22:29).
- Communicate.
- Obey spiritual leadership.
- Pray for spiritual leadership that they wouldn't fall.
- Be pleasing to God in all areas of life.

JAMES
Themes: Testings. Good works. Tongues. Exhortations.

James 1:2-3. I choose to have joy in spite of circumstances. What I am going through may not be joyful, but I am to define it as joy! Why? Because problems work on my character. I actually profit from trials! When I have joy internally, it will show externally. It's a matter of attitude. Jesus made it through the greatest trial of all times with joy (Hebrews 12:2). When the trial was over, He said, "It is finished" (John 19:30). My trial will be finished one day. I might as well have a good attitude about it and be joyful. (See also notes by Romans 5:2-4 above. See also essay entitled, "Troubles and Trials: Escape Route" in *It's Not Rocket Science, Volume 1*.)

James 1:4. Allow the trial run its course because you will be stronger, more patient, and closer to God when you are finished with it. When a trial is resisted, it is harder to endure. Surrender to it and allow it to happen.

James 1:6. Brother James loves similes! He is full of word pictures. Wavering faith is like an ocean wave. It is all over the place. Rooted and grounded faith gets results. Wavering faith is grasping at every new thought or idea that comes along. It is much like trying all of the new diet fads. They don't work and do damage to the body. Wavering faith doesn't work and does damage to my spiritual life. My faith is in Jesus. It is not in religious superstition. It is not in the "name it and claim it" preachers. It is not in politics or the economy. My faith is in Jesus. He didn't promise we wouldn't have troubles. In fact, he promised the opposite (John 16:33)! He did promise He would take care of us in spite of our troubles. I may not know how He will see me through my trial, but I know He will (Hebrews 13:5; Matthew 28:20).

James 1:7. I am guilty of this verse. I need to remember I shouldn't assume God knows what I want. Being God, He does know (Matthew 6:8), but He wants me to ask (Matthew 21:22; John 16:24). If I don't ask, I won't receive.

James 1:8. Have convictions! The wishy-washy person flip flops around and can't make a decision. My taste buds may change some over time, but my convictions and my life for God is settled! Even if the people I respect the most change their doctrine, I will cling to what the scriptures teach (Galatians 1:8).

James 1:9-11. Being rich isn't all it is cracked up to be. Riches don't last. It is the inward character and a life lived for God that matters. The ultimate analysis is this: is it temporal or eternal? My decisions must be made in light of eternity. When I humble myself, God will exalt me in due time. I don't need to pat myself on the back or bring attention to myself.

James 1:13-15. God does not tempt us. He may test us, but He does not tempt us to do evil. I cannot prevent evil thoughts that come crashing in my head, but I *can* control what I do with them. I must not dwell on them (vs 15; Psalm 7:14). When I dwell on my temptations, a strong desire is created. It is very hard to say no to strong desire. It is better to nip my temptation in the bud and not dwell on it. There are some things I don't even need to consider. I am not going to voluntarily allow temptation to dwell in my mind.

James 1:17. Is there anything good happening in my life (Psalm 84:11)? That's from God. Is there anything bad happening in my life? That's from the other guy. Sometimes I have to mentally take a piece of paper and draw a line down the middle. I categorize the good things on one side and the bad things on the other side. Oh yeah, the good always outweighs the bad. God is good to *all* (Psalm 145:9).

James 1:19-21. Patience is a virtue to be desired and cultivated. It is through patience that I will win life (Luke 21:19)! My daddy drilled Luke 21:19 in my head as a child. I am a red-head and all of the stereotypes fit! I have to force myself to be calm and patient. I have discovered most things take care of themselves if I back away and be patient. My anger serves no useful purpose. My lack of patience is characterized in verse 21 as being filthy!

James 1:22-25. It is not enough to hear the Word. Faith, real faith, demands action. If I really believe the word of God, I will take action upon it and do what it tells me to do. This ***ISN'T ROCKET SCIENCE.*** This doesn't take a whole lot of analyzing. It takes childlike acceptance (Matthew 18:3). Simply do what God tells us to do! I have to force myself to stop trying to figure out the rhyme and reason for things. God's ways are not mine (Isaiah 55:8). I'll have to be content with trusting He knows what He is doing and that it is right.

James 1:26. A true Christian will control his/her mouth! It doesn't matter how religious I am. If I don't control my tongue, I'm not right with God.

James 1:27. Pure religion is love in action and holiness. My "works" are a by-product of my faith (James 2:18-20, 24). Faith requires action. I am not saved by my works, but my works prove my faith. Faith and works go hand in hand (Hebrews 11:6; II Timothy 1:9; Ephesians 2:8-9). I believe this chair will hold me up, therefore I sit in it. I believe my car will get me to work safely, therefore I drive it. I believe in God; therefore, I obey His word. It's that simple. ***IT'S NOT ROCKET SCIENCE.***

James 2:1-6. I need to watch my motives. Do I give someone preferential treatment because they have a "position"? If so, why? *Everyone* matters to God. *Everyone* is important. I need to treat *everyone* with respect. Years ago, when I was much younger, I had a revelation! There was a lady in our church who sang VERY LOUDLY and very off-key. Ugh. I got irritated at her until my revelation. She was a worshiper! Her face glowed when she sang and she sang unto the Lord. I realized that whereas I was offended at her off-key screeching, God was loving it! God was basking in her adoration but was offended with my attitude. I had to repent. Preferential treatment is a sin (vs 9).

James 2:10-11. This scripture seems to contradict other scriptures. Since it is impossible for scripture to contract itself, I must analyze what this scripture means. As discussed previously, there is a moral law of God and in the Old Testament, a ceremonial law. The ceremonial law was fulfilled by Jesus (Matthew 5:17). The moral law of God stands. God basic character doesn't change (Malachi 3:6; Hebrews 13:8). He may change His methods of dealing with mankind, but His basic character doesn't change. I can't just pick and choose what I want to keep and make a doctrine out of it. I must obey God even if I don't like what He wants! Actually, if the *trajectory of my heart* is right, I WILL like what He wants. His ways become my ways and my desire will be His desires.

James 2:12-18. I cannot obtain mercy without showing mercy to others. Works is a by-product of faith. Faith requires action. I am not saved because of my works, but my works prove my faith. Lip service does not prove anything. Proclaiming a love for God and godly things means nothing. The *trajectory of my heart* is revealed by my works.

James 2:19. The devils believe in one God (Luke 4:41). This belief causes them to tremble because they know what their judgment will be. This verse is sandwiched between verses that talk about our works. Therefore, it is reasonable to deduct that my belief in one God should produce works.

James 2:20-26. In keeping with the theme of works completing or rounding out our faith, James gives the examples of Abraham and Rahab. Their faith produced actions or works. Proclaimed faith, without works, is just hot air. It was the works ascribed (imputed) to Abraham which resulted in him being called a friend of God. I can't say I am a friend of God if my works don't support my claim. Faith and works go hand in hand (vs 18; Hebrews 11:6).

James 3:1-2. We all stumble. Leaders are perceived to be perfect and thus, held to a higher standard, but no one is perfect. Understand that. My leadership will probably offend me at some point. If I understand they are flawed humans, I will not take offence. When I take offence, I open up a pandora's box for myself. (See essay entitled "Offence/Forgiveness" in *It's Not Rocket Science, Volume 1.*)

James 3:3-8. James' discourse on the tongue makes me think I know the reason God chose the utterance of unknown tongues to symbolize the infilling of the Holy Spirit (Acts 2:4). Who can tame the tongue? It is only when I have surrendered *everything*, even my tongue, that God can speak through me. There is power in the spoken word to speak good or to speak evil (Psalm 140:3). There is the potential for both. Will I surrender control of my mouth and words to God? Yes! I want God to guard my tongue, since I can't do a very good job guarding it myself (Psalm 141:3)!

James 3:9-14. When I talk badly about someone else, I am really talking badly about God, because we are all made in God's image. The old adage, "If you can't say anything nice, don't say anything at all" comes from this passage. When I talk out of both sides of my mouth, the ugly side prevails. The *trajectory of my heart* is revealed by my speech. Am I envious? Am I contentious? Am I angry? These negative traits are revealed by my tongue. To deny this is in my heart when these things come out of my mouth is lying to myself.

James 3:17-18. What is wisdom? We tend to think it means "smart". Not according to scripture! Wisdom is:
- Pure.
- Peaceable.
- Gentle.
- Accessible.
- Mercy.
- Good fruits.
- Without partiality.
- Without hypocrisy.
- Fruit of righteousness.

James 4:1-3. Why don't some prayers get answered? One reason is because they are prayed with the wrong motives! It's all about the *trajectory of the heart*. Am I praying for a new boat which will ultimately take me away from God? Am I praying for a raise on the job so I can take more vacations or am I praying for that raise so I can give more to missions? Most of my battles are because my *trajectory* is a little off. When my eyes get on others, I get jealous, I worry, I want to compete, etc. I've got to keep my eyes on Jesus. I don't need to scramble to achieve worldly success, but concentrate on pleasing Him! Oh, by the way, when I put first things first, He will take care of the rest (Matthew 6:33)! When my motives are right, God enjoys blessing me. [PS: Other reasons my prayers aren't answered is because I have abused my body (I Corinthians 3:17) or I have taken the sacrament without repenting (I Corinthians 11:30).] (See essay entitled "Is God Deaf?" in *It's Not Rocket Science, Volume 1*.)

James 4:4-5. I can't two-time God. He won't put up with that.

James 4:6-10. When I submit to God and humble myself before Him, He will give me the power to overcome my fleshly desires. I have to study the scriptures to see how God wants me to live and submit to Him. Pride causes me to rebel. Pride tells me my way is better and I can live for God MY way. Cain offered a sacrifice, but it was on his terms and not on God's terms. God rejected Cain (Genesis 4:1-15). How can I expect God to give me a free pass when I do things my way instead of His? If God turns a blind eye to my antics, He is going to have to apologize to Cain! He will be merciful with me; just has he was with Cain. He gave Cain several opportunities to repent. When Cain didn't, judgment came and was harsh. When I don't accept the opportunity to repent, my judgment will be harsh as well.

James 4:11-12. When I talk badly about someone, I become their self-appointed judge. Judging is God's job. He doesn't like it when I usurp authority and take over His job.

James 4:13-15. This old saying comes to mind as I read this passage: "Good Lord willin' and the creek don't rise!" We can plan future events all day long, but the truth of the matter is, we might not live long enough to accomplish those goals. When I remember it only takes one stroke or even one car wreck to change my life forever, I am humbled and ask God to guide me each day and make each day count for Him. I do want God's PERFECT will in my life ~ not just His permissive will. I don't want to nag Him to the point He just lets me do my thing. I want to trust HIM and trust He knows what is best for me. Even though I might not understand the circumstances. I trust His decisions and direction.

James 4:17. There is a sin of omissions. When I know to do good and I just refuse to do it, I have sinned. (Oh, dear!)

James 5:1-6. The rich who live for themselves and not for God will only enjoy their riches for a season. If God can trust me with riches, of course I want it! However, if God, in His infinite wisdom, knows that He cannot trust me with riches, it is better for me to struggle financially and be saved than to bask in my riches and be lost.

James 5:7-11. Our time is not God's time. God has a schedule, but it is not defined by a 24-hour day, such as ours. I have heard all of my life the second coming of Jesus could be any day. I still believe that! In my human eyes, it seems like He is taking forever to return. In reality, He may not return in my lifetime, BUT He sure could! I will be patient and be ready whenever His time is right. The prophets of old are my examples. They patiently preached and waited for the coming of the Messiah. None of them actually lived to see the day Jesus was born, but they still believed, and even endured persecution because of their beliefs. Likewise, I will believe.

James 5:13-15. Sometimes, a public step of faith is called for.

James 5:16. Prayer partners give power to prayers ... (just make sure to pick a trusted person!) When I admit my faults to another person, I have a greater realization and understanding of myself. I have a clearer vision of what to pray for. When I admit my shortcomings, I pray with a fervency to get those areas fixed. My fervency carries a lot of weight with God.

James 5:19-20. Unfortunately, from time to time, people backslide. Some go into false doctrine and ultimately apostasy, but others just go into sin. Once someone has denied truth, there's not much hope (II Thessalonians 2:11), but since God is the judge, it is my job to still work with anyone who has erred. If they have just gotten off course, but their *trajectory* can be corrected, I have a part in their soul's salvation. God will forgive a multitude of sins when the sinner is converted. As a soul winner, I play a part of this "hiding" process. This scripture does NOT mean that I should turn a blind eye to sin.

I PETER
Themes: Salvation. Christian living. Stand firm in suffering.

I Peter 1:2. The plan of salvation is once again, outlined by Peter. We must be born of the Spirit and the water, and we must obey the word of God. I suppose this is the scripture people use to sprinkle water on others as a form of baptism. To interpret it such, however, would be in contradiction to all other scriptures which declare baptism is by immersion. Does the Bible contradict itself? No! That is impossible. To accept the Bible contradicts itself is to declare the Bible null and void. In some Old Testament ceremonies people were sprinkled with blood for times of consecration or purification. This is a type of what Christ has done for us through His atonement and is not the same as baptism, which is a washing away of sins.

I Peter 1:3-7. Heaven will be worth all of the temporary trials I have to go through! Trails are for a season. Trials are for reason. **Why do I have trials?**
- To humble me (Deuteronomy 8:2).
- To prove the *trajectory of my heart* (Deuteronomy 8:2; Judges 2:22).
- Teach me to lean on God (Deuteronomy 8:3).
- For chastisement (Deuteronomy 8:5).
- To refine me (Isaiah 48:10; Job 23:10; Psalm 66:10; I Peter 4:12).
- To perfect, establish, strengthen & settle me (I Peter 5:10; Hebrews 2:10).
- To work patience (Romans 5:3-4; James 1:4).
- To soften us and teach me compassion (II Corinthians 1:4-6).
- I cannot enter Heaven w/o trials (Acts 14:22; Hebrews 12:5-11).
- To learn to obey God (Psalm 119:67, 71).
- To know the Lord better (Philippians 3:10).
- For my salvation (II Corinthians 1:6). I will come at a crossroads where I must

decide, once and for all, if I am going to live for God. This "trial of my faith" will challenge everything I believe. It will define the true ***trajectory of my heart***. (See essay entitled "Troubles and Trials: Escape Route" in *It's Not Rocket Science, Volume 1* for in depth discussion on trials.*)*

I Peter 1:8. Faith is defined here. By the time this was written, there were Christians who had never physically seen Jesus.

I Peter 1:10-13. The experience the New Testament believers (including us today) receive was thought about, wondered about, and longed for by the prophets of the Old Testament. What a privilege to live in the era of the new birth experience! The glory of God was:
- Inquired about & searched for by the prophets,
- Desired by the angels, and
- Received by US.

Therefore, I need to get a grip and be serious about my salvation!!

I Peter 1:13-14. I can't allow my imaginations to go wild. The human mind is capable of thinking far beyond the moment. It is capable of creating possible scenarios and make decisions. *Example:* We think beyond the moment every day while driving. We look at the car ahead on the shoulder and decide what we will do if the driver decides to merge into our lane of traffic. There is a danger of allowing my mind to explode into thought. The KJV says, "gird up the loins of your mind." The "loin" is the reproductive part of the body. I have to reign in my imagination and not allow my mind to go places the scripture doesn't go. A simple example is this: There is no mention in the Bible about the salvation of infants. I can logically argue both sides of the issue! The truth of the matter is: God is in control. What God says will be. God is just and fair. I'll let Him be God! I will focus on obeying the scriptures regardless of popular public opinion at the time. I will not allow my mind to be persuaded by the philosophies of mankind. The Bible will be my guide. I will be as a child and just obey without bringing in the rationale of my humanity.

I Peter 1:15-17. God is holy. He is pure. 100%. Why would I think that He would allow a smidgen of unholiness in me? I understand I have human failings, but by the power of the Holy Spirit, I can live a holy life. My every action should be governed by whether or not it is pleasing to God. My daily decisions should be based with eternity in mind. If I have a reverence for God and Heaven, I will make that my practice (vs 15).

I Peter 1:18-21. I was freed from the bonds of sin. I was set free. I was rescued, not by money, but by the blood of Jesus (Luke 24:21)! Therefore, when Jesus was on the cross, it <u>seemed</u> as though He could not redeem Israel, but with His resurrection, the redemption process was accomplished. *Example:* I am handcuffed to a fence and I am stuck there. If someone comes along and gives me the key, I can be free

BUT, I have to take the cuffs off. If I don't use the key, I stay cuffed to the fence. If I do use the key, unlock the cuffs but fail to take them off, I can easily re-cuff myself. If I squirm around without removing the cuffs, they will lock back up. I have to shake off those cuffs to be totally free. Jesus has provided the key to my salvation. I have to use it. Will I break free completely or will I squirm around and fall back into sin? I must take action!

I Peter 1:22-25. How is my soul purified? By obedience to the word of God. The word of God is the incorruptible seed (Luke 8:11). In recent history, scientists have planted seeds found in the ancient Egyptian pyramids. Those seeds still had life in them and once planted and watered, grew! The life of the seed had not been corrupted or compromised, even though it had been dormant and in a dark place for thousands of years. God's word is even more incorruptible. It is forever settled (Psalm 119:89). The tide of public opinion changes with each generation. Just look at fashion! Don't throw away your clothes! Your grandchildren will love them!! God's word does not change because God does not change (Malachi 3:6).

I Peter 2:1-2. Because of the preceding verses, I put down all ungodly feelings and behaviors and eagerly gobble up the word of God. I have to ingest and digest the word of God. My goal is not to go to Heaven, but my goal is to be like Jesus. If I emulate Him, I'll make it to Heaven without a problem! My attitude cannot be, "What do I have to do to be saved", but rather, "How closely can I emulate Jesus".

I Peter 2:3. Try Jesus! You'll like it. Living for Jesus 100% is a wonderful life. God is good (Psalm 34:8). He has my best interests at heart. Therefore, I trust Him with my life, even when trials that come my way.

I Peter 2:4-5. My emulation of Jesus will not be popular by worldly standards. The priesthood and sacrifices of the Old Testament are now experienced in a spiritual format. Those of old were a physical example of a spiritual act: an object lesson (Hebrews 8:5). My spiritual sacrifice is my daily living for God. It is a lifestyle. It is not limited to a Sunday event. It is a daily commitment.

I Peter 2:9. I belong to God. I am His "possession" by:
- Creation. He made me.
- Purchase. He bought me back from Satan. I am twice His.
- Calling. He gives me a choice. He calls out to me to willingly be His, even though I am rightfully His. He will allow me to make the choice to go back to Satan, if I so choose.

I Peter 2:11. I cannot give into the carnal desires which war against me. It is not just a "for the moment" situation. My soul is involved. My actions have long-lasting consequences. There are some things which may not be an outright sin, but if it might lead me to a sinful path, I have to resist. I should resist even the *appearance* of evil (I Thessalonians 5:22).

I Peter 2:12-19. My good citizenship will be a light to unbelievers. I am to obey the laws of the land (as long as they don't conflict with God's law).

I Peter 2:20-23. Remember, God will eventually avenge me (Romans 12:19).

I Peter 2:24-25. At the forefront of my mind, I realize I was wandering around lost and Jesus paid the price for my salvation and healing (Isaiah 53:5). I won't go back to sin.

I Peter 3:1-2. Unbelieving husbands can possibly be won just by the godly behavior of the wife! Please note: Verse 1 tells wives to be subject to their *own* husband, not every male. Some men take this verse as a license to be a tyrant. This verse always must be coupled with Ephesians 5:25, which explains the role of the husband.

I Peter 3:3-5. The *trajectory of my heart* will shine through in my outward appearance. PS: "Plaiting" (KJV) means elaborate adorning and is not the same as braiding. In Biblical times, elaborate hair styles were customary. People inserted all manner of ornaments. Remember, modesty is the rule of thumb. Anything which is "over the top" and draws attention to oneself instead of drawing attention to Jesus is to be avoided (I Timothy 2:9). I wonder about some of the ostentatious hair decorations I see in modern times. I wonder what God thinks of them. I'm glad I'm not God!

I Peter 3:7. Prayers are hindered when the chain of authority is broken. When I feel like my prayers aren't going anywhere, I need to check my submit/love relationship. The wife is to submit to the leadership of the husband; HOWEVER, the husband is to love the wife as much as Christ loved the church. Love is a more powerful bond than the bond of submission. Love demands more. Love requires submission! Jesus submitted to the will of the people because of love (Mark 5:17, 20). Jesus submitted to Calvary because of love (Philippians 2:8). Conclusion: The marital relationship is one of submission one to the other ~ with the man bearing the ultimate responsibility for decisions made for the family, and for the spiritual direction the family takes.

I Peter 3:9-11. When I am like Jesus, I will repay insults with a blessing! I am to be a blessing to others. If I repay a curse with a curse, how I am, as a Christian, any different than the sinner? I had a neighbor who, to make a very long story short, was just jealous of us. They did many malicious things over the course of several years to try and run us out of the neighborhood. One day, there was a death in their family. I took over a cake and expressed my condolences. Since that time, we became friends. We no longer live in that neighborhood, but these people come into my store and chit-chat like there was never any issues in the past! Being kind to someone who isn't kind to you never hurts: it just might help (Proverbs 26:21-

22)!

I Peter 3:15. I want to be prepared to be an instant witness. Going out and knocking on doors is not my cup of tea! That type of evangelism has been successful in some areas, but being a personal witness is very powerful. Do I have an intelligent, spiritual, and kind answer for the questions people ask me regarding my beliefs? Do I stumble around and just say "my religion says ..."? Do I even know why I act/dress/speak the way I do? When I am prepared for these questions, I garner respect and make the other person stop and think. I should be ready for a quick, short answer and I should be ready to give a Bible study for those who are interested in the long answer!

I Peter 3:16-18. Sometimes we suffer for doing right. That's ok! Suffering is only for a season. Jesus suffered for doing right as well and look what He accomplished by His suffering: my salvation! I may never know the consequences of my suffering, but God does (vs 12). A friend of mine was a waitress. She was angry at the world and close to being suicidal. A group of Pentecostal young people came in. The happier they were and the more fun they had just fueled her depression. She intentionally gave them horrible service. They still gave her a good tip and invited her to church. She was intrigued by their kindness to her and visited their church. She is now a pastor's wife! These teenagers repaid the suffering she gave them with kindness and the result is not only *her* salvation, but the salvation of all of those she has won to the Lord!

I Peter 3:20. God actually waits and withholds His judgment for "just a few" whose *trajectory of the heart* is pointed in the right direction. He waited for: Abraham to negotiate for Sodom and for Noah to finish the ark! Will God withhold judgment from my community for my benefit?

I Peter 3:21. Repentance is not enough. Baptism is important too! We experience the resurrection of Jesus by the in filling of the Holy Spirit (Romans 6:4). These three steps (Acts 2:38) are necessary to (1) give us a clean slate and to (2) get us on the right *trajectory*. Of course, living a holy, separated life on a daily basis is also paramount to salvation!

I Peter 4:1. Suffering brings the most important things in life into focus: that I have the same mind as Jesus and stop my sinning. I can strengthen myself by having the same mind as Jesus. My suffering is for my soul's salvation and to help me learn to love others. Suffering produces character (Ecclesiastes 7:3). How I respond to the suffering determines whether the character produced is a good one or not!

I Peter 4:2-6. This world is not my home. I am merely passing through a testing ground. This testing ground will prove the *trajectory of my heart*. Do I love God enough to say focused on eternal matters? Will I get sidetracked by the things of this world?

I Peter 4:7-9. Everything is either temporal or eternal. *Example:* If I am diagnosed with cancer, I do want you to pray for me. However, whether I die of cancer now or live another 20 years and die of something else is really a temporal matter. What really will matter 50 years from now? What will matter is not how long I lived on earth, but whether or not I lived for God! Pleasing people is a temporal thing. Pleasing God is eternal. How do I please God? By loving Him enough to obey His word and by loving others. Loving others doesn't mean to cover up their sins (vs 8), but it means to love them *in spite* of their sins.

I Peter 4:10-11. Our ministries or giftings are not all the same. I need to figure out what I am good at and do it to the very best of my abilities. I don't need to worry about being like someone else. Our talents are different. We all play different roles in the body of Christ. Each role is dependent upon another. If I neglect my role, the whole body of Christ will suffer (Romans 12:4-6; I Corinthians 12:26-28).

I Peter 4:12-16. Why are we surprised when we go through a trial? Trials are common and not a strange phenomenon. I can avoid many trials by living right (vs 15). Some trials, however, are because Satan is fighting for my soul. Those trials are actually a compliment (vs 16)! I sure hope I can see it that way and rejoice when I go through one!

I Peter 4:17. This is a spoof on Amos 5:15. "The Judgment Day" is in the future, but the daily choices we make means we bring judgment upon ourselves daily (Ezekiel 6:9). I must make the right choices each day because I will reap what I sow and there is a Judgment Day coming.

I Peter 4:18. No one is going to just squeak by. I'm either saved or not. There is no middle ground. I am either living for God 100% or I'm not living for Him at all.

I Peter 5:1-5. This passage is specifically addressing pastors. (See notes at Jeremiah 23 and Ezekiel 34 in *It's Not Rocket Science, Volume 3.*)
- Pastors are to teach the word of God without regard to their finances.
- Pastors are not demi-gods, but are loving care-takers of, and examples to, the children of God.
- Pastors have a special reward.
- Younger ministers, submit to a mentor.
- Be humble.

I Peter 5:6. We all have talents, but they are God-given talents and can be taken away at any moment. My talents are not something I can be proud of. They are something I am grateful for. When I recognize the source of my talents, I am humbled. When I recognize others have talents I don't possess, I am humbled. Pride and overconfidence played a huge part in Samson's downfall. My weaknesses are the true me. My strengths and talents are all God-given. I might as well humble myself. If I don't, God will.

I Peter 5:7. Jesus cares for me! The sparrow is His creation, but He died for me (not the sparrow). I have value to God (Matthew 10:31; Luke 12:7). Of course, He cares about the things which bother me! He has a listening ear to my troubles and a large shoulder for me to cry on! He even has solutions for my troubles, if I will just bring them to Him (Matthew 11:28)!

I Peter 5:8. Mosquitos love me. When I go outside in the summer time, I take precautions and put on mosquito repellent. Hunters are vigilant to take precautions against ticks. Those who go out in the jungles watch out for leeches. Likewise, I take precautions against the attacks of Satan. Satan is a parasite. This is why I stay away from even the appearance of evil (I Thessalonians 5:22). I am on guard. I know my own weaknesses and I will not allow myself to intentionally be tempted.

I Peter 5:9-10. We all experience trials. That is a given (Matthew 5:45; John 16:33; Job 14:1). *However*, after our trial, God completes us.

II PETER

Themes: Day of the Lord ~ Call to holiness ~ Warnings against apostates ~ Spiritual growth and maturity.

II Peter 1:1-2. This faith is precious. It comes from and grows by the word of God (Romans 10:17). I will guard it and not dilute it. Through Jesus, I can be in good standing with God (I Corinthians 1:30). Why would I want to jeopardize my good standing by being disobedient or by trying to twist God's word into saying what I want it to? Grace and peace both come via the knowledge of God. I need both of those: grace and peace! I must study and know God more.

II Peter 1:3-4. Through my knowledge of God, I am given *all* things pertaining to life and godliness. I need that! *Therefore*, I need to *know* God. The Israelites in the wilderness knew God's actions, but Moses knew God's *ways* (Psalm 103:7). It is not enough for me to hear the testimony of others. It is not enough for me to hear what someone else has to say about God's word. In an American court of law, that is considered "heresy evidence" and is not admissible! If a secular court would not admit heresy testimony into evidence, what makes me think God would be okay with it? I have to get to know God for <u>myself</u>. I have to have my own good relationship with Him.

II Peter 1:5-7. I should grow spiritually after I have been initially saved. I cannot stagnate. I must grow. As a babe in Christ, I hunger for more of His word (I Peter 2:2). I should not stay on the same level of spirituality. I must grow. The scripture uses an analogy of milk and meat to depict levels of spiritual growth (I Corinthians 3:2; Hebrews 5:12-13). The steps to spiritual maturity are:
- Faith,
- Knowledge,
- Temperance (balance),
- Patience,
- Godliness,
- Kindness, and
- Love.

II Peter 1:8-11. If I have the above virtues, I will grow and bring forth fruit. If not, I will digress to the point of even losing my salvation. There is no stagnant place with God. I'm either in or out (Revelation 3:16). My salvation is contingent upon my spiritual growth. Eternal security, as some preach, is not guaranteed. I must grow. This letter was not written to unbelievers or even new Christians. It was written to seasoned believers. I've seen some new Christians .more mature than some who have been attending church for decades! That ought not be.

II Peter 1:12-15. It is always good to be reminded of old truths and to reaffirm my faith and belief (3:1). I am human and need to be reminded. This is why I continue to return to the word of God. As the news of current events and changes in popular opinion come about, I have to go back to the basics of God's word and strengthen my grip on my faith.

II Peter 1:16-19. Peter and the other apostles didn't just cook up a new religion. They didn't have a fantasy dream or go into a trance. They didn't sit down and plot out a set of beliefs to con people out of money. They had an *experience* with God. They met Him face-to-face in the form of Jesus! Their writings are qualified to be used by me as a blueprint and reference for my life. Their writings will light my spiritual pathway to Heaven.

II Peter 1:20-21. Prophecies (or, forth telling) were and are inspired of God. God is not going to contradict Himself. I am not allowed to twist what He says to suit my fancy.

II Peter 2:1-3. False prophets abound (I Timothy 4:1). Many people follow false prophets and are deceived. How do I detect a false prophet? Here are some characteristics:
- Doctrines are heresy, meaning they are not Biblical and might even be anti-Biblical.

- In it for personal gain (Micah 3:11; Titus 1:7). Religion can be a money-making business!
- Lax and unrestrained (Isaiah 28:7-8; Jeremiah 23:14, 32).
- Want to be popular (II Timothy 4:3-4).
- Lead men further from God (Deuteronomy 13:1-5; II Timothy 3:13).
- Glory in their own wisdom (Colossians 2:18; Philippians 3:18-19).
- Boastful & deceptive (II Corinthians 11:12-15; Jude 12-15).
- Corrupt & unmerciful (vs 14; II Timothy 3:1-9; Jude 4-19; Revelation 13).

II Peter 2:4-6. Judgment will ultimately come. If God doesn't judge them, He will have to apologize to Satan, Noah's generation, Sodom & Gomorrah, etc.! Judgment will come! I cannot get side-tracked and hood-winked into thinking these false preachers are right because they are prospering at the moment. I will stay the course and keep my eyes on Jesus!

II Peter 2:7-9. God knows how to protect me and deliver me! He knows how. When I don't know how to get myself out of a sticky situation, He does. I take comfort in that.

II Peter 2:10-11. The angels know not to badmouth anyone to God. Unfortunately, humans aren't so smart. Those who allow their flesh to rule feel free to badmouth others. It's all about the *trajectory of the heart*. If my heart is right, I won't speak evil of others. If I feel the urge to talk badly about someone, it is time to tune-up my heart.

II Peter 2:12-18. The subject matter of this chapter is false teachers. However, there is an underlying principle here. People who say negative things about others don't just stop there. Their negativity breeds discontent. It spreads to those who will listen. Peter holds nothing back as he calls them out. I think he was rather upset as he penned these words! How dare negative people contaminate the body of Christ!! The negative spirit creates the atmosphere for all types of sins and hypocrisy.

II Peter 2:19-22. Oh my, how many times have I heard of people being "liberated" from the "bondage" of living a life pleasing unto God! Freedom is being *able* to live a life pleasing unto God. "Bondage" is not having a choice, but to be sinful. Peter is calling out those who have once believed and obeyed, but since rejected living a holy life and allowed their fleshly desires to rule again. Judgment is harsh for those who have experienced God and have rejected Him (Matthew 12:45; Hebrews 6:4-6; 10:26-29). I can't live for God my way. I must live for Him *His* way.

II Peter 3:1-2. The subject of this letter is this: to remind the church of the core doctrines.

II Peter 3:3-9. People get impatient. God is very patient. It's sometimes hard to get on the same page as God. I have to trust Him when it appears He is not doing what He said He would do. That's hard for me as a human. I have to condition my mind to sit back, relax, just trust and wait on God. He is coming back. There will be a judgment. I may not see it in my lifetime, but I will live as though it will happen any minute. God is not confined to a 24-hour day, a 365.25-day year. God is timeless. Therefore, what was promised cannot be measured by human time. There will always be those who scoff and disregard the warnings in the scriptures. I'm not one of them.

II Peter 3:10-14. *All* things as we know it will ultimately be dissolved. Why do I want to hang on to things which will not be? It pains me to see bumper stickers which say something to the effect of "My friend busted hell wide open - I might as well join the party." I want to go bang on the door of the vehicle and scream, "Are you insane? Do you honestly think hell is going to be a huge party that appeals to all of the human senses?" No! Hell is a depravation of all those things. That which I refuse to give up here on earth to live for God will be surrendered at the door of hell. I might as well give it up now, live for God, and enter Heaven! Hell is not a place for friends to get together. It is a place of torment. Torment and torture are separate things. Torture is bodily pain. I believe hell will contain torture, because of the fire and brimstone element. However, worse than that will be the torment of the mind. To be able to remember the chances I had to live right and didn't would be mental torment. To remember the times I refused to repent would be torment. I feel my blood pressure rising just typing these words! Suffice it to say that for me, personally, I do not intent to go to hell. I will go overboard to insure my destination is Heaven. What little bit I may have to give up during the few years I have here on earth will be well worth the sacrifice!

II Peter 3:15-16. Peter officially endorsed Paul's ministry and writings. It is good to work together. We are all on the same team. We should not be building our own kingdoms. This is GOD's church, and not Pastor XYZ's church! Peter acknowledged Paul was a little more cerebral in his writings which make them a little more difficult for the uneducated to understand. However, we all have our place and we all have a ministry. Together, we will present a church to God.

II Peter 3:17. Peter leaves us with one last admonition not to backslide.

I JOHN
Themes: Love ~ Knowing the Truth ~ Fellowship.

The crux of I John is LOVE. It's that simple. ***It's not Rocket Science!***
- If I don't have love and show love to others, God does NOT dwell in me (I

John 4:8, 10, 13, 16).
- If I love God, I will love to please Him and obey His word (I John 5:3).
- Living godly is not hard when I'm in love with Jesus. It is only hard when I love myself more than Him (I John 5:3).

I John 1:1-3. What was from the beginning? God in spirit form. God then manifest Himself in flesh. John and the others physically saw that manifestation in the body form of Jesus Christ. There are not multiple gods. Neither does God have a split personality. There is one God, who manifested Himself in the fleshly form we call Jesus (Genesis 1:1; John 1:1-5; 14; Colossians 1:18). The godhead isn't complicated. *It isn't rocket science.*

I John 1:6-8. Hypocrisy is a sin (I John 2:4)! I must have the right attitude on the inside of me (Psalm 51:6). Even though I am saved and live a godly life, I still have a sinful nature. The sinful nature is passed down through the father's blood line. This is why Jesus could not have a human father. Jesus did not have a sinful nature. (See notes on Gnosticism above at "Colossians, Social Climate".)

I John 1:9; 2:1; 3:6-9. Just because I have a sinful nature, doesn't mean I have to keep on sinning. I cannot stay a sinner and be saved. True, if I do slip up and sin, I can receive forgiveness, but the availability of forgiveness does not give me license to live a life of sin (Hebrews 10:26). I cannot be a habitual sinner. The King James Version of the Bible uses the word "froward" to describe a habitual sinner. I must not love the world system (I John 2:15).

I John 2:3-6. To really know God is to keep His commandments. **THIS ISN'T ROCKET SCIENCE.** Nike had a slogan "Just do it". That's what I want to scream out to people. Don't argue with the Bible, JUST DO IT! Do the Word. You say you love God, then do His word. Obey! When I keep God's commandments, His love is perfected or completed in me. If I say I am a Christian, but don't act like Christ, I am not a Christian!

I John 2:7. The message of love isn't anything new.

I John 2:8-11. I have to practice Christianity. I can't live one way during the hour or so of a church service and think I am okay. I have to practice love. It takes practicing! We don't get it right on the first try - or the second, for that matter! Just as a master surgeon must practice years before achieving master status, I must practice love. When I do, my salvation won't be a question. Remember: to love means to obey (I John 5:3). When I love God, I will obey His commandments (one of which is to love others). God is love (I John 4:16). When I have difficulty loving others, I am lacking in God.

I John 2:12-14. How encouraging to know there was a group of believers who overcame! I will meet them someday. We'll swap testimonies!

I John 2:15-16. I can't love the world system. It is not godly. I'm all for voting in elections, but I must understand that the political system is not a godly one. The world system consists of three categories and <u>*ALL*</u> sins fall under one of these:
- Lust of the flesh,
- Lust of the eyes, or
- Pride of life.

I John 2:17-18. What will I have or what will matter 50 years, 75 years from now? Nothing, except for my life for God! At some point, everything as I know it will pass (or I will pass)!

I John 2:19-20. There will be backsliders. The spirit of the Antichrist was around in John's day and in my day. The Antichrist is a man who claims to be the Christ, but the spirit of the Antichrist is anyone against Christ. Anyone who refuses to obey is against Jesus. That is a harsh statement, but it is true.

I John 2:20. The Holy Spirt will discern the real from the sham. I need to:
- receive the Holy Spirit,
- recognize its voice, and
- allow it to operate in my life by obeying it!

I John 2:21-24. People tend to forget the epistles were written to people who had *already* heard the truth. These were not written to unbelievers, but to believers. Apparently, the early church had just as much of a problem with backsliders and people twisting the truth around to fit their own theology as we do today! There is no gospel other than what was preached by Jesus and the apostles. The disciples had walked and talked with Jesus for three years. The highlights of His teachings/ministry were recorded in His biographies, but the details and application of His teachings were written in letter form (epistles). Jesus spent the days from the resurrection to the ascension teaching (Acts 1:2). Those teachings are revealed through the epistles. Years after the apostles had died, other teachings came into existence. Many denominations accept those teachings (outside of apostolic teaching) as being from God. Unfortunately, many of those teachings are in conflict with what was set forth by the apostles. God will not contradict Himself. I have to go back to the root. I have to obey scripture first.

I John 2:26. The world is trying to seduce me. Seduction is a process to make me do that which I know not to do. Seduction appeals to my senses. Seduction nags and wears me down at my weak spot. Seduction uses logic and human rationalization.

I John 2:27. I know of a man who uses this scripture to say he doesn't need a pastor. God gave us the five-fold ministry, so to interpret this passage as such would be in conflict with Ephesians 4:11. This scripture is not against human teachers, but is against human philosophy. Human reasoning is not a basis for understanding truth. There is no new doctrine; only that preached by Jesus as applied by the apostles.

I John 2:28-29. If I just obey the Bible, I don't have to be worried about my condition when Jesus comes back or when I die, whichever comes first! I have confidence in my salvation if I will live right! ***IT'S NOT ROCKET SCIENCE!***

I John 3:1-3. I can't expect the world to fully accept me. I am not really a part of this world (system). I am very involved in my community, both as a business owner and a volunteer, however, I am different. They know I am different. My dress is different. My speech is different. My actions are different. Being different is good! If I blend in with the world, something is wrong. People should be able to point me out and say, "There goes a real Christian!"

I John 3:4. Definition of sin: disobedience, insubordination.

I John 3:6-11. If I am a Christian, I will not habitually sin. I may slip up from time to time and commit a sin. I am, after all, human! *Example:* From time to time, I will buy a donut. However, I don't go to the donut shop every day. I don't make a habit of buying donuts! Likewise, I don't make a habit of sinning! If I do commit a sin, I must be quick to repent and fix the problem. My habits must be to do right and love others. (Thankfully, buying an occasional donut is not a sin!)

I John 3:12-21. Compassion for others is not just lip service. Do I put my actions and money where my mouth is? It is not enough to *say*, "I love you". I must *do*. Loving others means I put my own wants aside to help someone out. I will put my plans aside and drive someone to the doctor. I will set aside my "Starbucks" money and fill up someone's car with gas so they can get to work. I will forgo a restaurant meal and buy groceries for someone in need. Perhaps I need to forgo desert in order to give a decent tip to the waitress! John starts off with Cain as an example. Everyone knows and accepts murder is wrong. How does someone get to the point of murder? They hate so much they commit murder. How does someone get to the point of hatred? They are selfish. A big sin starts out very small. The opposite of selfishness is love. If I make sure my love-o-meter is on full, I will not sin. How do I stay full of love? Since God is love (I John 4:8), I must stay full of God. It's that simple. *It's not rocket science!* (See essay entitled, "Did Jesus Get It Wrong?" in *It's Not Rocket Science, Volume 1*.)

I John 3:22-24. On the heels of the admonishment to love others with actions is the statement that my prayers would be answered because (1) I obey and (2) I love. Hmmmm. That means, conversely, that my prayers are hindered if I don't (1) obey and don't (2) love.

I John 4:1-3. There are different spirits: (1) heavenly, (2) Satanic, and (3) human. I must prove a spirit to see if it is of God or not. What is the test of truth? It is acknowledging Jesus is God in the flesh. This is not mere lip service, because even the devil believes this (James 2:19).

I John 4:4-13. Love defines a Christian. If I don't have and show love to others, God does NOT dwell in me. It's that simple. ***This isn't Rocket Science!*** This type of love is not natural love one has for a family member. This kind of love is supernatural. We can't conjure up this kind of love on our own. It is imparted to us when we are filled with His spirit (vs 13). This is why I need the Holy Spirit! I can't love the way God wants me to without it!

I John 4:16. God = Love. It's a mathematical equation. There are no variables. God is love.

I John 4:17-20. If I don't love, I don't have God. It's that simple. ***IT'S NOT ROCKET SCIENCE!*** There is no if, ands, or buts. I have to love others REGARDLESS and without prejudice: racial, social, economic, etc.

I John 5:1-3. To believe is to love. To love is to obey. For me to say that I believe in Jesus as my personal savior to be true, I must obey His word. When I'm in love with God, pleasing Him is not an issue (Psalm 119:44-45). Living godly is not hard when I am in love with Jesus. It is only difficult when I love myself more than I love Him. If I love God, I will love to please Him and obey His word.

I John 5:12. This verse tells us Christ is in us. I John 4:13 tell us the Spirit is in us. I John 4:16 tells us God is in us. Are there three? No! There is just one Spirit (Deuteronomy 6:4).

I John 5:16-17. There is an unpardonable sin, and there are pardonable sins. In my opinion, an unpardonable sin is any sin that is not dealt with. If I don't repent, I won't be pardoned. If I am deceived into thinking I am not sinning, I won't repent.

I John 5:21. What is an idol? Anything elevated above God.

II JOHN
Theme: Walk in truth ~ Warning against false teachers.

The crux of II John is:
- The Law of Christ is (vs 5-6):
    - divine love via the Holy Spirit (Romans 5:5; Hebrews 10:16; I John 4:7).
    - Life changing (II Corinthians 5:14-20; I Thessalonians 2:7-8)
    - fulfills the Law of Moses, which "forced" love (James 1:25; 2:12; Leviticus 19:18; Deuteronomy 6:5; Luke 10:27; Romans 13:10; Galatians 5:14)
- The Doctrine of Christ (vs 7) is God in the flesh (II John 7-11; John 6:35, 41, 48, 58; I John 5:20). To reject Christ is to reject God.

THEREFORE (vs 8-11):
- I must not lose this truth.
- I must guard myself!
- He who doesn't believe, sins.
- Don't receive, or hang out with he who does not believe.
- Be careful who you bless!

II John 1. Was this written to a lady pastor? Some scholars believe it was a daughter work of another church. Some scholars point out the other epistles were addressed to a group of people. This is specific. I think she was the pastor of the congregation.

II John 3.
- Grace means divine favor & good will
- Mercy means free pardon and forgiveness
- Peace means tranquility of spirit
- God the Father means fountain of blessing
- Lord Jesus means communicator of the blessing

II John 5. If we diagram this sentence, we understand the base sentence says, "I BEG you to love each other!" It's that simple. ***THIS ISN'T ROCKET SCIENCE!***

II John 8. I am determined not to lose my reward and gains. I can't lose ground. There is no option but to keep moving forward.

II John 9. To reject Christ is to reject God.

II John 10-11. I need to be careful whom I bless! I must be on guard. In our modern church culture, we use the phrase, "God bless you", instead of "Goodbye". This scripture cautions me to be careful whom I bless. There was a lady who came to talk to us. She had been a faithful member for many years, but had coped an attitude. She felt she was more spiritual than everyone else and decided that she was going to go to another church. My husband just listened to her rant for a while and merely replied, "Ok, God bless you." She exclaimed, "You mean I have your blessing? You are blessing me?" He hastily explained, "No. You are making a big mistake. However, I see that your mind is made up so there is no point in reasoning with you." She hissed at our daughter, who was cleaning a table, and slammed the door on her way out. I think of that incident when I read this scripture. As it turns out, she did make a huge mistake.

II John 12. I think I am going to take John up on his offer to talk with him face-to-face! I know this scripture is specifically telling the "Elect Lady" he has plenty to discuss when he would later visit, but I'll see John one day and I'll get to talk with him face-to-face. I want to go to the same Heaven Jesus and His disciples are in. Therefore, I am going to obey their teachings.

III JOHN
Themes: Goodness, blessing & worldly doctrines.

The crux of III John is: Blessings! God will bless, but I must make myself available for blessings by living right.

III John 1-3.
- Prosper (Joshua 1:5-9; I Samuel 2:7-8; Job 36:11; Psalm 1:1-3; Matthew 7:7-11; Mark 9:23; Philippians 4:19; II Corinthians 9:6-8).
- Be in health (Exodus 15:25; Isaiah 58:8; Matthew 8:17).
- Soul to prosper (Matthew 1:21; Romans 1:16; 10:9-10; Ephesians 1:7).
- My physical prosperity and my soul's prosperity go hand in hand (Proverbs 28:13).

III John 4. I pray for my physical and spiritual children. In 50-75 years, what will matter? Not how nice my car or house is. Not how many vacations I was able to take. Nothing but my soul's salvation. I want my children to live comfortably, but above all, they (and I) must be saved.

III John 9-12. Some people are God's kingdom minded. Others are out to build their own kingdoms. This is not a new phenomenon in my generation! John dealt with that attitude 2,000 years ago.

JUDE
Theme: Warnings against heresy.

Jude is packed with warnings against heresy. There are deceivers who look and talk the part (vs 4) BUT are against authority (vs 8, 16). They ARE sometimes admired (vs 16) and corrupt the church (vs 12), SO GOD WILL judge them (vs 15).

Jude 3. The complete doctrine has already been given. I cannot get off the path, nor can I cause anyone else to stray (Jeremiah 18:15). There is no new doctrine given to an individual in a trance or during some other type of meditation. God will not contradict His own word. Therefore, if someone tells me they heard from God, and it does not match up with God's word, I automatically know they are a false prophet. I don't even have to pray about it. If it creates a conflict with God's word, it's wrong. Period. ***It's not rocket science!***

Jude 5-7. God has a track record of destroying those who don't believe. He may be patient and long-suffering, but that doesn't mean He won't bring judgment upon those who don't obey. God's mercy does not mean He condones an activity or doctrine. His track record speaks for itself!

Jude 8. The path to apostacy begins with dreams or revelations which do not line up with scripture. A revelation is not going to contradict scripture (Galatians 1:8-9; Revelation 22:18-19). These anti-Biblical dreams open up the door to defiling the body, which is the temple of God (I Corinthians 6:18-19); rejection of authority; and speaking against the angels (II Peter 2:10)-11. Those who are rebellious and are anti-authority will receive their judgment. Those who "live for God" on their own terms and not on God's terms will be judged just as Cain was judged.

Jude 9. Michael, the archangel, didn't feel comfortable rebuking Lucifer, a fellow archangel, albeit a fallen one. Instead, Michael stated the Lord God would rebuke him. I, in and of myself, have no authority. I cannot take dominion over anything. This is why I need the Holy Spirit. When I have God's spirit inside of me, I have the power to overcome. God's spirit has the dominion over all. When I go to rebuke, it must be in Jesus' name and not mine.

Jude 11.
- Way of Cain
    - own self
    - own religion
    - jealousy, murder, self-will
    - rebelled against the revelation of the word
- Error of Balaam
    - compromiser
    - hireling (II Peter 2:15)

- material gain
- rebelled against spoken Word
- doctrine of Balaam (Revelation 2:14): Taught others how to be a stumbling block.
- Gainsaying of Korah (Core)
  - rebellion against authority of the Word
  - murmured and complained against ministry (Numbers 16:1-3, 32)

Jude 12-13. Uses picture words
- Spots = blemishes
- Feeding without fear = refers to the "bring your own food" potlucks. The rich didn't share food with the poor, so there was a big difference between them
- Clouds without water
  - Not refreshed, dry (Deuteronomy 32:2)
  - Evil spirits wander in dry places (Matthew 12:43)
- Clouds obscure view of the sunlight
- Barren trees, twice dead = without spiritual fruit, I will be plucked out (Matthew 15:13; Proverbs 2:22)
- wild waves = wasted effort (Isaiah 57:20-21; Psalm 18:4)
- wandering star = no direction

Jude 17-19. We have been duly warned of false doctrines sneaking into the church. If it happened then, it will happen now. On Guard! (Acts 20:29; I Timothy 4:1; II Timothy 3:1; II Peter 3:1-3).

Jude 20. Ways of praying in the Spirit
- Tongues
- 2-way communication
- Holy Spirit praying through me, making intercession (Ephesians 6:18)
- God talking to me
- Building up my inheritance (Acts 20:32)

Jude 21-23. Christian Duties
- Mutual exhortation and prayer
- Love God and trust Him
- Win souls

Jude 24. The Holy Spirit will
- Keep me from falling
- Present me faultless

(There is only one God. He plays different roles in my life. As the creator, He is my father. As the redeemer, He is the son of God. As One who dwells within me, He is the Holy Spirit.)

REVELATION
The Revelation of who Jesus Christ is.

Note:
- Rome put John on Patmos for punishment. Heaven put John on Patmos for revelation and privilege.
- Some scriptures are parenthetical (in parenthesis).
- God tells His people His secrets.

Revelation 1:1. Bear in mind the book of Revelation is to reveal who Jesus is. All of the other verses serve to support this point. John tries to describe the vision(s) he saw. Those visions revealed Jesus. Up to that point, John had only seen Jesus in the flesh on this earth. His vision allowed him to see Jesus in His heavenly habitat. The key verse is Revelation 1:19 which divides world events into past, present, and the future. A lot of people want to dwell on the future. That is a tactic of Satan. If he can deflect my attention off of who Jesus is and get me to speculate on the future, he knows I will think I have plenty of time to get right with God. There is so much contention within Christianity about when (and even, if) the rapture will take place. Some people split hairs over a pre-tribulation, mid-tribulation, or post-tribulation rapture. I am pan-tribulation. I believe it will all pan out in the end. I do have somewhat of an opinion on when the rapture will take place, but it doesn't really matter what my opinion is. God is going to do what He will regardless of my interpretation of scriptures. I will just be ready whenever He decides to take me out of here. If I must live through some or all of the tribulation, His grace will be sufficient (II Corinthians 12:9). I'm sure the Christians burned in Nero's gardens thought that was the great tribulation and the coming of the Lord was nigh! I need to have a general knowledge of the future, but I must work on my present self.

IN THE BOOK OF REVELATION, JESUS IS PORTRAYED AS:
1. **God**. Revelation 1:1. Revelation which God gave to John. God made known by His angel. According to Revelation 22:16, God is called Jesus Christ whose angel was sent. Two angels were not sent, but Jesus and God are the same!
2. Salutations from Him **"Who is, was and is to come"** ... and "from 7 spirits" (vs 1:4). The one who is, was, and is to come is the Almighty (1:8; 4:8). The Alpha and Omega is the beginning and the end, the Creator (Genesis 1:1; Revelation 4:11). The Almighty is the son (Isaiah 9:6). Therefore, Jesus is portrayed as the "Alpha & Omega", the Almighty, the Creator, and the Son.
3. Revelation 1:5. **"Faithful witness"** or Prophet. Jesus is the faithful witness; that is, our prophet. Hebrews 1:1-2 states Jesus is a prophet and He is greater than any other prophet.
4. Revelation 1:5. Jesus is portrayed as the **First born of the Dead**. In this we find He is the sacrifice, the propitiation. That is, the only sacrifice acceptable for the plan of God. The blood of goats and bulls was not the propitiation for

sin. Hebrews 10:4-5. It was only temporary. John 1:29 calls Jesus "the Lamb to take away the sins of the world." I Peter 1:18-19. God's plan before the foundation of the world called for a lamb ... blood. Jesus is not only portrayed as a sacrifice, but as a priest-sacrifice as He did both works.

5. Revelation 1:5. Jesus is revealed as **Prince of Kings** (Revelation 19:16) "King of Kings and Lord of Lord" - none greater!
6. Revelation 1:7. Revealed as the **One to come** and all will see Him. Zechariah 12:9-10 teaches this is JHVH.
7. Revelation 1:1, 13, 18. "**Alpha & Omega**". The meaning is all inclusive - all in all - complete, everything. He appears AS LIKE the Son of Man. Daniel 7:9 explains He is the Ancient of Days. His garments teach he is a Judge, since His girdle is around the chest. He came to Judge the Churches (Chapter 2 & 3). He is therefore the Son of Man, Ancient of Days, and Judge of the Churches.
8. Revelation 4:8, 11. **The Creator**. The Alpha & Omega is the Creator and is the one "which was, and is, and is to come"(compare 1:8)
9. Revealed as being **the authority** (head) of the churches since He holds the ministers (stars) in His hand and is in the midst of the candles (church). I Corinthians 11 teaches Christ is the head of everyone. He is the head of the church.
10. Revelation 4:2, 8, 10, 11. Jesus Christ, the Creator, the Alpha & Omega is the **occupant of the throne**.
11. Revelation 5:1-4, 9. He is revealed as the only one who had qualifications to redeem. There was none on earth, under, or above, who had these qualifications. He is **the kinsman redeemer** of the Old Testament.
12. Revelation 5:5. **Lion of tribe of Judah**. Their earthly-Human-Jewish-Eternal King. (Lion is symbolic of kingship). This qualifies Him to rule the Jews in the Millennium. He is qualified as Messiah. It proves He is of the flesh-part of the qualifications of Kinsman redeemer, whose one qualification demanded that he be kin. By the flesh Jesus Christ became part of humanity.
13. **Root of David** (Revelation 5:5). Jesus is thus revealed as the Creator of David. David's ancestor. This was a great problem to the Jews, who could not answer the question put forth by Jesus as just who the Son of David was (Matthew 22:42-46; Revelation 22:16). Jesus is both the offspring of David, or David's creator as well as being David's son. Before David, as JHVH. Jesus put on flesh becoming David's descendent and salvation, savior.
14. Revelation 5:6. Revealed as **Lamb** with 7 eyes, 7 spirits. The number 7 denotes completeness (7 dispensations, 7 festivals in Old Testament). For after 7 comes 8, which is the perfect, everlasting. For it was the 8th day when one was circumcised and name was given him after birth. It means "something new". In the lamb was all completeness of the Godhead (Colossians 2:2, 9; I Timothy 3:16). Fullness of God (Zechariah 3:9, 4:6, 10). There is only one spirit. There is only one who sits on the throne. The 7 spirits which denote fullness teach that the "spirit of Old" (Micah 1:3; 5:2) was to come down to

Bethlehem. We know He came and His name was Jesus (compare John 1:1, 14)

15. Jesus appears as the **all in all** (Revelation 5:14; Exodus 20; Deuteronomy 6:4). There is only One God. This was the Great commandment to the Jews. Since all the Godhead dwelled in Jesus bodily (Colossians 2:9), therefore those redeemed worshiped the Lamb (or the manifestation - the way He was portrayed), for if He would not have come in the form of sacrifice, no one could be saved!
16. The **Avenger-Angel-Priest** (Revelation 8:1-5). Only the priest could use the censors. This part of Revelation considers the wrath of the Lamb. He is avenging (Revelation 6:16).
17. Jesus appears as a **roaring Lion with seven thunders** (Revelation 10:1-6). The Messenger Angel who proclaims Satan's era is about finished, and Genesis 3:15 is about to be completed and the reason for the Mystery of Godliness (I Timothy 3:16; Colossians 2:2, 9). The Messenger Angels states the Redeemer ready to take Possession.
18. Appears in Revelation 14:14-16 as the **Master of Reapers of World**
19. **Bridegroom** of saved (Revelation 19:7).
20. Appears as **Faithful and Truth** and as **Judge and Avenger of War** (Revelation 19:11).
21. Name revealed. He is "**Word of God**" (Revelation 19:13; John 1:1, 14)
22. Comes forth as **King of Kings and Lord of Lords** (Revelation 17:14).
23. **Ruler of Millennium** of Kings and Priests (Revelation 20:6).
24. He is temple of New Jerusalem **(light)** (Revelation 21:22).
25. **Judge** of all Wicked Dead (Revelation 20:11).

Revelation 1:4. The churches specifically mentioned in Revelation were real, individual churches, but also appear to designate church "ages". Most Bible scholars agree on with the following chart. Bear in mind that dates can't be precise as there are many characteristics which overlap. In fact, each and every local church probably bears some or all of these characteristics. It is interesting to me that the church in Philadelphia was told God had opened the door and no man could shut it (Revelation 3:8), however to the Laodicean church, God complained He had to stand at the door and knock (Revelation 3:20). What was the difference? Who shuts the door? I can shut the door in God's face and tie His hands when I don't have (1) love, (2) am not true to God's word, and (3) am lukewarm or passive!

Church	Church Age (A.D.)	Jesus Revealed as ….	Characteristic	Promise to Overcomers
Ephesians	33-100	Mighty God holding 7 stars and walking in midst of 7 candlesticks	doctrinally sound, but lacking in love	Eat of the tree of life
Smyrna	100-312	Resurrected One	persecuted & poor	Will not die spiritually
Pergamos	313-600	One with a sharp, 2-edged sword	full of heresy	Manna, white stone with a new name
Thyatira	600-1517	Eyes like fire; feet like brass	rise of false prophetess	Power over nations
Sardis	1517-1648	7 spirits of God and 7 stars	dying church	Be clothed in white raiment and name in book of Life (Matthew 17:2; Revelation 4:4; 7:9; 19:8)
Philadelphia	1649-1900	Holy; true; possesses key of David; power to open and shut	love for missions, loyal to the word	Receive crown; make pillar in temple; given new name
Laodicea	1900-present	Faithful & true witness; beginning of creation of God	lukewarm	Sit with God in throne (Psalm 91:14)

Revelation 1:19. This is the key verse. John is instructed to:
- tell who Christ is and
- tell of the events after the "church age".

Revelation 2:1-6. The church in Ephesus went through a lot. They had to endure persecution. They had to ward off false doctrine. Perhaps that made them a little harsh. God commended them for standing for truth and hating false doctrine, but His problem with them was they had left their first love. I suppose we could debate forever over what the "first love" is, but I wonder if they lost their worship and love for souls and became more legalistic in their approach. I wonder if they became introverted and reactive instead of proactive and reaching out to others. Did they lose sight of the great commission of "go ye into all the world, preaching" (Matthew 28:19)? The longer we live for God, the more prone we are to turn into an Ephesus Saint. Lord, help me to stir up what is in me (II Timothy 1:6). I want to keep the Holy Spirit fresh in my life. I don't want to become a stagnant Christian. To do so, I must maintain a healthy, *daily*, relationship with God. Much like the Israelites gathering manna fresh every day (Exodus 16:16-20), I have to keep my love for God and a love for others fresh.

Revelation 2:7. If the church in Ephesus corrected its ways, they would have abundance. The "name it and claim it" preachers have one thing right. God wants to bless me abundantly (Ezekiel 34:14; John 6:51; Ephesians 3:20; Isaiah 55:2). What those preachers don't understand is blessings come with obedience and not just because I'm claiming it as mine. I don't demand blessings from God. God responds to my love. My love for Him is not just lip service, but is expressed through my obedience to Him.

Revelation 2:8-11. The church in Smyrna had to deal with both poverty and persecution. They really had it rough. Their endurance and faith earned them a spot in Heaven! I can't say I have been through anything like this church went through. Nevertheless, God knows where I am. God knows and cares. I have had times of (mild) persecution. I have been taunted for my stand. I have had a saxophone ripped out of my mouth in an effort to stop a church service. I have had times when I barely had enough coins to buy a few groceries. I've had to make do with hand-me-downs and garage sale items. God has always provided for me. God really does know and care about us.

Revelation 2:12-17. Pergamos was a church that kept some doctrine and even had martyrs, but they compromised some doctrine. Compromise never ends well. I've talked to pastors who have compromised "a little". They insist they will never lose their grip on core doctrines. Unfortunately, they always do. It may take a few years, but in every case, without fail, once they start compromising, there is no stopping. Ultimately, they compromise on all doctrines. Once the older generation dies off, the church becomes more of a social club and not a church. The membership blends in with the world. Their worship is fun, but no longer anointed. God promises if Pergamos would turn themselves around, He would give them a new name. Jacob and Saul both received new names when they turned their lives around. I don't want to compromise. I don't want to run the risk of slipping into false doctrine.

Revelation 2:18-29. Thyatira was a generous church. They did many good things in a social setting. Unfortunately, they didn't do many good things in a spiritual setting. They allowed the spirit of Jezebel into their church. Jezebel (in the Old Testament) was known for her make-up (II Kings 9:30), her seductive prowess (I Kings 21:25; II Kings 9:22), and her allegiance to a false god (I Kings 18:19) to the point of wanting to destroy everything of God (I Kings 18:13; 19:2). I must not forget my main focus on this earth is winning souls. Community service is a good thing, but not the main thing. Community service should be a means to make contact with people I can win to the Lord. When I push the Lord's work aside in favor of community service, I run the risk of allowing the spirit of Jezebel to enter my heart. God promises those who would hold on to spiritual works would be rulers in the millennial reign (I Corinthians 6:2).

Revelation 3:1-5. Sardis was dead and didn't know it. They had a glimmer of truth in them, but for the most part had become just another social club. God told them to repent and strengthen their grip on what they had, or they would be lost and not even know it. That is a sad state of affairs. How many people think they are saved, but will be surprised when the rapture takes place and they are still sitting on the church pew? I had a tenant who was having an affair with a married man. This lady was a Sunday school teacher at a well-known church in my city. The man refused to leave his wife and my tenant got mad and slashed his tires. She also slashed the tires of the neighbor so it would look like a random act. Another tenant couple I had were members of the praise team at their church. The woman was the lead singer and the man was the drummer. They were not married. I am amazed at the amount of open sin allowed in churches. God is not pleased. Remember Achan (Joshua 7)? God punished the entire nation of Israel because sin, although unknown to leadership, was in the camp.

Revelation 3:7-13. The Philadelphia church was commended for keeping God's word. Because of their loyalty, God promised to be loyal to them and keep them from temptation. He exhorted them to hold on.

Revelation 3:14-22. Laodicea was so-so. They didn't have a backbone and were neither on fire for God nor were they cold in sin. They were prosperous and had lost sight of winning the lost. They were satisfied in their little group. They didn't realize they no longer had the anointing. They were "professional Christians" who went through the motions of church, but weren't really living for God. Much like Samson (Judges 16:20), they didn't know God had departed from their midst. God was still merciful and asked them to open the door. He was standing by just waiting for them to let Him in.

Revelation 4:2. Contrary to the testimony of a well-known televangelist, there is only one throne in heaven and only one sits upon that throne! My husband heard this evangelist's radio broadcast one night. The man said he saw two thrones in heaven. Red flag! This man is a false prophet.

Revelation 4:6-8. There are worship leaders in heaven! I find it interesting the faces of these worship leaders bear the same image as the lead tribe (from north, south, east, west) of the encampment in the wilderness. God has a people from the four corners of the earth.

Revelation 4:11. The reason for creation is found here ... for HIS pleasure and for HIS glory (Isaiah 43:7)!

Revelation 5:8. My prayers do make it to heaven, after all! Sometimes I think they only hit the ceiling of my room and bounce right back down to me. This verse lets me know my prayers not only make it to heaven, but are preserved.

Revelation 6 - 19:21. This segment goes hand-in-hand with Daniel's 70th week (See also Zechariah 1:8). Nothing nice will be going on down here on earth. I don't intend to be here to witness any of it.

Revelation 7:9-14. There will be a redeemed people in heaven. John saw me in heaven, because I intend to end up there!

Revelation 8:1-3. There will be silence in heaven while my prayers and the prayers which have been prayed throughout the ages are released.

Revelation 8:11. The word "wormwood" parallels to a situation like termites, a wood eating worm which weakens the "backbone" (Proverbs 5:4; Deuteronomy 29:18).

Revelation 9:20-21. It boggles my mind to think with all of the troubles and bad things happening on earth, there *still* would be people who refuse to repent. I suppose I shouldn't be too surprised. There are plenty of people who refuse to repent today. How can God get my attention? How can God chastise me? The only way He can is to allow bad things to happen. I want to always evaluate my situation and see if there is something I need to get right. When bad things come my way, it is time to do some soul searching. Is this just "life" happening, or is God chastising me? Do I need to repent?

Revelation 10:6. There will come a day when time, as we know it, will cease.

Revelation 11:9, 13. How will the whole world witness these things? I'm sure John didn't have an answer to that question. With television, satellites, cell phone cameras, and the internet today, we understand. People disbelieve the Bible because they can't prove it scientifically. The Bible is true. Science hasn't completely caught up with it yet. In Christopher Columbus' day, science thought the earth was flat, even though the Bible declared it was round (Isaiah 40:22). If there are scientifically unexplainable things in the Bible, I am confident, in due time, we will come to understand them.

Revelation 16. Seven vials will be poured out during the tribulation. I do **not** want to be anywhere around when all of this goes down! I've heard people say if they didn't make the rapture, they would be sure not to take the mark of the beast. I'm not so sure that's going to work out very well for them. If I can't live for God right now, when God's presence is available and living for God is relatively easy, what makes me think I will be able to live for God during the tribulation? Now is the day of salvation (II Corinthians 6:2). I must make my salvation sure today (II Peter 1:10).
- Sores (boils?) (vs 2).
- Ocean water turns to blood (vs 3).
- Fresh water turns to blood (vs 4).
- Scorching heat (vs 8).
- Darkness and pain (so much pain they will gnaw their tongues) (vs 10).
- Euphrates will dry up (vs 12; Isaiah 27:12).
- Voice declaring "the end" & Natural disasters multiplied (vs 17-18).

Revelation 17. A "woman" is identified.
- She is called the "great whore" (vs 1).
- Nations have built a political alliance with her (vs 2).
- She is identified as "mystery Babylon", which denotes she adheres to the same religious doctrine as the old Babylonian religion: same song, second verse (vs 5).
- She has martyred many of the true saints of God (vs 6).
- She rides on a beast with 7 heads and 10 horns, which is probably a type of some political entity (vs 7, 10-13). These political super powers will join together.
- She sits in the midst of 7 mountains (vs 9).
- The politicians will ultimately turn on her (vs 16).
- Politicians will be used by God to punish the religion which distorted God's truth so much and caused so many people to believe falsehoods (vs 17).
- This woman is a city (vs 18).

Revelation 18. *Finally*, after centuries of existence, the religious ideology of Babylon will be completely destroyed! This religion has had many names, but its core doctrine has been consistence throughout time: imitation of the true church, a counterfeit. This ideology is not only prevalent in "pagan" cultures, but has seeped into Christianity as well. I **must** make sure I turn to the Bible for truth and not to man's opinion. The patience of God amazes me. The ideology of this religion has been in place since Genesis (Tower of Babel and Nimrod). God has allowed it to

exist for thousands of years, but He will ultimately destroy it. Just because God hasn't judged me immediately for my sin doesn't mean He never will. Just because God lets an individual or nation continue to exist doesn't mean He is ignoring their sin. Judgment will come in God's timing and judgment will be harsh. I must make sure my heart and life are clean so God won't have a need to judge me. Here are the facts concerning the demise of this religious system.
- Full of evil spirits (vs 2).
- Alliance with nations. This religion is a political machine (vs 3).
- God calls individuals, with a pure *trajectory of heart* (with a heart that wants to please God and live for Him), to come out of this religion (vs 4). This tells me there are people who really do want to live for God, but who have been deceived by this religion.
- Rich and opulent (vs 7).
- Judgment, when it finally comes, will be swift and harsh (vs 8).
- Politicians will mourn its demise (vs 9-10).
- Its demise will be detrimental to international commerce (vs 11-19).
- Heaven will rejoice. A grievous false doctrine has finally been judged (vs 20).
- All good things in it will be destroyed because this religion has deceived so many and even fought against the true church of God (vs 21-24).

Revelation 20.
- It will only take one angel to lock up Satan and all his devils (vs 1-3)! If I live for God, I am surrounded by angels (Psalm 34:7). Why should I be afraid of the devil?
- There will be some saved through the tribulation. These people did not take the mark of the beast and will be martyred (vs 4).
- It is far better to qualify for the rapture of the saints than to go through the tribulation (vs 6). The saints will be rulers (mayors, governors, etc.) during the millennial reign of Jesus on earth.
- After 1,000 years, Satan will be loosed again (vs 7-8). Why? For a blissful 1,000 years, there will be no evil on earth, thus no temptations and no death. Those born during this time won't have a choice whether or not to live for God. After Satan is loosed, they will face temptation and be allowed the privilege of choosing to live for God or not. Mankind has always had a choice.
- My name must be in the Book of Life! I will be measured according to my works recorded there (vs 12). The Bible is the plumb line whereby all things are measured (Deuteronomy 6:18). Nothing else matters. After that judgment, the 2nd death, which is eternal punishment, is handed to those whose name is not in that book (Revelation 20:14). After that, time will cease to exist and things will be as it was in the Garden of Eden before man's fall into sin.
- The "2nd Death" is eternal punishment (vs 14).
- My name **must** be in the Book of Life (vs 15). I will do whatever I need to do to make sure it is in there. If the Bible told me I must wear green socks on

Thursdays, I would do it. **I must be saved.**

Revelation 21. How wonderful the new heaven and new earth will be! This is what we know about Heaven:
- It is beautiful (vs 2).
- God will dwell there (vs 3).
- God will wipe away our tears (vs 4).
- No more crying, no death, no sorrow, no pain (vs 4).
- All things are new (vs 5).
- Nothing that is abominable to God (something God hates) will be allowed in Heaven (vs 8, 27). I must be careful not to entertain abominable things in my home, or I will be cursed along with it (Deuteronomy 7:26). If I truly have the "mind of Christ", I will hate what God hates. If I truly have God's holy spirit dwelling in me, I will hate what God hates. When the things that repulse God do not repulse me, I need to take a good look at my spiritual self. If my flesh is overpowering the spirit of God, I am in danger of God's spirit departing from my life like it did from Jerusalem (See notes at Ezekiel 10 in *It's Not Rocket Science, Volume 3.*)
- Full of the glory of God and very opulent (vs 11-21). The streets will be pure gold! Here on earth, gold is very precious. We pave our streets with asphalt or concrete, the cheapest, but most durable material we can find! God will use the things most precious on earth to pave the streets of Heaven!
- The foundation of the city is the doctrine of the 12 apostles (vs 14). I can't go wrong if I believe and obey what the 12 apostles preached.
- God is the light (vs 23) and there will be no night (vs 25). I really will need a glorified body to live there (I Corinthians 15:51-52)!

Revelation 22.
- The curse will finally be over (vs 3).
- God sent His angel (vs 6) but then, Jesus sent the angel (16). Are these scriptures contradicting themselves? No! Jesus is the name of God. God came in flesh and that manifestation is called Jesus (John 1:1; 14). There are not two gods.
- In the meantime, until that day, I must be on fire for God (vs 11). There is no middle ground. When cement is freshly poured, it is easily moldable into any shape, but it begins to dry out quickly. There is but a short window of opportunity in which initials can be carved before it sets. Once it sets, it is impossible to alter. Such is our lives. The choices we make while we are young set the stage for our adult lives (Ecclesiastes 12:1).

Revelation 22:17. The offer stands. Jesus offers me the opportunity to make the right choices. God is not sneaky about the consequences of sin. It is all very, very clear. If I go to hell, it will be because of the choices *I* make and not because God is mean and hateful. God has an open invitation to us all, regardless of economic status, race, social positions, etc. (Acts 10:34). I only need to obey His word and heaven is mine. God will not send anyone to hell. Hell is a consequence of disobedience. People send themselves to hell by their disobedience to the word of God.

Revelation 22:18-19. It's not about what I think or what anyone else can talk me in to. I am not allowed to add or subtract from the word of God (Deuteronomy 12:32; Joshua 1:7). His word is forever settled (Psalm 119:89). God's word is the "owner's manual". I can't go wrong if I live by the Bible. I don't argue with the gasoline gauge in my car. When it hits "E" for empty, I know I have a very short time before I will run out of gasoline and my car will not move. It does me no good to complain that (1) I'm too tired to stop and pump gas; (2) I don't want to get out in the rain to pump gas; (3) I will be late for my appointment if I have to pump gas; etc. It is what it is and if I don't heed the gauge, I will be stopped. There is no negotiating for extra time. So it is with the Bible. There is no negotiating with God's word. It's just that simple. ***IT'S NOT ROCKET SCIENCE!*** It is not required of me to understand all things, but it is required that I obey. It's nice of God to open up my understanding, but He is not obligated to do so. I just obey and do what He wants if I want to get into Heaven. Heaven is a privilege and not a "right".

Revelation 22:21. The last message of the New Testament is **GRACE** (unmerited favor)!

PS: The last message of the Old Testament was "cursed"! What a difference Calvary makes! I'm thankful I live on this side of Calvary.

VOCABULARY

In order to understand the scriptures (especially from the King James Version of the Bible), a basic understanding of some words we don't use in modern, everyday language is required.

Sin:	Insubordination (to God)
Atone:	To make amends and to bring in harmony with God
Just:	One who is in correct legal standing with God. "Justify" means to get into a correct legal standing with God. To be "justified" means to be counted righteous in God's sight.

Propitiation:	Removal of a wrath by an offering.
Grace:	Undeserved favor (privilege) This is what caused Jesus to leave the riches of Heaven and dwell in the poverty of earth (II Corinthians 8:9)
Mercy:	The extension of grace to someone. Mercy compels a sinner to be loved. Mercy causes judgment to be restrained.
Impute:	Charge to account.
Conversation:	Behavior.
Predestination:	Comes from the word "pro-orizo". "Pro" means before and "Orizo" means determined. Hence: The medium of salvation has been predetermined from the foundation of the world (Calvary).
Perfect:	Mature, complete.
Repent:	To make a U-turn. Repentance is NOT *saying* "sorry"; it is *making a change*. There are times where the Bible states God "repented" (Exodus 32:14). God does not have to be "sorry" about anything or apologize to anyone. God did, however, change His course of action and took another course of action. Repentance for my sins is *being* sorry. *Being* sorry means I'm going to take corrective action so I don't do this again (II Corinthians 7:9).
Repent (2):	to change your mind; to return to your right mind. Sin makes humanity a little "crazy". We need to come to our senses and return to our right state of mind!
Remission	To expunge (totally erase and do away with); to destroy all evidence; an expungement of my record of sin. This is only through the shedding of blood (Hebrews 9:22). The blood sacrifices of the Old Testament were not enough for remission. They only served to delay judgment until innocent blood could be shed (Hebrews 9:12). The blood of Jesus is applied to my heart at baptism (Acts 2:38). Expungement is not the same as a pardon. A pardon means I am forgiven. This expungement is what enables me, a sinful person, to be allowed in the presence of Almighty God (Ephesians 2:13; Hebrews 10:19). Expungement means all evidence against me is destroyed and I no longer have a "rap sheet" with God. Remember Hurricane Katrina in 2005? Crime labs were either contaminated or destroyed by flood waters. Consequently, many criminals were released because there was no evidence to make a case against them. When I am baptized in Jesus' name, His blood contaminates the evidence of sin against me and there is no case! YAY!
And:	The Greek word "kai" is most often translated in the King James Version of the Bible as "and". A more accurate translation is "even". Example: "God the father and the Lord Jesus Christ" should read "God the father EVEN the Lord Jesus Christ". In these instances, "and" does not mean "in addition to", but rather is used for a fuller explanation.
Froward:	Habitually disposed to disobedience. Inclined to be rebellious. Sounds

	like a _**trajectory of the heart**_ problem, doesn't it?
Prophesy:	To tell forth. Sometimes in the scriptures, this means to tell forth the future, but not always. In today's language, we might just use the word "preach" or "teach" instead.
Debate:	strife
Malignity:	evil minded
Clamor:	loud uproar, usually a voice of dissatisfaction
Implacable:	unforgiving
Blessed:	to be envied; empowered to succeed
Iniquities:	undisciplined spirit
Judgment:	(of God) when judgment overrides mercy.
Guile:	refraining from the WHOLE truth
Hearing:	also means obey
Fear:	reverence, not feeling afraid (fear/revere God)

Made in the USA
Monee, IL
08 March 2025